Rifle, Blanket and Kettle
Selected Indian Treaties and Laws

by
Frederick E. Hosen

McFarland & Company, Inc., Publishers
Jefferson, North Carolina, and London

Library of Congress Cataloguing-in-Publication Data

Main entry under title:

Rifle, blanket, and kettle.

  Includes index.
  1. Indians of North America — Treaties. 2. Indians of
North America — Legal status, laws, etc. I. Hosen,
Frederick E., 1938 —
KF8202   1985   349.73′08997   [347.3008997]   84-43208

ISBN 0-89950-153-2

Printed in the United States of America.

McFarland   Box 611   Jefferson NC 28640

CONTENTS

Introduction   1
First Indian Deed to William Penn, 1682   5
Treaty with the Indians of Ohio, 1747   9
Treaty with the Chickesaws, Creeks, Chactaws, Cherokees, and
    Catawba, 1763   16
Treaty with the Delawares, 1778   20
Treaty with the Six Nations, 1784   24
Treaty with the Wyandot, Etc., 1785   26
Treaty with the Choctaw, 1786   29
Treaty with the Six Nations, 1789   33
Treaty with the Oneida, Etc., 1794   36
Treaty with the Passamaquaddy, 1794   39
Treaty with the Six Nations, 1794   42
Treaty with the Mohawk, 1797   47
Treaty with the Sioux of the Lakes, 1815   49
Treaty with the Cherokee, 1817   51
Treaty with the Seminole, 1833   57
Treaty with the Chickasaw, 1834 [First]   59
Treaty with the Chickasaw, 1834 [Second]   67
Treaty with the Cherokee, 1835   69
Treaty with the Choctaw and Chickasaw, 1837   84
Treaty with the Utah, 1849   87
Treaty of Fort Laramie with Sioux, Etc., 1851   90
Treaty with the Nisqualli, Puyallup, Etc., 1854   94
Treaty with the Blackfeet, 1855   99
Treaty with the Western Shoshoni, 1863   105
Treaty with the Creeks, 1866   108
Treaty with the Navaho, 1868   116
Treaty with the Sioux — Brulé, Oglala, Miniconjou, Yanktonai,
    Hunkpapa, Blackfeet, Cuthead, Two Kettle, Sans Arcs, and
    Santee — and Arapaho, 1868   123

Treaty with the Nez Percés, 1868	138
Act of First Congress, Second Session, 1790	140
Act of Twenty-First Congress, First Session, 1830	142
General Laws Regulating Indian Affairs, 1871	144
Act of Forty-Fourth Congress, Second Session, 1877	145
Act of Forty-Ninth Congress, Second Session, 1887	151
Act of Fiftieth Congress, Second Session, 1889	156
Act of Fifty-First Congress, Second Session, 1891	160
Act of Fifty-Ninth Congress, First Session, 1906	163
Act of Sixty-Eighth Congress, First Session, 1924	165
Act of Seventy-Third Congress, Second Session, 1934	166
Act of Seventy-Ninth Congress, Second Session, 1946	172
Act of Eighty-Sixth Congress, First Session, 1959	182
Index	185

INTRODUCTION

These treaties and laws have been gathered together to provide a cross-section of documented agreements and statutes of historical significance, first between the European settlers of the New World and the Indians and, later, between the descendents of those settlers and the Indians. The overall focus is not on a particular tribe. Neither is a time period nor type of treaty the center of attention. The chronological order may provide the reader with a sense of evolutionary or social movement.

At the time of the creation of the United States of America, and even before then, Indian tribes were viewed as foreign nations, with whom therefore, treaties were to be made. Treaty-making with the Indians formally ended when a rider inserted in the Indian Appropriations Act of March 3, 1871, provided,

> that hereafter no Indian nation or tribe within the territory of the United States shall be acknowledged or recognized as an independent nation, tribe, or power with whom the United States may contract by treaty: Provided, further, That nothing herein contained shall be construed to invalidate or impair the obligations of any treaty heretofore lawfully made and ratified with any such Indian nation or tribe.

The United States government continued for many more years to draft agreements with the Indians. Those documents, however, remain unratified by the United States Congress.

Today, and in recent years, Indian rights and past treatment are issues of national importance and impact. Various fishing and hunting rights claims and land claims have been, are, or will be before the courts and the legislative bodies of the country. This work includes selected treaties and statutes upon which some of those actions are based.

The following chart illustrates some of the more active claims in recent years, most of which are still on-going.

State	Tribe	Issue	Treaty/Statute
Maine	Passamaquoddy & Penobscot	Claim to a significant amount of land in the State of Maine (about sixty percent of the land area of the State).	Treaty with the Passamaquoddy, 1794. Act of First Congress — Second Session, 1790 (Chap. 33).
Nevada	Western Shoshoni	Claim to a significant amount of land in the State of Nevada (about one-third of the land area of the State).	Treaty with the Western Shoshoni, 1863.
North Carolina	Eastern Band of Cherokee	The right to self-government without interference from the State of North Carolina.	Treaty with the Cherokee, 1835.
South Carolina	Catawba	Claim to about 144,000 acres of land in the State of South Carolina.	Act of Eighty-Sixth Congress-First Session, 1959 (Chap. 322).
South Dakota	Sioux Nation	Claim to the Black Hills area of the State of South Dakota.	Treaty with the Brulé, Oglala, Miniconjou, Yanktonai, Hunkpapa, Blackfeet, Cuthead, Two Kettle, Sans Arcs, and Santee-and Arapaho, 1868. Act of Forty-Fourth Congress-Second Session, 1877 (Chap. 72).
Washington	Nisqualli, Puyallup, Nez Percés and others.	Fishing rights,	Treaty with the Nisqualli, Puyallup, etc., 1854. (This is only one of several treaties of significance in the fish-rights issue).

A treaty might contain any of the following provisions:

There would be mutual forgiveness, by the parties, of all offenses.

There would be peace and perpetual friendship between the parties.

Neither party was to protect enemies, criminals, or fugitives of the other party.

The United States would guarantee to the Indians all territorial rights of former treaties.

The Indians would give the United States hostages until prisoners held by the Indians were turned over.

Boundaries were to be set.

No citizen of the United States was to settle on Indian lands.

Distribution of goods was to be made by the United States to the Indians for humanitarian purposes.

Indians were to recognize the title of the United States to certain lands.

The Indians were to acknowledge the protection of the United States.

The United States was to regulate trade.

Monies would be given to the Indians by the United States as restitution.

Mills, millers, schools, churches etc. would be given to the Indians by the United States.

Lands would be ceded by the Indians to the United States in exchange for other lands.

Reservations would be established for the Indians.

Indians would be removed from their lands.

Hostilities between the Indians and the United States would cease.

The Indians would allow the people of the United States free passage through their territory.

United States' military posts and agencies would be established.

The Indians were to stay within designated boundaries.

The United States would be able to build roads and telegraph lines in and across Indians lands.

The use of intoxicating liquor by Indians would be banned.

Slavery by the Indians would be banned.

A census of the Indians would be taken.

Scalping by the Indians would be prohibited.

An Indian would be penalized for leaving the Reservation.

Indian hunting and fishing rights were acknowledged and specified.

Some of the treaties have very poignant passages, such as the one found in the Treaty with the Chickasaw, 1834:

The Chickasaws are about to abandon their homes, which they have long cherished and loved; and though hitherto unsuccessful, they still hope to find a country, adequate to the wants and support of their people, somewhere west of the Mississippi and within the territorial limits of the United States....

Little of the general literature or history about the Indians present treaties in their entirety. Usually, only small portions of treaties are occasionally quoted to support an author's particular point or position. Complete treaties provide valuable insights not often gained from other sources.

Two publications of the U.S. Government Printing Office are essential to the subject of Indian treaties. Many of the treaties can be found in Volume II of the five-volume work first published in 1904 and entitled *Indian Affairs, Laws and Treaties*, compiled and edited by Charles J. Kappler. It is the likely source for putting together an anthology or a listing or other grouping of treaties. The work entitled *Federal Indian Law* (Department of the Interior) provides, mainly from a legal standpoint, the history of treaty-making with the Indians. A third publication that can provide valuable pre–Revolutionary information about treaties, including some complete treaties, was published in 1938 by the Historical Society of Pennsylvania. Its title is *Indian Treaties Printed by Benjamin Franklin 1736–1762* and includes an extensive Introduction as well as extensive Historical Bibliographical Notes.

A few last comments: Every effort has been made to be true to the sources of this anthology. To the extent possible, with the type of print used and the space available on the pages of this anthology, the format of the source material has been followed. The capitalization of words is as capitalized in the source document and the spelling is as spelled in the source document. There are a number of treaties with apparent spelling errors and inconsistencies. This is not surprising since it is doubtful that many of them were subjected to professional editorial review at the time they were originally written. Of course the problem, in some cases, might be with their later publication.

FIRST INDIAN DEED
TO WILLIAM PENN, 1682

This Indenture, made the ffifteenth day of July, in the years of o^R Lord, according to English Accompt, one Thousand Six Hundred Eightye Two, Between Idquahon, Ieanottowe, Idquoquequon, Sahoppe for himselfe and Okonikon, Merkekowon Orecton for Nannacussey, Shaurwawghon, Swanpisse, Nahossey, Tomakhickon, Westkekitt & Tohawsis, Indyan Sachamakers of ye one pte, And William Penn, Esq^R, Chief Proprieto^R of the Province of Pennsylvania of the other pte: Witnesseth that for and in Consideracon of the sumes and particulars of Goods, merchandizes, and vtensills herein after mentioned and expressed, (That is to say,) Three Hundred and ffifty ffathams of Wampam, Twenty white Blankits, Twenty ffathams fo Strawd waters, Sixty ffathams of Duffields, Twenty Kettles, ffower whereof large, Twenty Gunns, Twenty Coates, fforty Shirts, fforty payre of Stockings, fforty Howes, fforty Axes, Two Barrells of Powder, Two Hundred Barres of Lead, Two Hundred Knives, Two Hundred small Glasses, Twelve payre of Shooes, fforty Copper Boxes, fforty Tobacco Tonngs, Two small Barrells of Pipes, fforty payre of Sissors, fforty Combes, Twenty ffower pounds of Red Lead, one Hundred Aules, Two handfulls of ffish-hooks, Two handfulls of needles, fforty pounds of Shott, Tenne Bundles of Beads, Tenne small Saws, Twelve drawing knives, ffower anchers of Beere, And Three Hundred Gilders, by the said William Penn, anchers of Beere, And Three Hundred Gilders, by the said Willliam Penn, his Agents or Assigns, to the said Indyan Sachmakers, for the use of them and their People, at and before Sealing and delivery hereof in hand paid and delivered, whereof and wherewith they the said Sachemakers doe hereby acknowledge themselves fully satisfyed, Contented and paid. The said Indyan Sachamakers (parties to these presents,) As well for and on behalf of themselves as for and on the behalfe of their Respective Indyans or People for whom they are concerned, Have Granted, Bargained, sold and delivered, And by these presents doe fully, clearly and absolutely Grant,

5

bargayne, sell and deliver vnto the sayd William Penn, his Heirs and Assignes forever, All that or Those Tract or Tracts of Land lyeing and being in the Province of Pennsylvania aforesaid, Beginning at a certaine white oake in the Land now in the tenure of John Wood, and by him called the Gray Stones over against the ffalls of Dellaware River, And soe from thence up by the River side to a corner marked Spruce Tree with the letter P at the ffoot of a mountayne, And from the sayd corner marked Spruce Tree along by the Ledge or ffoot of the mountaines west north west to a corner white oake, marked with the letter P standing by the Indyan Path that Leads to an Indyan Towne called Playwickey, and near the head of a Creek called Towsissinck, And from thence westward to the Creek called Neshammonys Creek, And along by the sayd Neshammonyes Creek unto the River Dellaware, alias Makeriskhickon; And soe bounded by the sayd mayne River to the Sayd first mentioned white oake in John Wood's Land; And all those Islands called or knowne by the severall names of Mattinicunk Island, Sepassincks Island, and Orecktons Island, lying or being in the sayd River Dellaware, Togeather alsoe with all and singular Isles, Islands, Rivers, Rivoletts, Creeks, Waters, Ponds, Lakes, Plaines, Hills Mountaynes, Meadows, Marrishes, Swamps, Trees, Woods, Mynes, minerals and Appurtennces whatsoever to the sayd Tract or Tracts of Land belonging or in any wise Apperteyning; And the reverson and reversons, Remaindr. and remaindrs. thereof, And all the Estate, Right, Tytle, Interest, vse, pperty, Clayme and demand whatsoever, as well as them the sayd Indyan Sachamakers (Ptyes to these presents) as of all and every other the Indyans concerned therein or in any pte. or Pcel. thereof. To have and to hold the sayd Tract or Tracts of Land, Islands, and all and every other the sayd Granted premises, with their and every of their Appurtennces vnto the sayd William Penn, his Heirs and Assignes, forever, To the only pper vse & Behoofe of the sayd William Penn, his Heires and Assignes, forevermore. And the sayd Indyan Sachamakers and their Heirs and successors, and every of them, the sayd Indyan Sachamakers and their Heires and successors, and every of them, the sayd Tract or Tracts of Land, Islands, and all and every other the sayd Granted pmisses, with their and every of their Appurtennces unto the sayd William Penn, his Heires and Assignes forever, against them the sayd Indyan Sachamakers, their Heires and successors, and against all and every Indyan and Indyans and their Heires and successors, Clayming or to Clayme, any Right, Tytle or Estate, into or out of the sayd Granted prmisses, or any pte. or prcel. thereof, shall and will warrant and forever defend by these presents; In witness whereof the said Prtves. to these present Indentures Interchangeably have sett their hands and seals the day and yeare ffirst above written, 1682.

The (x) mark of
Kowockhickon

The (x) mark of
Attoireham,
Wm Markham,
Deputy Gov^R. to Wm. Penn, Esq^R.

Sealed and Delivered in ye presence of

Lasse Cock
Pieowjicom
Rich. Noble
Thos. Revell

First day of August, 1682.

Att ye house of Capt. Lasse Cock.

Wee, whose names are underwritten, for our Selves and in name and behalfe of the rest of the within mentioned Shackamachers, in respect of a mistake in the first bargaine betwixt us and the within named Wm. Penn, of the number of tenn gunns more than are mentioned in the within deed when we should then have received, doe now acknowledge the receipt of the saide tenn gunns from the said Wm. Penn; And whereas in the said deed there is certaine mention made of three hundred and fifte fathom Wampum, not expressing the quality thereof, wee yrfore for our Selves, and in behalfe also do declare the same to be one halfe whyt wampum and the other halfe black wampum; And we, Peperappamand, Pyterhay and Eytepamatpetts, Indian Shachamakers, who were the first owners of ye Land called Soepassincks, & of ye island of ye same name, and who did not formerlie Sign and Seal ye within deed, nor were present when the same was done, doe now by signing and sealing hereof Ratefie, approve and confirm ye within named deed and the ye partition of ye Lands within mentioned writen and confirm thereof in all ye points, clauses, and articles of ye same, and doe declare our now sealing hereof to be as valid, effectual and sufficient for ye conveyance of ye whole Lands, and of here within named to ye sd.

Wm. Penn, his heirs and assigns, for evermore, as if we had their with the other named Shachamakers signed and sealed in ye same.

The (x) mark of
Nomne Soham.
Wm. Markham.

Signed and Sealed and delivered in p^{R}nce of us,
    Redtharnvelleon,
    Lass Cock.

A TREATY, &C
[WITH THE INDIANS OF OHIO, 1747]

At a Council held at Philadelphia, the 13th of November, 1747.

PRESENT: The Honourable ANTHONY PALMER, Esq; President

Thomas Lawrence,	Samuel Hassell,	
Willliam Till,	Abraham Taylor,	Esqrs.
Robert Strettell,	Benjamin Shoemaker,	
Joseph Turner,	William Logan,	

THE Indian Warriors from Ohio, having arriv'd in Town on Wednesday, the President sent them a Message Yesterday, by Mr. Weiser, the Interpreter, to bid them welcome: And understanding that they were desirous to be heard To-day, he summon'd the Council for this Purpose. Mr. Weiser attending, he was sent to tell the Indians the Council was sitting, and ready to receive them. They immediately came. The President inform'd them, the Council were glad to see their Brethren, took their Visit very kindly, and desired to know what they had to communicate.

After a Pause, the principal Warrior rose up, and spoke as follows: Brethren, the English, the Governor of York, the Commissioners at Albany, the Governor and Councellors of Pennsylvania,

We who speak to you are Warriors, living at Ohio, and address you on Behalf of ourselves, and the rest of the Warriors of the Six Nations.

You will, perhaps, be surprized at this unexpected Visit; but we cou'd not avoid coming to see you, the Times are becoming so critical and dangerous. We are of the Six Nations, who are your ancient Friends, having made many Treaties of Friendship with the English, and always preferv'd the Chain bright. You know when our Father, the Governor of Canada, declar'd War against our Brethren, the English, you the Governor of New-York, the Commissioners of Indian Affairs at Albany, the Commissioners for this Province, sent to inform the Council at Onondago of it, and to desire that they wou'd not meddle with the War; that they wou'd only look on, and see what wou'd be done; that we, the Indians, wou'd let you fight it out by yourselves, and not pity either Side; and that we would send to all the Nations in Alliance with us, to do the same: And accordingly the Indians did send to all their Friends and Allies, and particularly to the Indians about the Lakes, and in the Places where we live, requesting they wou'd not engage on either Side; and they all stood Neuters, except the French Praying Indians, who, tho' they promis'd, yet were not as good as their Words. This is the first Thing we have to say to our Brethren, and we hope they will receive this in good Part, and be willing to hear what we have further to say.

Brethren

When the Indians received the first Message from the English, they thought the English and French would fight with one another at Sea, and not suffer War to made on the Land: But some Time after this, Messengers were sent by all the English to Onondago, to tell us that the French had begun the War on the Land in the Indian Countries, and had done a great deal of Mischief to the English, and they now desired their Brethren, the Indians, would take up the Hatchet against the French, and likewise prevail with their Allies to do the same. The old Men at Onondago however refus'd to do this, and would adhere to the Neutrality; and on their declaring this, the English sent other Messengers again and again, who pressed earnestly that the Indians would take up their Hatchet, but they were still denied by the old Men at the Fire at Onondago, who, unwilling to come into the War, sent Message after Message to Canada and Albany. to desire both Parties would fight it out at Sea. At last the young Indians, the Warriors, and Captains, consulted together, and resolved to take up the English Hatchet against the Will of their old People, and to lay their old People aside, as of no Use but in Time of Peace. This the young Warriors have done, provoked to it by the repeated Applications of our Brethren the English; and we now come to tell you, that the French have hard Heads, and that we have nothing strong enough to break them. We have only little Sticks, and Hickeries, and such Things, that will do little or no Service against the hard Heads of the French: We therfore present this Belt, to desire that we may be furnished with better Weapons, such as will knock the French down; and in Token that we are hearty for you, and will do our best if you put better Arms into our Hands, we give you this Belt.

Here they gave a Belt of Seven Rows

Brethren,

When once we, the young Warriors, engaged, we put a great deal of Fire under our Kettle, and the Kettle boil'd high, and so it does still (meaning they carried the War on Briskly) that the Frenchmens Heads might soon be boil'd. But when we look'd about us, to see how it was with the English Kettle, we saw the Fire was almost out, and that it hardly boil'd at all; and that no Frenchmens Heads were like to be in it. This truly surprizes us, and we are come down on Purpose to know the Reason of it. How comes it to pass, that the English, who brought us into the War, will not fight themselves? This has not a good Appearance, and therefore we give you this String of Wampum to hearten and encourage you, to desire you wou'd put more Fire under your Kettle.

Here they presented the String of Wampum of Seven Strings

Brethren,

We have now done with general Matters; but old Scaiohady desires to inform the Council, that he was here in James Logan's Time, a long Time ago, when he had but one Child, and he a little one: That he was then employed in the Affairs of the Government: That James Logan gave him this String, to assure him, if ever he should come to want, and apply to this Government, they wou'd do something for him. Scaiohady is now grown old and infirm, and recommends himself to James Logan's and the Council's Charity.

Here he laid down a String of Wampum.

The Indians withdrew, and the Council adjourn'd to To-morrow Morning, Eleven a Clock.

In the Council-Chamber, 14th November 1747.

PRESENT,

Thomas Lawrence,   Robert Strettell,
Benjamin Shoemaker,   William Logan,

The President being indispos'd, and the other Members not attending, there could be no Council; the Members present, judg'd that before the Heads of an Answer to the Speech of the Indians could be considered, it was necessary previously to learn from Mr. Weiser, the particular History of these Indians, their real Disposition towards us, and their future Designs; and accordingly sent for him. He said the Indians, had in Part told him their Mind, and he thought they might be brought to tell him more; and when they did, he would inform the Council. The Members likewise judg'd, that it might be of Service to know Mr. Logan's Sentiments about what might be proper to be said to the Indians, and requested Mr. Weiser and the Secretary to wait on him for that Purpose.

At a Council held at Philadelphia, 16th November 1747

PRESENT,

The Honourable the President,

Thomas Lawrence,	Samuel Hassel,	
William Till,	Abr. Taylor,	
Robert Strettell,	Benj. Shoemaker,	Esqrs.
Thomas Hopkinson,	William Logan,	

Mr. Weiser attending was called in, and inform'd the Council, that he had learn'd the following Particulars from the Indians, viz. That last Summer the Governor of Canada had sent the Hatchet to the Indians about the Lakes, and on the Branches of Ohio; that one Nation took it up; and that these Indians, and the Indians in those Quarters, consisting principally of Warriors, being afraid others would do the like, to prevent this took up the English Hatchet, and proclaim'd War against the French; which had a good Effect, no more daring after this to meddle with the French Hatchet: That these Indians on Ohio, had concluded to kindle a Fire in their Town, and had invited all the Indians at a considerable Distance round about them to come to their Fire in the Spring; and that they had consented to it. Mr. Weiser added, that the Indians in the Parts these People came from, were numerous, not less than Five Hundred Men, and had many Allies more numerous than themselves: That it was always the Custom in War Time, to put the Management into the Hands of the young People; and that it would be of the most pernicious Consequence not to give them Encouragement at this Time; and particularly he thought the Council should at least tell them, they approv'd of their taking up the Hatchet; and aknowledge the Service done to the English by their seasonable Declaration in their Favour: He thought Providence had furnished this Province with a fine Opportunity of making all the Indians about the Lakes their Friends, and warm Friends too. — Mr. Weiser being asked what Sort of a Present should be given them at this Time, He said Goods were now so dear, that the Value of 100 Pounds would appear but small, that they should have so much given them at least, and Half as much to the Canayiahaga Indians. Not that this was by any Means sufficient, but would be a good Salutation-Present, and preparatory to a larger to be sent in the Summer. This he judged necessary to be done, and that they should now be told of this future Present: And, tho' he had never been in those Parts, yet he judged the attaching these Indians and their Friends to the English Cause to be so necessary, that he would, if the Council pleased, and his Health should permit, go with the Present himself, and see with his own Eyes what Number of Indians was there, and in what Disposition. He said further, that he accompanied the Secretary to Mr.

Logan's Yesterday, and that the Secretary had informed Mr. Logan of all these Particulars, and taken his Sentiments in Writing, and on them form'd the Plan of an Answer. The Board ordered the Secretary to read what he had wrote; and on considering this, and Mr. Weiser's Information, and Answer was agreed to, and the Presents settled. The Council adjourned to Four o'Clock in the Afternoon, and directed that the Indians should be told to be there, in order to receive the Answer of the Council to their Speech.

At a Council held at Philadelphia, the 16th of November, 1747. P.M.

PRESENT,

The Honourable ANTHONY PALMER, Esq; President;
And the same Members as in the Forenoon

The Indians having taken their Seats, the President spoke as follows:
Brethren Warriors of the Six Nations,
We the President and Council of the Province of Pennsylvania, have taken what you said to us into Consideration, and are now going to give you an Answer.

We are always glad to see our Brethren, and are particularly pleased at this critical Time, with your present Visit. You are sensible of the constant Friendship this Government has always shewn to the Indians of the Six Nations; and that, from their first Settlement in the Country, their Interest has been put on the same Foot with our own. And as long as you shall act up to your Engagements, you will never want the most substantial Proofs that we can give of our Regard for your Nations.

You tell us, that at the Beginning of the War, you receiv'd a Message from all the English, to stand neuter, and to prevail with your Allies to do the same; that in Compliance therewith, you did stand neuter, and all your Allies, except the Praying Indians, who promis'd, but broke their Word: That the French commencing Hostilities, you received repeated Messages from the English to continue neuter no longer, but to take up their Hatchet against the French; and that you and your Allies have accordingly done this. Brethren, You did well to hearken to the Messages sent by the English. Your Allies so readily concurring with you, shews you keep up a good Understanding with them; for which you are to be commended. You live in small Tribes at a Distance from one another: Separate, you will be easily overcome; united, it will be difficult, if not impossible, to hurt you: Like the Strings on which you put your Wampum, a single Thread is soon snapp'd, a few require more Strength; but if you weave them into a Belt, and fasten them tight together, it must be a strong Hand that can break it.

We are pleased to hear, that at the pressing Instances of the Govenors of New-York and New-England, you have taken up the Hatchet against the French; who you know, notwithstanding their fair Speeches, have been from the Beginning your inveterate Enemies: And in Confirmation that we approve of what you have done, we give you this Belt.

By your String of Wampum you tell us, that you observe the English Kettle does not boil high, and you give the String to all the English, to encourage them to put more Fire under their Kettle.

As you address this to all the English, we shall send your String to the other Governors: But to lessen your Concern on this Account, we are to apprize you, that the French were sending large Forces in big Ships, well arm'd with great Cannon, over the Seas to Canada; that the English pursued them, attack'd them, took their Men of War, killed a Number of their Men, and carried the rest Prisoners to England. This Victory put a Stop for the Present to the Expedition intended against Canada: You are therefore not to judge by the Appearance Things make now, that the English Fire is going out; but that this is only accidental, and it will soon blaze again.

As this is the first Visit paid us by our Brethren the Warriors living on the Branches of Ohio, to shew that we take it kindly of them, and are desirous to cultivate and improve the Friendship subsisting between the Six Nations and us, we have provided a Present of Goods; a List whereof will be read to you at the Close of our Answer. They are at John Harris's, and the Interpreter will go along with, and deliver them to you there. In the Spring we propose to send Mr. Weiser to you, and he will be furnished with a proper Present to be distributed to all the Indians at Ohio, at Canayiahaga, and about the Lake Erie. In Confirmation of what we say, we give you this String of Wampum.

Having receiv'd by the Traders a kind Message from the Canayiahaga Indians, to let them see we are pleased with it, we have sent them a small Present of Powder and Lead, by Mr. Croghan, which you will inform them of, and likewise of our further Intentions in their Favour, with this String of Wampum, which is given you for that Purpose.

The President and Council at your Recommendation will take Care to give Scaiohady a Present for his own private Use, and his old Friend Mr. Logan will do the same.

A String of Wampum.

The Indian Speaker having consulted with Scaiohady, took up the Belt and Strings of Wampum in the Order they were presented, and repeating the Substance of every Paragraph, express'd high Satisfaction at what the Council had said, and promis'd to send the String of Wampum to the Canayiahaga Indians, who being their own Flesh and Blood, they were pleased with the Regards shewn to them. And in Testimony of their intire

Satisfaction and Devotion to the English Interest, they gave the Indian Marks of Approbation, and danc'd the Warrior Dance.

A true Copy,

Nov. 25. 1747   Richard Peters, Secretary.

Compiler's Note: The above treaty is known as the "Treaty between the President and Council of the Province of Pennsylvania, and the Indians of Ohio, held at Philadelphia, November 13, 1747," and was "Printed and Sold by B. Franklin, at the New Printing-Office, near the Market. MDCCXLVIII." This treaty was republished in facsimile by The Historical Society of Pennsylvania, in 1938, as part of a book entitled INDIAN TREATIES Printed By Benjamin Franklin 1736-1762.

TREATY WITH THE CHICKESAWS, UPPER AND LOWER CREEKS, CHACTAWS, CHEROKEES, AND CATAWBA, 1763

At a Congress held at Augusta in the Province of Georgia on the 10th of Nov: in the year of our Lord God 1763. by their Excellencies

James Wright.		Georgia
Arthur Dobbs.	Esq^{Re} Governors	N° Carolina
Thos Boone		S° Carolina

The Honble Francis Fauqier Esq^{Re} Lieut: Gov: of Virginia and John Stuart Esq^{Re} Agent and Superintendant of Southern Indian Affairs.

A Treaty for the Preservation and continuance of a firm and perfect Peace and Friendship Between His most sacred Majesty George the Third by the Grace of God of Great Britain France and Ireland King Defender of the Faith and so forth and the several Indian Chiefs herein named who are authorized by the King's Head Men and Warriors of the Chickesaws Upper and Lower Creeks Chactaws Cherokees and Catawbas for and in behalf of themselves and their several Nations and Tribes

Article 1st

That a Perfect and perpetual Peace and sincere Friendship shall be continued between His Majesty King George the Third and all his subjects and the several Nations and Tribes of Indians herein mentioned that is to say the Chickesaws, Upper and Lower Creeks, Chactaws & Catawbas and each Nation of Indians hereby respectively engages to give the utmost attention to preserve and maintain Peace and Friendship between their People and the King of Great Britain and his subjects and shall not commit or permit any kind of Hostilities injury or Damage whatever against them from henceforth and from any cause or under any Pretence whatsoever And for laying the strongest and purest foundation for a perfect and perpetual Peace and Friendship His most sacred Majesty has been graciously pleased to pardon and forgive all past offences and injuries And hereby declares there shall be a general Oblivion of all Crimes Offences and Injuries that may have been heretofore committed or done by any of the said Indian Parties.

Art: 2nd

The Subjects of the Great King George and the aforesaid several Nations of Indians shall forever hereafter be looked upon as one People and the several Governors and Superintendent engage that they will encourage Persons to furnish and supply the several Nations and Tribes of Indians aforesaid with all sorts of Goods usually carried amongst them in the manner in which they now are and which will be sufficient to answer all their Wants.

In consideration whereof the Indian Parties on their Part severally engage in the most solemn manner that the Traders and others who may go amongst them shall be perfectly safe and secure in their several persons and Effects and shall not on any account or pretence whatsoever be molested or disturbed whilst in any of the Indian Towns or Nations or on their journey to or from the Nations.

Art: 3d

The English Governors and Superintendent engage for themselves and their successors as far as they can that they will always give due attention to the Interest of the Indians and will be ready on all Occasions to do them full and ample justice. And the several Indian Parties do expressly promise and engage for themselves severally and for their several Nations and Tribes pursuant to the full Right and Power which they shall have so to do that they will in all cases and upon all occasions do full and ample justice to the English and will use their utmost endeavours to prevent any of their People from giving any disturbance or doing any damage to them in the Settlements or elsewhere as aforesaid either by stealing their Horses killing their Cattle or otherwise or by doing them any Personal hurt or injury And that if any damage be done as aforesaid satisfaction shall be made for the same to the Party injured and that if any Indian or Indians whatever shall hereafter murder or kill a White Man the Offender or Offenders shall without any delay excuse or pretence whatsoever be immediately put to death in a public manner in the Presence of at least two of the English who may be in the Neighborhood where the offence is committed.

And if any White Man shall kill or murder an Indian such White Man shall be tried for the offence in the same manner as if he had murdered a

White Man and if found guilty shall be executed accordingly in the presence of some of the relations of the Indians who may be murdered if they choose to be present.

Art: 4th

Whereas Doubts and Disputes have frequently happened on account of Encroachments or supposed encroachments committed by the English Inhabitants of Georgia on the lands or hunting grounds reserved and claimed by the Creek Indians for their own use.

Wherefore to prevent any mistakes Doubts or Disputes for the future and in consideration of the great marks of Clemency and Friendship extended to us the said Creek Indians. We the King's Head Men and Warriors of the several Nations and Towns of both Upper and Lower Creeks by Virtue and in Pursuance of the full Right and Power which we now have and are possessed of Have consented and agreed that for the future the Boundary between the English Settlements and our Lands and hunting Grounds shall be known and settled by a Line extending up Savannah River to Little River and back to the Fork of Little River to the Ends of the South Branch of Briar Creek and down that Branch to the Lower Creek Path and along the Lower Creek Path to the Main Stream of Ogeechee River and down the Main Stream of that River just below the Path leading from Mount Pleasant and from thence in a Line cross to Santa Savilla on the Matamaha River and from thence to the Southward as far as Georgia extends or may be extended to remain to be regulated agreeable to former Treaties and His Majesty's Royal Instruction a copy of which was lately sent to you.

And We the Catawba Head Men and Warriors in Confirmation of an Agreement heretofore entered into with the White People declare that we will remain satisfied with the Tract of Land of Fifteen Miles square a Survey of which by our consent and at our request has been already begun and the respective Governors and Superintendent on their Parts promise and engage that the aforesaid survey shall be compleated and that the Catawbas shall not in any respect be molested by any of the King's subjects within the said Lines but shall be indulged in the usual Manner of hunting Elsewhere.

And we do by these Presents give grant and confirm unto his most sacred Majesty King George the Third all such Lands whatsoever as we the said Creek Indians have at any time heretofore been possessed of or claimed as our hunting grounds which lye between the sea and the River Savannah and the Lines herein before mentioned and described to hold the same unto the Great King George and his successors for ever. And we do fully and absolutely agree that from henceforth the above Lines and Boundary shall be the mark of Division of Lands between the English and Us the Creek

Indians notwithstanding any former agreement or boundary to the contrary. And that we will not disturb the English in their Settlements or otherwise within the Lines aforesaid.

In consideration whereof it is agreed on the Part of his Majesty King George that none of His subjects shall settle upon or disturb the Indians in the Grounds or Lands to the Westward of the Lines herein before described and that if any shall presume to do so, then on complaint made to the Indians the party shall be proceeded against for the same and punished according to the Laws of the English.

In Testimony whereof we the underwritten have signed this present Treaty and put to it the Seals of our Arms the day and year above written And the several Kings and Chiefs of the several Nations and Tribes of Indians have also sent their Hands and Seals to the same at the Time and Place aforesaid.

Ja. Wright Govenor of Georgia		L. S.		
Arthur Dobbs Govenor of North Carolina		L. S.		
Tho⁵ Boone Govenor of South Carolina		L. S.		
Frans Fauquier Lt. Gov. of Virginia		L. S.		
John Stuart Supert South District		L. S.		
Pia Matta his Mark	L. S.		Col Ayres' Mark	L. S.
Capt Ellick his Mark	L. S.		*	
Sampiafi his Mark	L. S.		*	
*			*	
*			*	
*			The Wolfes Mark	L. S.
*			*	
Attakullakulla's mark	L. S.		*	
*			*	
*			*	

* indicates signers whose names were not legible enough, or could not be confirmed by another document, for the compiler of this work to attempt quoting.

By Command of these

Excellences   James Wright
Arthur Dobbs   Esquires
Thomas Boone

The Honble Francis Fauquier &.
John Stuart Esq^Re Superintendent
Fenwicke Bull Secretary

TREATY WITH THE DELAWARES, 1778

Articles of agreement and confederation, made and entered into by Andrew and Thomas Lewis, Esquires, Commissioners for, and in Behalf of the United States of North-America of the one Part, and Capt. White Eyes, Capt, John Kill Buck, Junior, and Capt. Pipe, Deputies and Chief Men of the Delaware Nation of the other Part.

ARTICLE I.

That all offences or acts of hostilities by one, or either of the contracting parties against the other, be mutually forgiven, and buried in the depth of oblivion, never more to be had in remembrance.

ARTICLE II.

That a perpetual peace and friendship shall from henceforth take place, and subsist between the contracting parties aforesaid, through all succeeding generations: and if either of the parties are engaged in a just and necessary war with any other nation or nations, that then each shall assist the other in due proportion to their abilities, till their enemies are brought to reasonable terms of accommodation: and that if either of them shall discover any hostile designs forming against the other, they shall give the earliest notice thereof, that timeous measures may be taken to prevent their ill effect.

ARTICLE III.

And whereas the United States are engaged in a just and necessary war, in defence and support of life, liberty and independence, against the King of England and his adherents, and as said King is yet possessed of several posts and forts on the lakes and other places, the reduction of which is of great importance to the peace and security of the contracting parties, and as the most practicable way for the troops of the United States to some of the posts and forts is by passing through the country of the Delaware nation, the aforesaid deputies, on behalf of themselves and their nation, do hereby stipulate and agree to give a free passage through their country to the troops aforesaid, and the same to conduct by the nearest and best ways to the posts, forts or towns of the enemies of the United States, affording to said troops such supplies of corn, meat, horses, or whatever may be in their power for the accommodation of such troops, on the commanding officer's, &c. paying, or engageing to pay, the full value of whatever they can supply them with. And the said deputies, on the behalf of their nation, engage to join the troops of the United States aforesaid, with such a number of their best and most expert warriors as they can spare, consistent with their own safety, and act in concert with them; and for the better security of the old men, women and children of the aforesaid nation, whilst their warriors are engaged against the common enemy, it is agreed on the part of the United States, that a fort of sufficient strength and capacity be built at the expense of the said States, with such assistance as it may be in the power of the said Delaware Nation to give, in the most convenient place, and advantageous situation, as shall be agreed on by the commanding officer of the troops aforesaid, with the advice and concurrence of the deputies of the aforesaid Delaware Nation, which fort shall be garrisoned by such a number of the troops of the United States, as the commanding officer can spare for the present, and hereafter by such numbers, as the wise men of the United States in council, shall think most conducive to the common good.

ARTICLE IV.

For the better security of the peace and friendship now entered into by the contracting parties, against all infractions of the same by the citizens of either party, to the prejudice of the other, neither party shall proceed to the infliction of punishments on the citizens of the other, otherwise than by securing the offender or offenders by imprisonment, or any other competent means, till a fair and impartial trial can be had by judges or juries of both parties, as near as can be to the laws, customs and usages of the contracting parties and natural justice: The mode of such trials to be hereafter fixed by the wise men of the United States in Congress assembled, with the assistance of such deputies of the Delaware nation, as may be appointed to act in concert with them in adjusting this matter to their mutual liking. And it is further agreed between the parties aforesaid, that neither shall entertain or give countenance to the enemies of the other, or protect in their respective states, criminal fugitives, servants or slaves, but the same to apprehend, and secure and deliver to the State or States, to which such enemies, criminals, servants or slaves respectively belong.

ARTICLE V.

Whereas the confederation entered into by the Delaware nation and the United States, renders the first dependent on the latter for all the articles of clothing, utensils and implements of war, and it is judged not only reasonable, but indispensably necessary, that the aforesaid Nation be supplied with such articles from time to time, as far as the United States may have it in their power, by a well-regulated trade, under the conduct of an intelligent, candid agent, with an adequate salary, one more influenced by the love of his country, and a constant attention to the duties of his department by promoting the common interest, than the sinister purposes of converting and binding all the duties of his office to his private emolument: Convinced of the necessity of such measures, the Commissioners of the United States, at the earnest solicitation of the deputies aforesaid, have engaged in behalf of the United States, that such a trade shall be afforded said nation, conducted on such principles of mutual interest as the wisdom of the United States in Congress assembled shall think most conducive to adopt for their mutual convenience.

ARTICLE VI.

Whereas the enemies of the United States have endeavored, by every artifice in their power, to possess the Indians in general with an opinion, that it is the design of the States aforesaid, to extirpate the Indians and take possession of their country: to obviate such false suggestion, the United States do engage to guarantee to the aforesaid nation of Delawares, and their heirs, all their territorial rights in the fullest and most ample manner, as it hath been bounded by former treaties, as long as they the said Delaware nation shall abide by, and hold fast the chain of friendship now entered into. And it is further agreed on between the contracting parties should it for the future be found conducive for the mutual interest of both parties to invite any other tribes who have been friends to the interest of the United States, to join the present confederation, and to form a state whereof the Delaware nation shall be the head, and have a representation in Congress: Provided, nothing contained in this article to be considered as conclusive until it meets with the approbation of Congress. And it is also the intent and meaning of this article, that no protection or countenance shall be afforded to any who are at present our enemies, by which they might escape the punishment they deserve.

In witness whereof, the parties have hereunto interchangeably set their hands and seals, at Fort Pitt, September seventeenth, anno Domini one thousand seven hundred and seventy-eight.

Andrew Lewis,	L. S.
Thomas Lewis,	L. S.
White Eyes, his x mark,	L. S.
The Pipe, his x mark,	L. S.
John Kill Buck, his x mark,	L. S.

In presence of—

Lach'n McIntosh, brigadier-general, commander the Western Deparment.
Daniel Brodhead, colonel Eighth Pennsylvania Regiment,
W. Crawford, colonel,
John Campbell,
John Stephenson,
John Gibson, colonel Thirteenth Virginia Regiment,
A. Graham, brigade major,
Lach. McIntosh, jr., major brigade,
Benjamin Mills,
Joseph L. Finley, captain Eighth Pennsylvania Regiment,
John Finley, captain Eighth Pennsylvania Regiment.

TREATY WITH THE SIX NATIONS, 1784

Articles concluded at Fort Stanwix, on the twenty-second day of October, one thousand seven hundred and eighty-four, between Oliver Wolcott, Richard Butler, and Arthur Lee, Commissioners Plenipotentiary from the United States, in Congress assembled, on the one Part, and the Sachems and Warriors of the Six Nations, on the other.

The United States of America give peace to the Senecas, Mohawks, Onondagas and Cayugas, and receive them into their protection upon the following conditons:

ARTICLE I.

Six hostages shall be immediately delivered to the commissioners by the said nations, to remain in possession of the United States, till all the prisoners, white and black, which were taken by the said Senecas, Mohawks, Onondagas and Cayugas, or by any of them, in the late war, from among the people of the United States, shall be delivered up.

ARTICLE II.

The Oneida and Tuscarora nations shall be secured in the possession of the lands on which they are settled.

ARTICLE III.

A line shall be drawn, beginning at the mouth of a creek about four miles east of Niagara, called Oyonwayea, or Johnston's Landing-Place, upon the lake named by the Indians Oswego, and by us Ontario; from thence southerly in a direction always four miles east of the carrying-path, between Lake Erie and Ontario, to the mouth of Tehoseroron or Buffaloe Creek on Lake Erie; thence south to the north boundary of the state of Pennyslvania;

thence west to the end of the said north boundary; thence south along the west boundary of the said state, to the river Ohio; the said line from the mouth of the Oyonwayea to the Ohio, shall be the western boundary of the lands of the Six Nations, so that the Six Nations shall and do yield to the United States, all claims to the country west of the said boundary, and then they shall be secured in the peaceful possession of the lands they inhabit east and north of the same, reserving only six miles square round the fort of Oswego, to the United States, for the support of the same.

ARTICLE IV.

The Commissioners of the United States, in consideration of the present circumstances of the Six Nations, and in execution of the humane and liberal views of the United States upon the signing of the above articles, will order goods to be delivered to the said Six Nations for their use and comfort.

Oliver Wolcott,	L. S.	Oneidas:	
Richard Butler,	L. S.	Otyadonenghti, his x mark,	L. S.
Arthur Lee,	L. S.	Dagaheari, his x mark,	L. S.
Mohawks:		Cayuga:	
Onogwendahonji, his x mark,	L. S.	Oraghgoanendagen, his x	
Touighnatogon, his x mark,	L. S.	mark,	L. S.
Onondagas:		Tuscaroras:	
Oheadarighton, his x mark,	L. S.	Ononghsawenghti, his x mark,	L. S.
Kendarindgon, his x mark,	L. S.	Tharondawagon, his x mark,	L. S.
Senekas:		Seneka Abeal:	
Tayagonendagighti, his x mark,	L. S.	Kayenthoghke, his x mark,	L. S.
Tehonwaeaghrigagi, his x mark,	L. S.		

Witnesses:

Sam. Jo. Atlee,
Wm. Maclay,
Fras. Johnston,
    Pennsylvania Commissioners.
Aaron Hill,
Alexander Campbell,
Saml. Kirkland, missionary,

James Dean,
Saml. Montgomery,
Derick Lane, captain,
John Mercer, lieutenant,
William Pennington, lieutenant,
Maholn Hord, ensign,
Hugh Peebles.

TREATY WITH
THE WYANDOT, ETC., 1785

Articles of a treaty concluded at Fort M'Intosh, the twenty-first day of January, one thousand seven hundred and eighty-five, between the Commissioners Plenipotentiary of the United States of America, of the one Part, and the Sachems and Warriors of the Wiandot, Delaware, Chippawa and Ottawa Nations of the other.

The Commissioners Plenipotentiary of the United States in Congress assembled, give peace to the Wiandot, Delaware, Chippewa and Ottawa nations of Indians, on the following conditions:

ARTICLE I.

Three chiefs, one from among the Wiandot, and two from among the Delaware nations, shall be delivered up to the Commissioners of the United States, to be by them retained till all the prisoners, white and black, taken by the said nations, or any of them, shall be restored.

ARTICLE II.

The said Indian nations do acknowledge themselves and all their tribes to be under the protection of the United States and of no other sovereign whatsoever.

ARTICLE III.

The boundary line between the United States and the Wiandot and Delaware nations, shall begin at the mouth of the river Cayahoga, and run thence up the said river to the portage between that and the Tuscarawas branch of Meskingum; then down the said branch to the forks at the crossing place above Fort Lawrence; then westerly to the portage of the Big

26

Miami, which runs into the Ohio, at the mouth of which branch the fort stood which was taken by the French in one thousand seven hundred and fifty-two; then along the said portage to the Great Miami or Ome river, and down the south-east side of the same to its mouth; thence along the south shore of lake Erie, to the mouth of Cayahoga where it began.

ARTICLE IV.

The United States allot all the lands contained within the said lines to the Wiandot and Delaware nations, to live and to hunt on, and to such of the Ottawa nation as now live thereon; saving and reserving for the establishment of trading posts, six miles square at the mouth of Miami or Ome river, and the same at the portage on that branch of the Big Miami which runs into the Ohio, and the same on the lake of Sanduske where the fort formerly stood, and also two miles square on each side of the lower rapids of Sanduske river, which posts and the lands annexed to them, shall be to the use and under the government of the United States.

ARTICLE V.

If any citizen of the United States, or other person not being an Indian, shall attempt to settle on any of the lands alloted to the Wiandot and Delaware nations in this treaty, except on the lands reserved to the United States in the preceding article, such person shall forfeit the protection of the United States, and the Indians may punish him as they please.

ARTICLE VI.

The Indians who sign this treaty, as well in behalf of all their tribes as of themselves, do acknowledge the lands east, south and west of the lines described in the third article, so far as the said Indians formerly claimed the same, to belong to the United States; and none of their tribes shall presume to settle upon the same, or any part of it.

ARTICLE VII.

The post of Detroit, with a district beginning at the mouth of the river Rosine, on the west end of lake Erie, and running west six miles up the southern bank of the said river, thence northerly and always six miles west of the strait, till it strikes the lake St. Clair, shall be also reserved to the sole use of the United States.

ARTICLE VIII.

In the same manner the post of Michillimachenac with its dependencies, and twelve miles square about the same, shall be reserved to the use of the United States.

ARTICLE IX.

If any Indian or Indians shall commit a robbery or murder on any citizen of the United States, the tribe to which such offenders may belong, shall be bound to deliver them up at the nearest post, to be punished according to the ordinances of the United States.

ARTICLE X.

The Commissioners of the United States, in pursuance of the humane and liberal views of Congress, upon this treaty's being signed, will direct goods to be distributed among the different tribes for their use and comfort.

SEPARATE ARTICLE

It is agreed that the Delaware chiefs, Kelelamand or lieutenant-colonel Henry, Hengue Pushees or the Big Cat, Wicocalind or Captain White Eyes, who took up the hatchet for the United States, and their families, shall be received into the Delaware nation, in the same situation and rank as before the war, and enjoy their due portions of the lands given to the Wiandot and Delaware nations in this treaty, as fully as if they had not taken part with America, or as any other person or persons in the said nations.

Go. Clark,	L. S.	Talapoxic, his x mark,	L. S.
Richard Butler,	L. S.	Wingenum, his x mark,	L. S.
Arthur Lee,	L. S.	Packelant, his x mark,	L. S.
Daunghquat, his x mark,	L. S.	Gingewanno, his x mark,	L. S.
Abraham Kuhn, his x mark,	L. S.	Waanoos, his x mark,	L. S.
Ottawerreri, his x mark,	L. S.	Konalawassee, his x mark,	L. S.
Hobocan, his x mark,	L. S.	Shawnaqum, his x mark,	L. S.
Walendightun, his x mark,	L. S.	Quecookkia, his x mark,	L. S.

Witness:

Sam'l J. Atlee,
Fras. Johnston,
   Pennsylvania Commissioners.
Alex. Campbell,
Jos. Harmar, lieutenant-colonel commandant.
Alex. Lowrey,
Joseph Nicholas, interpreter.

I. Bradford,
George Slaughter,
Van Swearingen,
John Boggs,
G. Evans,
D. Luckett,

TREATY WITH THE CHOCTAW, 1786

Articles of a treaty concluded at Hopewell, on the Keowée, near Seneca Old Town, between Benjamin Hawkins, Andrew Pickens and Joseph Martin, Commissioners Plenipotentiary of the United States of America, of the one part; and Yockonahoma, great Medal Chief of Soonacoha; Yockehoopoie, leading Chief of Bugtoogoloo; Mingohoopoie, leading Chief of Hashoogua; Tobocoh, great Medal Chief of Congetoo; Pooshemastubie, Gorget Captain of Senayazo; and thirteen small Medal Chiefs of the first Class, twelve Medal and Gorget Captains, Commissioners Plenipotentiary of all the Choctaw Nation, of the other part.

The Commissioners Plenipotentiary of the United States of America give peace to all the Choctaw nation, and receive them into the favor and protection of the United States of America, on the following conditions:

ARTICLE I

The Commissioners Plenipotentiary of all the Choctaw nation, shall restore all the prisoners, citizens of the United States, or subjects of their allies, to their entire liberty, if any there be in the Choctaw nation. They shall also restore all the negroes, and all other property taken during the late war, from the citizens, to such person, and at such time and place as the Commissioners of the United States of America shall appoint, if any there be in the Choctaw nation.

ARTICLE II

The Commissioners Plenipotentiary of all the Choctaw nation, do hereby acknowledge the tribes and towns of the said nation, and the lands within the boundary allotted to the said Indians to live and hunt on, as mentioned in the third article, to be under the protection of the United States of America, and of no other soverign whosoever.

ARTICLE III

The boundary of the lands hereby allotted to the Choctow nation to live and hunt on, within the limits of the United States of America, is and shall be the following, viz. Beginning at a point on the thirty-first degree of north latitude, where the Eastern boundary of the Natches district shall touch the same; thence east along the said thirty-first degree of north latitude, being the southern boundary of the United States of America, until it shall strike the eastern boundary of the lands on which the Indians of the said nation did live and hunt on the twenty-ninth of November, one thousand seven hundred and eighty-two, while they were under the protection of the King of Great-Britain; thence northerly along the said eastern boundary, until it shall meet the northern boundary of the said lands; thence westerly along the said northern boundary, until it shall meet the western boundary thereof; thence southerly along the same to the beginning: saving and re-serving for the establishment of trading posts, three tracts or parcels of land of six miles square, at such places as the United [States] in Congress assembled shall think proper; which posts, and the lands annexed to them, shall be to the use and under the government of the United States of America.

ARTICLE IV

If any citizen of the United States, or other person not being an Indian, shall attempt to settle on any of the lands hereby allotted to the Indians to live and hunt on, such person shall forfeit the protection of the United States of America, and the Indians may punish him or not as they please.

ARTICLE V

If any Indian or Indians, or persons, residing among them, or who shall take refuge in their nation, shall commit a robbery or murder or other capital crime on any citizen of the United States of America, or person under their protection, the tribe to which such offender may belong, or the nation, shall be bound to deliver him or them up to be punished according to the ordinances of the United States in Congress assembled: Provided, that the punishment shall not be greater than if the robbery or murder, or other capital crime, had been committed by a citizen on a citizen.

ARTICLE VI

If any citizen of the United States of America, or person under their pro-tection, shall commit a robbery or murder, or other capital crime, on any

Indian, such offender or offenders shall be punished in the same manner as if the robbery or murder, or other capital crime, had been committed on a citizen of the United States of America; and the punishment shall be in presence of some of the Choctaws, if any will attend at the time and place; and that they may have an opportunity so to do, due notice, if practicable, of the time such intended punishment, shall be sent to some one of the tribes.

ARTICLE VII

It is understood that the punishment of the innocent, under the idea of retaliation, is unjust, and shall not be practiced on either side, except where there is a manifest violation of this treaty; and then it shall be preceded, first by a demand of justice, and if refused, then by a declaration of hostilities.

ARTICLE VIII

For the benefit and comfort of the Indians, and for the prevention of injuries or oppressions on the part of the citizens or Indians, the United States in Congress assembled, shall have the sole and exclusive right of regulating the trade with the Indians, and managing all their affairs in such manner as they think proper.

ARTICLE IX

Until the pleasure of Congress be known, respecting the eighth article, all traders, citizens of the United States of America, shall have liberty to go to any of the tribes or town of the Choctaws, to trade with them, and they shall be protected in their persons and property, and kindly treated.

ARTICLE X

The said Indians shall give notice to the citizens of the United States of America, of any designs which they may know or suspect to be formed in any neighboring tribe, or by any person whosoever, against the peace, trade or interest of the United States of America.

ARTICLE XI

The hatchet shall be forever buried, and the peace given by the United States of America, and friendship re-established between the said states on the one part, and all the Choctaw nation on the other part, shall be universal; and the contracting parties shall use their utmost endeavors to maintain the peace given as aforsaid, and friendship re-established.

In witness of all and every thing herein determined, between the United States of America and all the Choctaws, we, their underwritten commissioners, by virtue of our full powers, have signed this definitive treaty, and have caused our seals to be hereunto affixed.

Done at Hopewell, on the Keowee, this third day of January, in the year of our Lord one thousand seven hundred and eighty-six.

Benjamin Hawkins,	L. S.	Yockenahoma, his x mark,	L. S.
Andrew Pickens,	L. S.	Yockehoopoie, his x mark,	L. S.
Jos. Martin,	L. S.	Mingohoopoie, his x mark,	L. S.
Tobocoh, his x mark,	L. S.	Cshecoopoohoomoch, his x mark,	L. S.
Pooshemastuby, his x mark,	L. S.	Stonakoohoopoie, his x mark,	L. S.
Pooshahooma, his x mark,	L. S.	Tushkoheegohta, his x mark,	L. S.
Tuscoonoohoopoie, his x mark,	L. S.	Teshuhenochloch, his x mark,	L. S.
Shinshemastuby, his x mark,	L. S.	Pooshonaltla, his x mark,	L. S.
Yoopahooma, his x mark,	L. S.	Okanconnooba, his x mark,	L. S.
Stoonokoohoopoie, his x mark,	L. S.	Autoonachuba, his x mark,	L. S.
Tehakuhbay, his x mark,	L. S.	Pangehooloch, his x mark,	L. S.
Pooshemastuby, his x mark,	L. S.	Steabee, his x mark,	L. S.
Tuskkahoomoih, his x mark,	L. S.	Tenetchenna, his x mark,	L. S.
Tushkahoomock, his x mark,	L. S.	Tushkementahock, his x mark,	L. S.
Yoostenochla, his x mark,	L. S.	Tushtallay, his x mark,	L. S.
Tootehooma, his x mark,	L. S.	Cshnaangehabba, his x mark,	L. S.
Toobenahoomoch, his x mark,	L. S.	Cunnopoie, his x mark,	L. S.

Witness:

    Wm. Blount,
    John Woods,
    Saml. Taylor,
    Robert Anderson,
    Benj. Lawrence.
    John Pitchlynn,
    James Cole,
        Interpreters

TREATY WITH THE SIX NATIONS, 1789

Articles of a treaty made at Fort Harmar, the ninth day of January, in the year of our Lord one thousand seven hundred and eighty-nine, between Arthur St. Clair, esquire, governor of the territory of the United States of America, nort-west of the river Ohio, and commissioner plenipotentiary of the said United States, for removing all causes of controversy, regulating trade, and settling boundaries, between the Indian nations in the northern department and the said United States, of the one part, and the sachems and warriors of the Six Nations, of the other part;

ART 1. WHEREAS the United States, in congress assembled, did, by their commissioners, Oliver Wolcott, Richard Butler, and Arthur Lee, esquires, duly appointed for that purpose, at a treaty held with the said Six Nations, viz: with the Mohawks, Oneidas, Onondagas, Tuscaroras, Cayugas, and Senekas, at fort Stanwix, on the twenty-second day of October, one thousand seven hundred and eighty-four, give peace to the said nations, and receive them into their friendship and protection: And whereas the said nations have now agreed to and with the said Arthur St. Clair, to renew and confirm all the engagements and stipulations entered into at the beforementioned treaty at fort Stanwix: and whereas it was then and there agreed, between the United States of America and the said Six Nations, that a boundary line should be fixed between the lands of the said Six Nations and the territory of the said United States, which boundary line is as follows, viz: Beginning at the mouth of a creek, about four miles east of Niagara, called Onwnwayea, or Johnston's Landing Place, upon the lake named by the Indians Oswego, and by us Ontario; from thence southerly, in a direction always four miles east of the carrying place, between lake Erie and lake Ontario, to the mouth of Tehoseroton, or Buffalo creek, upon lake Erie; thence south, to the northern boundary of the state of Pennsylvania; thence west, to the end of the said north boundary; thence south, along the west boundary of the said state to the river Ohio. The said line, from the mouth of Onwnwayea to the Ohio, shall be the western boundary of the lands of the Six Nations, so that the Six Nations shall and do yield to the United

States, all claim to the country west of the said boundary; and then they shall be secured in the possession of the lands they inhabit east, north, and south of the same, reserving only six miles square, round the fort of Oswego, for the support of the same. The said Six Nations, except the Mohawks, none of whom have attended at this time, for and in consideration of the peace then granted to them, the presents they then received, as well as in consideration of a quantity of goods, to the value of three thousand dollars, now delivered to them by the said Arthur St. Clair, the receipt whereof they do hereby acknowledge, do hereby renew and confirm the said boundary line in the words beforementioned, to the end that it may be and remain as a division line between the lands of the said Six Nations and the territory of the United States, forever. And the undersigned Indians, as well in their own names as in the name of their respective tribes and nations, their heirs and descendents, for the considerations beforementioned, do relaese, quit claim, relinquish, and cede, to the United States of America, all the lands west of the said boundary or division line, and between the said line and the strait, from the mouth of Onowayea and Buffalo Creek, for them, the said United States of America, to have and to hold the same, in true and absolute propriety, forever.

ART. 2. The United States of America confirm to the Six Nations, all the lands which they inhabited, lying east and north of the beforementioned boundary line, and relinquish and quit claim to the same and every part thereof, excepting only six miles square round the fort of Oswego, which six miles square round said fort is again reserved to the United States by these presents.

ART. 3. The Oneida and Tuscarora nations, are also again secured and confirmed in the possession of their respective lands.

ART. 4. The United States of America renew and confirm the peace and friendship entered into with the Six Nations, (except the Mohawks), at the treaty beforementioned, held at fort Stanwix, declaring the same to be perpetual. And if the Mohawks shall, within six months, declare their assent to the same, they shall be considered as included.

Done at Fort Harmer, on the Muskingum, the day and year first above written.

In witness whereof, the parties have hereunto, interchangeably, set their hands and seals.

Ar. St. Clair,	L. S.	Owenewa, or Thrown in the	
Cageaga, or Dogs Round the Fire,	L. S.	Water, his x mark,	L. S.
Sawedowa, or The Blast,	L. S.	Gyantwaia, or Cornplanter,	
Kiondushhowa, or Swimming Fish,	L. S.	his x mark,	L. S.
Oncahye, or Dancing Feather,	L. S.	Gyasota, or Big Cross, his	L. S.
Sohaeas, or Falling Mountain,	L. S.	x mark,	L. S.

Otachsaka, or Broken Tomahawk, his x mark, L. S.
Tekahias, or Long Tree, his x mark, L. S.
Onecnsetee, or Loaded Man, his x mark, L. S.
Kiahtulaho, or Snake, L. S.
Aqueia, or Bandy Legs, L. S.
Kiandogewa, or Big Tree, his x mark, L. S.

Kannassee, or New Arrow, L. S.
Achiout, or Half Town,
Anachout, or The Wasp, his x mark, L. S.
Chishekoa, or Wood Bug, his x mark, L. S.
Sessewa, or Big Bale of a Kettle, L. S.
Sciahowa, or Council Keeper, L. S.
Tewanias, or Broken Twig, L. S.
Sonachshowa, or Full Moon, L. S.
Cachunwasse, or Twenty Canoes, L. S.
Hickonquash, or Tearing Asunder, L. S.

In presence of—
  Jos. Harmer, lieutenant—colonel commanding First U.S. Regiment and brigadier— general by brevet,
  Richard Butler,
  Jno. Gibson,
  Will. M'Curdy, captain,
  Ed. Denny, ensign First U.S. Regiment,
  A. Hartshorn, ensign,
  Robt. Thompson, ensign, First U.S. Regiment,
  Fran. Leile, ensign,
  Joseph Nicholas.

SEPARATE ARTICLE

Should a robbery or murder be committed by an Indian or Indians of the Six Nations, upon the citizens or subjects of the United States, or any of them, upon any of the Indians of the said nations, the parties accused of the same shall be tried, and if found guilty, be punished according to the laws of the state, or of the territory of the United States, as the case may be, where the same was committed. And should any horses be stolen, either by the Indians of the said nations, from the citizens or subjects of the United States, or any of them, or by any of the said citizens or subjects from any of the said Indians, they may be reclaimed into whose possession soever they may have come; and, upon due proof, shall be restored, any sale in open market not withstanding; and the persons convicted shall be punished with the utmost severity the laws will admit. And the said nations engage to deliver the persons that may be accused, of their nations, of either of the beforementioned crimes, at the nearest post of the United States, if the crime was committed within the territory of the United States; or to the civil authority of the state, if it shall have happened within any of the United States.

Ar. St. Clair.

TREATY WITH
THE ONEIDA, ETC., 1794

A treaty between the United States and the Oneida, Tuscorora and Stockbridge Indians, dweeling in the Country of the Oneidas.

WHEREAS, in the late war between Great-Britain and the United States of America, a body of the Oneida and Tuscorora and the Stockbridge Indians, adhered faithfully to the United States, and assisted them with their warriors; and in consequence of this adherence and assistance, the Oneidas and Tuscororas, at an unfortunate period of the war, were driven from their homes, and their houses were burnt and their property destroyed: And as the United States in the time of their distress, acknowledged their obligations to these faithful friends, and promised to reward them: and the United States being now in a condition to fulfil the promises then made: the following articles are stipulated by the respective parties for that purpose; to be in force when ratified by the President and Senate.

ARTICLE I

The United States will pay the sum of five thousand dollars, to be distributed among individuals of the Oneida and Tuscorora nations, as a compensation for their individual losses and services during the late war between Great-Britain and the United States. The only man of the Kaughnawaugas now remaining in the Oneida country, as well as some few very meritorious persons of the Stockbridge Indians, will be considered in the distribution.

ARTICLE II

For the general accommodations of these Indian nations, residing in the country of the Oneidas, the United States will cause to be erected a complete grist-mill and saw-mill, in a situation to serve the present principal settlements of these nations. Or if such one convenient situation cannot be found, then the United States will cause to be erected two such grist-mills and saw-mills, in places where it is now known the proposed accommodation may be effected. Of this the United States will judge.

ARTICLE III

The United States will provide, during three years after the mills shall be completed, for the expense of employing one or two suitable persons to manage the mills, to keep them in repair, to instruct some young men of the three nations in the arts of the miller and sawyer, and to provide teams and utensils for carrying on the work of the mills.

ARTICLE IV

The United States will pay one thousand dollars, to be applied in building a convenient church at Oneida, in the place of the one which was there burnt by the enemy, in the late war.

ARTICLE V

In consideration of the above stipulations to be performed on the part of the United States, the Oneida, Tuscorora and Stockbridge Indians aforementioned, now acknowledge themselves satisfied, and relinquish all other claims of compensation and rewards for their losses and services in the late war. Excepting only the unsatisfied claims of such men of the said nations as bore commissions under the United States, for any arrears which may be due to them as officers.

In witness whereof, the chiefs of those nations, residing in the country of the Oneidas, and Timothy Pickering, agent for the United States, have hereto set their hands and seals, at Oneida, the second day of December, in the year one thousand seven hundred and ninety-four.

Timothy Pickering,   L. S.

Wolf Tribe:		Bear Tribe:	
Odotsaihte, his x mark,	L. S.	Lodowik Kohsauwetau, his x mark	L. S.
Konnoquenyau, his x mark,	L. S.	Cornelius Kauhiktoton, his x mark	L. S.
Head sachems of the Oneidas.			
John Skenendo, eldest chief,		Thos. Osauhataugaunlot, his x	
his x mark,	L. S.	mark,	L. S.
		War chiefs.	

Turtle Tribe:		Tuscaroras:	
Shonohleyo, war chief, his		Thaulondauwaugon, sachem, his	
x mark,	L. S.	x mark,	L. S.
Peter Konnauterlook, sachem,		Kanatjogh, or Nicholas Cusick,	
his x mark,	L. S.	war chief, his x mark,	L. S.
Daniel Teouneslees, son of			
Skenendo, war chief, his			
x mark,	L. S.		

Witnesses to the signing and sealing of the agent of the United States, and of the chiefs of the chiefs of the Oneida and Tuscarora nations:

      S. Kirkland

      James Dean, Interpreter.

Witnesses to the signing and sealing of the four chiefs of the Stockbridge Indians, whose names are below:

      Saml. Kirkland,

      John Sergeant.

Stockbridge Indians:

Hendrick Aupaumut,	L. S.
Joseph Quonney,	L. S.
John Konkapot,	L. S.
Jacob Konkapot,	L. S.

TREATY WITH
THE PASSAMAQUADDY, 1794
(Resolves of Massachusetts*)

To all People to whom this Present agreement Shall be made known, We Alexander Campbell, John Allan, & George Stillman Esquires a Committee appointed and Authorised by the General Court of the Commonwealth of Massachusetts, To Treat with and assign Certain lands to the Passamaquaddy Indians and Others Connected with them agreeable to a Resolve of Said General Court of ye Twentysixth of June in the year of our Lord one thousand Seven hundred & ninety four of the one part and the Subscribing Chiefs & Others For Themselves and in behalf of the said Passamaquady Tribe & Others Connected with them of the Other part, WITNESSETH, that the said Committee In behalf of the Commonwealth aforesaid and In Consideration of the said Indians Relinquishing all their Right Title Interest Claim or demand of any land or Lands lying and being within the said Commonwealth of Massachusetts and also engageing to be Peaceable & Quiet Inhabitanta of Said Commonwealth without Mollesting any Other of the settlers of the Commonwealth aforesaid in any way or means whatever. In Consideration of all which, the Committee aforesaid for and in behalf of the Comm: — wealth aforesaid do hereby assign[s] and Set of [f] to the aforsaid Indians the Following Tracts or Parcels of land lying & being within the Commonwealth of Massachusetts *Vizt.* all those Islands lying and being in Schoodic River† between The falls at the head of the Tide and the falls below the Forks of the said River where the north Branch and West Branch parts being fifteen in number Containing one hundred Acres more or less, also Township No. two in the first Range Surveyed by Mr. Samuel Titcomb in the year of our Lord one thousand seven hundred &

---

*In 1820 Maine separated from Massachusetts to become the 23rd State.
†Also known as the St. Crois River.

ninety four Containing about twenty three thousand Acres more or less being bounded as follows Easterly by Tomers River & Township No. one First Range Northerly by Township No. two Second Range Westerly by township No. three first Range, Southerly by the West Branch of Schoodic River & Lake, also Lues Island lying in Front of said Township Containing Ten Acres more or less Together with one hundred Acres of land lying on Nemcass point adjoining the West side of Said Township also Pine Island lying to the westward of said Nemcass Point Containing one hundred & fifty acres more or less also assign & Set off [f] to John Baptist Lacote a French Gentleman Now Settled among the said Indians one hundred Acres of Land as a Settler in Township No. one first Range lying at the falls at the Carrying Place on the North Branch of Schoodic River to be Intitled to have said land laid out to him in the same manner as Settlers in New Townships are Intitled, also assign to said Indians the privilege of Fishing on Both Branches of the River Schoodic without Hindrance or Molestation and the privilege of passing the said River over the deferent Carrying places theron all which Islands, Townships, Tracts or parcels of Land and privileges being marked with a Cross Thus X on the plan taken by Mr. Samuel Titcomb with the Reservation of all Pine Trees fit for Masts on said Tracts of land to Government they making said Indians a Reasonable Compensation therefor also assign & Set of [f] to the Said Indians Ten Acres of land more or less at Pleasant point purchased by said Committee In behalf of said Commonwea[l]th of John Frost being bounded as follows *Vizt.* beginning at a stake to the eastward of the dwelling house & Running North twenty five degrees west fifty four Rods from thence Running North fifty six degrees East thirty eight Rods to the Bay from thence by the shore to the first Bounds also a Privilege of Sitting down at the Carrying Place at West Passamaquady between the Bay of West Quady and the Bay of Fundy to Contain fifty acres the Said Islands Tracts of land, & Privileges to be Confirmed by the Commonwealth of Massachusetts to the said Indians & their Heirs Forever.

In Testimony of all which we the Said Alexander Campbell John Allan and George Stillman the Committee aforesaid and In behalf of the Commonwealth aforesaid, and the Chiefs & Other Indians aforesaid In behalf of themselves and those Connected with them as aforesaid Have hereunto Set our hands and Seals at Passamaquady the Twenty Ninth Day of September in the Year of our Lord one thousand seven Hundred & Ninety Four.

ALEX CAMPBELL
J. ALLAN
GEORGE STILLMAN

Signed Sealed   Samuel Titcomb
in Presence of   Jno. Frost, Junr.

                                       his
                  FRANCIS JOSEPH   X   NEPTUNE,   L. S.
                                       mark.

                                       his
                            JOHN   X   NEPTUNE,   L. S.
                                       mark.

                                       his
                            PIER   X   NEPTUNE,   L. S.
                                       mark.

                                       his
                          JOSEPH   X   NEPTUNE,   L. S.
                                       mark.

                                       his
                            PIER   X   DENNY,   L. S.
                                       mark.

                                       his
                         JONALE   X   DENNY,   L. S.
                                       mark.

                                       his
                          JOSEPH   X   DENNY,   L. S.
                                       mark.

TREATY WITH THE SIX NATIONS, 1794

A Treaty between the United States of America, and the Tribes of Indians called the Six Nations.

The President of the United States having determined to hold a conference with the Six Nations of Indians, for the purpose of removing from their minds all causes of complaint, and establishing a firm and permanent friendship with them; and Timothy Pickering being appointed sole agent for that purpose; and the agent having met and conferred with the Sachems, Chiefs and Warriors of the Six Nations, in general council: Now, in order to accomplish the good design of this conference, the parties have agreed on the following articles; which, when ratified by the President, with the advice and consent of the Senate of the United States, shall be binding on them and the Six Nations.

ARTICLE I.

Peace and friendship are hereby firmly established, and shall be perpetual, between the United States and the Six Nations.

ARTICLE II.

The United States acknowledge the lands reserved to the Oneida, Onondaga and Cayuga Nations, in their respective treaties with the state of New-York, and called their reservations, to be their property; and the United States will never claim the same, nor disturb them or either of the Six Nations, nor their Indian friends residing thereon and united with them, in the free use and enjoyment thereof: but the said reservations shall remain theirs, until they choose to sell the same to the people of the United States, who have the right to purchase.

ARTICLE III.

The land of the Seneka nation is bounded as follows: Beginning on Lake Ontario, at the north-west corner of the land they sold to Oliver Phelps, the line runs westerly along the lake, as far as O-yong-wong-yeh Creek, at Johnson's Landing-place, about four miles eastward from the fort of Niagara; then southerly up that creek to its main fork, then straight to the main fork of Stedman's creek, which empties into the river Niagara, above fort Schlosser, and then onward, from that fork, continuing the same straight course, to that river; (this line, from the mouth of O-yong-wong-yeh Creek to the river Niagara, above fort Schlosser, being the eastern boundary of a strip of land, extending from the same line to Niagara river, which the Seneka nation ceded to the King of Great-Britain, at a treaty held about thirty years ago, with Sir William Johnson:) then the line runs along the river Niagara to Lake Erie; then along Lake Erie to the north-east corner of a triangular piece of land which the United States conveyed to the state of Pennsylvania, as by the President's patent, dated the third day of March, 1792; then due south to the northern boundary of that state; then due east to the south-west corner of the land sold by the Seneka nation to Oliver Phelps; and then north and northerly, along Phelp's line, to the place of beginning on Lake Ontario. Now, the United States acknowledge all the land within the aforementioned boundaries, to be the property of the Seneka nation; and the United States will never claim the same, nor disturb the Seneka nation, nor any of the Six Nations, or of their Indian friends residing thereon and united with them, in the free use and enjoyment thereof; but it shall remain theirs, until they choose to sell the same to the people of the United States, who have the right to purchase.

ARTICLE IV.

The United States having thus described the acknowledged what lands belong to the Oneidas, Onondagas, Cayugas and Senekas, and engaged never to claim the same, nor to disturb them, or any of the Six Nations, or their Indian friends residing thereon and united with them, in the free use and enjoyment thereof: Now, the Six Nations, and each of them, hereby engage that they will never claim any other lands within the boundaries of the United States; nor ever disturb the people of the United States in the free use and enjoyment thereof.

ARTICLE V.

The Seneka nation, all others of the Six Nations concurring, cede to the United States the right of making a wagon road from Fort Schlosser to Lake Erie, as far south as Buffaloe Creek; and the people of the United States shall have the free and undisturbed use of this road, for the purposes of travelling and transportation. And the six Nations, and each of them, will forever allow to the people of the United States, a free passage through their lands, and the free use of the harbors and rivers adjoining and within their respective tracts of land, for the passing and securing of vessels and boats, and liberty to land their cargoes where necessary for their safety.

ARTICLE VI.

In consideration of the peace and friendship hereby established, and of the engagements entered into by the Six Nations; and because the United States desire, with humanity and kindness, to contribute to their comfortable support; and to render the peace and friendship hereby established, strong and perpetual; the United States now deliver to the Six Nations, and the Indians of the other nations residing among and united with them, a quanity of goods of the value of ten thousand dollars. And for the same considerations, and with a view to promote the future welfare of the Six Nations, and of their Indian friends aforesaid, the United States will add the sum of three thousand dollars to the one thousand five hundred dollars, heretofore allowed them by an article ratified by the President, on the twenty-third day of April, 1792;* making in the whole, four thousand five hundred dollars; which shall be expended yearly forever, in purchasing clothing, domestic animals, implements of husbandry, and other utensils suited to their circumstances, and in compensating useful artificers, who shall reside with or near them, and be employed for their benefit. The immediate application of the whole annual allowance now stipulated, to be made by the superintendent appointed by the President for the affairs of the Six Nations, and their Indian friends aforesaid.

ARTICLE VII.

Lest the firm peace and friendship now established should be interrupted by the misconduct of individuals, the United States and Six Nations agree, that for injuries done by individuals on either side, no private revenge or

*Charles J. Kappler, compiler and editor of Indian Affairs, Laws and Treaties states that "It appears that this treaty was never ratified by the Senate."

retaliation shall take place; but, instead thereof, complaint shall be made by the party injured, to the other: By the Six Nations or any of them, to the President of the United States, or the Superintendent by him appointed: and by the Superintendent, or other person appointed by the President, to the principal chiefs of the Six Nations, or of the nation to which the offender belongs: and such prudent measures shall then be pursued as shall be necessary to preserve our peace and friendship unbroken; until the legislature (or great council) of the United States shall make other equitable provision for the purpose.

NOTE. It is clearly understood by the parties to this treaty, that the annuity stipulated in the sixth article, is to be applied to the benefit of such of the Six Nations and of their Indian friends united with them as aforesaid, as do or shall reside within the boundaries of the United States: For the United States do not interfere with nations, tribes or families, of Indians elsewhere resident.

In witness whereof, the said Timothy Pickering, and the sachems and war chiefs of the said Six Nations, have hereto set their hands and seals.

Done at Konondaigua, in the State of New York, the eleventh day of November, in the year one thousand seven hundred and ninety-four.

Timothy Pickering,	L. S.	Tauhoondos, his x mark, or	
Onoyeahnee, his x mark,	L. S.	Open the Way,	L. S.
Konneatorteeoooh, his x mark, or		Twaukewasha, his x mark,	L. S.
Handsome Lake,	L. S.	Sequidongquee, his x mark,	
Tokenhyouhau, his x mark, alias		alias Little Beard,	L. S.
Captain Key,	L. S.	Kodjeote, his x mark, or	
Oneshauee, his x mark,	L. S.	Half Town,	L. S.
Hendrick Aupaumut,	L. S.	Kenjauaugus, his x mark,	
David Neesoonhuk, his x mark,	L. S.	or Stinking Fish,	L. S.
Kanatsoyh, alias Nicholas Kusik,	L. S.	Soonohquaukau, his x	
		mark,	L. S.
Sohhonteoquent, his x mark,	L. S.	Twenniyana, his x mark,	L. S.
Ooduhtsait, his x mark,	L. S.	Jishkaaga, his x mark, or	
Konoohqung, his x mark,	L. S.	Green Grasshopper, alias	
Tossonggaulolus, his x mark,	L. S.	Little Billy,	L. S.
John Skenendoa, his x mark,	L. S.	Tuggehshotta, his x mark,	L. S.
Oneatorleeooh, his x mark,	L. S.	Tehongyagauna, his x mark	L. S.
Kussauwatau, his x mark,	L. S.	Tehongyoowush, his x mark	L. S.
Eyootenyootauook, his x mark,	L. S.	Konneyoowesot, his x mark,	L. S.
Kohnyeaugong, his x mark, alias		Tioohquottakauna, his x	
Jake Stroud,	L. S.	mark, or Woods on Fire,	L. S.
Shaguiesa, his x mark,	L. S.	Taoundaudeesh, his x mark,	L. S.
Teeroos, his x mark, alias		Honayawus, his x mark,	
Captain Prantup,	L. S.	alias Farmer's Brother,	L. S.
Sooshaoowau, his x mark,	L. S.	Soggooyawauthau, his x	
Henry Young Brant, his x mark,	L. S.	mark, alias Red Jacket,	L. S.

Sonhyoowauna, his x mark, or		Konyootiayoo, his x mark,	L. S.
Big Sky,	L. S.	Sauhtakaongyees, his x	
Onaahhah, his x mark,	L. S.	mark, or Two Skies of a	
Hotoshahenh, his x mark,	L. S.	length,	L. S.
Kaukondanaiya, his x mark,	L. S.	Ounnashattakau, his x mark	L. S.
Nondiyauka, his x mark,	L. S.	Kaungyanehquee, his x mark,	L. S.
Kossishtowau, his x mark,	L. S.	Sooayoowau, his x mark,	L. S.
Oojaugenta, his x mark, or		Kaujeagaonh, his x mark,	
Fish Carrier,	L. S.	or Heap of Dogs,	L. S.
Toheonggo, his x mark,	L. S.	Soonoohshoowau, his x mark,	L. S.
Ootaguasso, his x mark,	L. S.	Thaoowaunias, his x mark,	L. S.
Joonondauwaonch, his x mark,	L. S.	Soonongjoowau, his x mark,	L. S.
Kiyauhaonh, his x mark,	L. S.	Kiantwhauka, his x mark,	
Ootaujeaugenh, his x mark, or		alias Cornplanter,	L. S.
Broken Axe,	L. S.	Kaunehshonggoo, his x	L. S.

Witnesses:

Israel Chapin.	Israel Chapin, jr.
William Shepard, jr.	Horatio Jones.
James Smedley.	Joseph Smith,
John Wickham.	Jasper Parish,
Augustus Porter.	Interpreters.
James K. Garnsey.	Henry Abeele.
William Ewing.	

TREATY WITH THE MOHAWK, 1797

Relinquishment to New York, by the Mohawk nation of Indians, under the sanction of the United States of America, of all claims to lands in that state.

At a treaty held under the authority of the United States, with the Mohawk nation of Indians, residing in the province of Upper Canada, within the dominions of the king of Great Britain, present the honorable Isaac Smith, commissioner appointed by the United States to hold this treaty; Abraham Ten Broeck, Egbert Benson, and Ezra L'Hommedieu, agent for the state of New York; captain Joseph Brandt, and captain John Deserontyon, two of the said Indians and deputies, to represent the said nation at this treaty.

The said agents having, in the presence, and with the approbation of the said commissioner, proposed to and adjusted with said deputies, the compensation as hereinafter mentioned to be made to the said nation, for their claim, to be extinguished by this treaty, to all lands within the said state: it is thereupon finally agreed and done, between the said agents, and the said deputies, as follows, that is to say: the said agents do agree to pay to the said deputies, the sum of one thousand dollars, for the use of the said nation, to be by the said deputies paid over to, and distributed among, the persons and families of the said nation, according to their usages. The sum of five hundred dollars, for the expenses of the said deputies, during the time they have attended this treaty: and the sum of one hundred dollars, for their expenses in returning, and for conveying the said sum of one thousand dollars, to where the said nation resides. And the said agents do accordingly, for and in the name of the people of the state of New York, pay the said three several sums to the said deputies, in the presence of the said commissioner. And the said deputies do agree to cede and release, and these presents witness, that they accordingly do, for and in the name of the said nation, in consideration of the said compensation, cede and release to the people of the state of New York, forever, all the right or title of the said nation to lands within the said state: and the claim of the said nation to lands within the said state, is hereby wholly and finally extinguished.

In testimony whereof, the said commissioner, the said agents, and the said deputies, have hereunto, and to two other acts of the same tenor and date, one to remain with the United States, one to remain with the said State, and one delivered to the said deputies, to remain with the said nation, set their hands and seals, at the city of Albany, in the said State, the twenty-ninth day of March, in the year one thousand seven hundred and ninety-seven.

Isaac Smith,	L. S.
Abm. Ten Broeck,	L. S.
Egbt. Benson,	L. S.
Ezra L'Hommedieu,	L. S.
Jos. Brandt,	L. S.
John Deserontyon,	L. S.

Witnesses:

Robert Yates,
John Tayler,
Chas. Williamson,
Thomas Morris,
The mark of x John Abeel, alias the Cornplanter, a chief of the Senekas.

TREATY WITH
THE SIOUX OF THE LAKES, 1815

A treaty of peace and friendship, made and concluded at Portage des Sioux between William Clark, Ninian Edwards, and Auguste Chouteau, Commissioners Plenipotentiary of the United States of America, on the part and behalf of the said States, of the one part; and the undersigned Chiefs and Warriors of the Siouxs of the Lakes, on the part and behalf of their Tribe, of the other part.

THE parties being desirous of re-establishing peace and friendship between the United States and the said tribe, and of being placed in all things, and in every respect, on the same footing upon which they stood before the late war between the United States and Great Britain, have agreed to the following articles:

ARTICLE 1. Every injury, or act of hostility, committed by one or either of the contracting parties against the other, shall be mutually forgiven and forgot.

ARTICLE 2. There shall be perpetual peace and friendship between all the citizens of the United States of America and all the individuals composing the said tribe of the Lakes, and all the friendly relations that existed between them before the war, shall be, and the same are hereby, renewed.

ARTICLE 3. The undersigned chiefs and warriors, for themselves and their said tribe, do hereby acknowledge themselves and their aforesaid tribe to be under the protection of the United States, and of no other nation, power, or soverign, whatsoever.

In witness whereof, the said William Clark, Ninian Edwards, and Auguste Chouteau, commissioners aforesaid, and the chiefs and warriors of the aforesaid tribe, have hereunto subscribed their names and affixed their seals this nineteenth day of July, in the year of our Lord one thousand eight hundred and fifteen, and of the independence of the United States the fortieth.

William Clark,	L.S.
Ninian Edwards,	L.S.
Auguste Chouteau,	L. S.
Tatangamania, the Walking Buffaloe, his x mark,	L. S.
Haisanwee, the Horn, his x mark,	L. S.
Aampahaa, the Speaker, his x mark,	L. S.
Narcesagata, the Hard Stone, his x mark,	L. S.
Haibohaa, the Branching Horn, his x mark,	L. S.

Done at Portage des Sioux, in the presence of—

R. Wash, secretary to the
commission,
John Miller, colonel Third
Infantry,
T. Paul, C.T. of the C.
Edmund Hall, lietenant late
Twenty-eighth Infantry,
Thomas Forsyth, Indian agent,
Jno. W. Johnson,

United States factor and
Indian agent,
Maurice Blondeaux,
Lewis Decouagne,
Louis Dorion,
John A. Cameron,
Jacques Mette,
John Hay.

TREATY WITH THE CHEROKEE, 1817

Articles of a treaty concluded, at the Cherokee Agency, within the Cherokee nation, between major general Andrew Jackson, Joseph M'Minn, governor or the state of Tennessee, and general David Meriwether, commissioners plenipotentiary of the United States of America, of the one part, and the chiefs, head men, and warriors, of the Cherokee nation, east of the Mississippi river, and the chiefs, head men, and warriors, of the Cherokees on the Arkansas river, and their deputies, John D. Chisholm and James Rogers, duly authorized by the chiefs of the Cherokees on the Arkansas river, in open council, by written power of attorney, duly signed and executed, in presence of Joseph Sevier and William Ware.

WHEREAS in the autumn of the year one thousand eight hundred and eight, a deputation from the Upper and Lower Cherokee towns, duly authorized by their nation, went on to the city of Washington, the first named to declare to the President of the United States their anxious desire to engage in the pursuit of agriculture and civilized life, in the country they then occupied, and to make known to the President of the United States the impracticability of inducing the nation at large to do this, and to request the establishment of a division line between the upper and lower towns, so as to include all the waters of the Hiwassee river to the upper town, that, by thus contracting their society within narrow limits, they proposed to begin the establishment of fixed laws and a regular government: The deputies from the lower towns to make known their desire to continue the hunter life, and also the scarcity of game where they then lived, and, under those circumstances, their wish to remove across the Mississippi river, on some vacant lands of the United States. And whereas the President of the United States, after maturely considering the petitions of both parties, on the ninth day of January, A.D. one thousand eight hundred and nine, including other subjects, answered those petitions as follows:

"The United States, my children, are the friends of both parties, and, as far as can be reasonably asked, they are willing to satisfy the wishes of both. Those who remain may be assured of our patronage, our aid, and good neighborhood. Those who wish to remove, are permitted to send an exploring party to reconnoitre the country on the waters of the Arkansas and White rivers, and the higher up the better, as they will be the longer unapproached by our settlements, which will begin at the mouths of those rivers. The regular districts of the government of St. Louis are already laid off to the St. Francis.

"When this party shall have found a tract of country suiting the emigrants, and not claimed by other Indians, we will arrange with them and you the exchange of that for a just portion of the country they leave, and to a part of which, proportioned to their numbers, they have a right. Every aid towards their removal, and what will be necessary for them there, will then be freely administered to them; and when established in their new settlements, we shall still consider them as our children, give them the benefit of exchanging their peltries for what they will want at our factories, and always hold them firmly by the hand."

And whereas the Cherokees, relying on the promises of the President of the United States, as above cited, did explore the country on the west side of the Mississippi, and made choice of the country on the Arkansas and White rivers, and settled themselves down upon United States' lands, to which no other tribe of Indians have any just claim, and have duly notified the President of the United States thereof, and of their anxious desire for the full and complete ratification of his promise, and, to that end, as notified by the President of the United States, have sent on their agents, with full powers to execute a treaty, relinquishing to the United States all the right, title, and interest, to all lands of right to them belonging, as part of the Cherokee nation, which they have left, and which they are about to leave, proportioned to their numbers, including, with those now on the Arkansas, those who are about to remove thither, and to a portion of which they have an equal right agreeably to their numbers.

Now, know ye, that the contracting parties, to carry into full effect the before recited promises with good faith, and to promote a continuation of friendship with their brothers on the Arkansas river, and for that purpose to make an equal distribution of the annuities secured to be paid by the United States to the whole Cherokee nation, have agreed and concluded on the following articles, viz:

ART. 1. The chiefs, head men, and warriors, of the whole Cherokee nation, cede to the United States all the lands lying north and east of the following boundaries, viz: Beginning at the high shoals of the Appalachy river, and running thence, along the boundary line between the Creek and Cherokee nations, westwardly to the Chatahouchy river; thence, up the Chatahouchy river, to the mouth of Souque creek; thence, continuing with the general course of the river until it reaches the Indian boundary line, and, should it strike the Turrurar river, thence, with its meanders, down said river to its mouth, in part of the proportion of land in the Cherokee nation east of the Mississippi, to which those now on the Arkansas and those about to remove there are justly entitled.

ART. 2. The chiefs, head men, and warriors, of the whole Cherokee nation, do also cede to the United States all the lands lying north and west of the following boundary lines, viz: Beginning at the Indian boundary line that runs from the north bank of the Tennessee river, opposite to the mouth of Hywassee river, at a point on the top of Walden's ridge, where it divides the waters of the Tennessee river from those of the Sequatchie river; thence, along the said ridge, southwardly, to the bank of the Tennessee river, at a point near to a place called the Negro Sugar Camp, opposite to the upper end of the first island above Running Water Town; thence, westwardly, a straight line to the mouth of Little Sequatchie river; thence, up said river, to its main fork; thence, up its northernmost fork, to its source; and thence, due west, to the Indian boundary line.

ART. 3. It is also stipulated by the contracting parties, that a census shall be taken of the whole Cherokee nation, during the month of June, in the year of our Lord one thousand eight hundred and eighteen, in the following manner, viz: That the census of those on the east side of the Mississippi river, who declare their intention of remaining, shall be taken by a commissioner appointed by the President of the United States, and a commissioner appointed by the Cherokees on the Arkansas river; and the census of the Cherokees on the Arkansas river, and those removing there, and who, at that time, declare their intention of removing there, shall be taken by a commissioner appointed by the President of the United States, and one appointed by the Cherokees east of the Mississippi river.

ART. 4. The contracting parties do also stipulate that the annuity due from the United States to the whole Cherokee nation for the year one thousand eight hundred and eighteen, is to be divided between the two parts of the nation in proportion to their numbers, agreeably to the stipulation contained in the third article of this treaty; and to be continued to be divided thereafter in proportion to their numbers; and the lands to be apportioned and surrendered to the United States agreeably to the aforesaid enumeration, as the proportionate part, agreeably to their numbers, to which those who have removed, and who declare their intention to remove, have a just right, including these with the lands ceded in the first and second articles of this treaty.

ART. 5. The United States bind themselves, in exchange for the lands ceded in the first and second articles hereof, to give to that part of the Cherokee nation on the Arkansas as much land on said river and White river as they have or may hereafter receive from the Cherokee nation east of the Mississippi, acre for acre, as the just proportion due that part of the nation on the Arkansas agreeably to their numbers; which is to commence on the north side of the Arkansas river, at the mouth of the Point Remove or Budwell's Old Place; thence, by a straight line, northwardly, to strike Chataunga mountain, or the hill first above Shield's Ferry on White river, running up and between said rivers for complement, the banks of which rivers to be the lines; and to have the above line, from the point of beginning to the point on White river, run and marked, which shall be done soon after the ratification of this treaty; and all citizens of the United States, except Mrs. P. Lovely, who is to remain where she lives during life, removed from within the bounds as above named. And it is further stipulated, that the treaties heretofore between the Cherokee nation and the United States are to continue in full force with both parts of the nation, and both parts thereof entitled to all the immunities and privilege which the old nation enjoyed under the aforesaid treaties; the United States reserving the right of establishing factories, a military post, and roads, within the boundaries above defined.

ART. 6. The United Stated do also bind themselves to give to all the poor warriors who may remove to the western side of the Mississippi river, one rifle gun and ammunition, one blanket, and one brass kettle, or, in lieu of the brass kettle, a beaver trap, which is to be considered as a full compensation for the improvements which they may leave; which articles are to be delivered at such points as the President of the United States may direct: and to aid in the removal of the emigrants, they further agree to furnish flat bottomed boats and provisions sufficient for that purpose: and to those emigrants whose improvements add real value to their lands, the United States agree to pay a full valuation for the same, which is to be ascertained by a commissioner appointed by the President of the United States for that purpose, and paid for as soon after the ratification of this treaty as practicable. The boats and provisions promised to the emigrants are to be furnished by the agent on the Tennessee river, at such time and place as the emigrants may notify him of; and it shall be his duty to furnish the same.

ART. 7. And for all improvements which add real value to the lands lying within the boundaries ceded to the United States, by the first and second articles of this treaty, the United States do agree to pay for at the time, and to be valued in the same manner, as stipulated in the sixth article of this treaty; or, in lieu thereof, to give in exchange improvements of equal value which the emigrants may leave, and for which they are to receive pay. And it is further stipulated, that all these improvements, left by the emigrants within the bounds of the Cherokee nation east of the Mississippi river, which add real value to the lands, and for which the United States shall give a consideration, and not so exchanged, shall be rented to the Indians by the agent, year after year, for the benefit of the poor and decrepid of that part of the nation east of the Mississippi river, until surrendered by the nation, or, to the nation. And it is further agreed, that the said Cherokee nation shall not be called upon for any part of the consideration paid for said improvements at any future period.

ART. 8. And to each and every head of any Indian family residing on the east side of the Mississippi river, on the lands that are now, or may hereafter be, surrendered to the United States, who may wish to become citizens of the United States, the United States do agree to give a reservation of six hundred and forty acres of land, in a square, to include their improvements, which are to be as near the centre thereof as practicable, in which they will have a life estate, with a reversion in fee simple to their children, reserving to the widow her dower, the register of whose names is to be filed in the office of the Cherokee agent, which shall be kept open until the census is taken as stipulated in the third article of this treaty. Provided, That if any of the heads of families, for whom reservations may be made, should remove therefrom, then, in that case, the right to revert to the United States. And provided further, That the land which may be reserved under this article, be deducted from the amount which has been ceded under the first and second articles of this treaty.

ART. 9. It is also provided by the contracting parties, that nothing in the foregoing articles shall be construed so as to prevent any of the parties so contracting from the free navigation of all the waters mentioned therein.

ART. 10. The whole of the Cherokee nation do hereby cede to the United States all right, title, and claim, to all reservations made to Doublehead and others, which were reserved to them by a treaty made and entered into at the city of Washington, bearing date the seventh of January, one thousand eight hundred and six.

ART. 11. It is further agreed that the boundary lines of the lands ceded to the United States by the first and second articles of this treaty, and the boundary line of the lands ceded by the United States in the fifth article of this treaty, is to be run and marked by a commissioner or commissioners appointed by the President of the United States, who shall be accompanied by such commissioners as the Cherokees may appoint; due notice thereof to be given to the nation.

ART. 12. The United States do also bind themselves to prevent the intrusion of any of its citizens within the lands ceded by the first and second articles of this treaty, until the same shall be ratified by the President and Senate of the United States, and duly promulgated.

ART. 13. The contracting parties do also stipulate that this treaty shall take effect and be obligatory on the contracting parties so soon as the same shall be ratified by the President of the United States, by and with the advice and consent of the Senate of the United States.

In witness of all and every thing herein determined, by and between the before recited contracting parties, we have, in full and open council, at the Cherokee Agency, this eighth day of July, A. D. one thousand eight hundred and seventeen, set our hands and seals.

Andrew Jackson,	L. S.	Young Davis, his x mark,	L. S.
Joseph McMinn,	L. S.	Souanooka, his x mark,	L. S.
D. Meriwether,	L. S.	The Locust, his x mark,	L. S.
United States Commiss'rs		Beaver Carrier, his x mark,	L. S.
Richard Brown, his x mark,	L. S.	Dreadful Water, his x mark,	L. S.
Cabbin Smith, his x mark,	L. S.	Chyula, his x mark,	L. S.
Sleeping Rabbit, his x mark,	L. S.	Ja. Martin,	L. S.
George Saunders, his x mark,	L. S.	John McIntosh, his x mark,	L. S.
Roman nose, his x mark,	L. S.	Katchee of Cowee, his x mark,	L. S.
Currohe Dick, his x mark,	L. S.	White Man Killer, his, x mark,	L. S.
John Walker, his x mark,	L. S.	Arkansas chiefs:	
George Lowry,	L. S.	Toochalar, his x mark,	L. S.
Richard Taylor,	L. S.	The Glass, his x mark,	L. S.
Walter Adair,	L. S.	Wassosee, his x mark,	L. S.
James Brown,	L. S.	John Jolly, his x mark,	L. S.
Kelachule, his x mark,	L. S.	The Gourd, his x mark,	L. S.
Sour Mush, his x mark,	L. S.	Spring Frog, his x mark,	L. S.
Chulioa, his x mark,	L. S.	John D. Chisholm	L. S.
Chickasautchee, his x mark,	L. S.	James Rogers,	L. S.
The Bark of Chota, his x mark,	L. S.	Wawhatchy, his x mark,	L. S.
The Bark of Hightower, his		Attalona, his x mark,	L. S.
x mark,	L. S.	Kulsuttchee, his x mark,	L. S.
Big Half Breed, his x mark,	L. S.	Tuskekeetchee, his x mark,	L. S.
Going Snake, his x mark,	L. S.	Chillawgatchee, his x mark,	L. S.
Leyestisky, his x mark,	L. S.	John Smith, his x mark,	L. S.
Ch. Hicks,	L. S.	Toosawallata, his x mark,	L. S.

In presence of—

J. M. Glassel, secretary to the
  commission,
Thomas Wilson, clerk to the
  commissioners,
Walter Adair,
John Speirs, interpreter, his
  x mark,
A. McCoy, interpreter,

James C. Bronaugh, hospital
  surgeon, U.S. Army,
Isham Randolph, captain First
  Redoubtables,
Wm. Meriwether,
Return J. Meigs, agent
  Cherokee Nation.

TREATY WITH THE SEMINOLE, 1833

WHEREAS, the Seminole Indians of Florida, entered into certain articles of agreement, with James Gadson, [Gadsden,] Commissioner on behalf of the United States, at Payne's landing, on the 9th day of May, 1832: the first article of which treaty or agreement provides, as follows: "The Seminoles Indians relinquish to the United States all claim to the land they at present occupy in the Territory of Florida, and agree to emigrate to the country assigned to the Creeks, west of the Mississippi river; it being understood that an additional extent of territory proportioned to their number will be added to the Creek country, and that the Seminoles will be received as a constituent part of the Creek nation, and be re-admitted to all the privileges as members of the same." And whereas, the said agreement also stipulates and provides, that a delegation of Seminoles should be sent at the expense of the United States to examine the country to be allotted them among the Creeks, and should this delegation be satisfied with the character of the country and of the favorable disposition of the Creeks to unite with them as one people, then the aforementioned treaty would be considered binding and obligatory upon the parties. And whereas a treaty was made between the United States and the Creek Indians west of the Mississippi, at Fort Gibson, on the 14th day of February 1833, by which a country was provided for the Seminoles in pursuance of the existing arrangements between the United States and that tribe. And whereas, the special delegation, appointed by the Seminoles on the 9th day of May 1832, have since examined the land designated for them by the undersigned Commissioners, on behalf of the United States, and have expressed themselves satisfied with the same, in and by their letter dated, March 1833, addressed to the undersigned Commissioners.

Now, therefore, the Commissioners aforesaid, by virtue of the power and authority vested in them by the treaty made with Creek Indians on the 14th day of February 1833, as above stated, hereby designate and assign to the Seminole tribe of Indians, for their separate future residence, forever, a tract of country lying between the Canadian river and the north fork thereof, and extending west to where a line running north and south between the main Canadian and north branch, will strike the forks of Little river, provided said west line does not extend more than twenty-five miles west from the mouth of said Little river. And the undersigned Seminole chiefs, delegated as aforesaid, on behalf of their nation hereby declare themselves well satisfied with the location provided for them by the Commissioners, and agree that their nation shall commence the removal to their new home, as soon as the Government will make arrangements for their emigration, satisfactory to the Seminole nation.

And whereas, the said Seminoles have expressed high confidence in the friendship and ability of their present agent, Major Phagen, and desire that he may be permitted to remove them to their new homes west of the Mississippi; the Commissioners have considered their request, and cheerfully recommend Major Phagan as a suitable person to be employed to remove the Seminoles as aforesaid, and trust his appointment will be made, not only to gratify the wishes of the Indians but as conducive to the public welfare.

In testimony whereof, the commissioners on behalf of the United States, and the delegates of the Seminole nation, have hereunto signed their names, this 28th day of March, A. D. 1833, at fort Gibson.

> Montfort Stokes,
> Henry L. Ellsworth,
> John F. Schermerhorn.

Seminole Delegates:
> John Hick, representing Sam Jones, his x mark.
> Holata Emartta, his x mark.
> Jumper, his x mark,
> Coi Hadgo, his x mark.
> Charley Emartta, his x mark.
> Ya-ha-hadge, his x mark.
> Ne-ha-tho-clo, representing Fuch-a-lusti-hadgo, his x mark,
> > On behalf of the Seminole
> > nation.

TREATY WITH
THE CHICKASAW, 1834 [First]

Articles of convention and agreement proposed by the Commissioners on the part of the United States, in pursuance of the request made, by the Delegation representing the Chickasaw nation of Indians, and which have been agreed to.

ART. I. It is agreed that perpetual amity, peace and friendship, shall exist between the United States, and the Chickasaw nation of Indians.

ART. II. The Chickasaws are about to abandon their homes, which they have long cherished and loved; and though hitherto unsuccessful, they still hope to find a country, adequate to the wants and support of their people, somewhere west of the Mississippi and within the territorial limits of the United States; should they do so, the Government of the United States, hereby consent to protect and defend them against the inroads of any other tribe of Indians, and from the whites; and agree to keep them without the limits of any State or Territory. The Chickasaws pledge themselves never to make war upon any Indian people, or upon the whites, unless they are so authorized by the United States. But if war be made upon them, they will be permitted to defend themselves, until assistance, be given to them by the United States, as shall be the case.

ART. III. The Chickasaws are not acquainted with the laws of the whites, which are extended over them; and the many intruders which break into their country, interrupting their rights and disturbing their repose, leave no alternative whereby restraint can be afforded, other than an appeal to the military force of the country, which they are unwilling to ask for, or see resorted to; and therefore they agree to forbear such a request, for prevention of this great evil, with the understanding, which is admitted, that the agent of the United States, upon the application of the chiefs of the nation, will resort to every legal civil remedy, (at the expense of the United States,) to prevent intrusion upon the ceded country; and to restrain and remove trespassers from any selected reservations, upon application of the owner of the same. And it is also agreed, that the United States, will continue some discreet person as agent, such as they now have, to whom they can look for redress of wrongs and injuries which may be attempted against them; and it is consented, that if any of their property, be taken by persons of the United States, covertly or forcibly, the agent on satisfactory and just complaint being made, shall pursue all lawful civil means, which the laws of the State permit, in which the wrong is done, to regain the same, or to obtain a just remuneration; and on failure or inability to procure redress, for the offended, against the offending party; payment for the loss sustained, on production of the record, and certificate of the facts, by the agent, shall be made by the United States; but in all such cases, satisfactory proof, for the establishing of the claim, shall be offered.

ART IV. The Chickasaws desire to have within their own direction and control, the means of taking care of themselves. Many of their people are quite competent to manage their affairs, though some are not capable, and might be imposed upon by designing persons; it is therefore agreed that the reservations hereinafter admitted, shall not be permitted to be sold, leased, or disposed of unless it appear by the certificate of at least two of the following persons, to wit; Ish-ta-ho-ta-pa the King, Levi Colbert, George Colbert, Martin Colbert, Isaac Alberson, Henry Love, and Benj. Love, of which five have affixed their names to this treaty, that the party owning or claiming the same, is capable to manage, and to take care of his or her affairs; which fact, to the best of his knowledge and information, shall be certified by the agent; and furthermore that a fair consideration has been paid; and thereupon, the deed of conveyance shall be valid provided the President of the United States, or such other person as he may designate shall approve of the same, and endorse it on the deed; which said deed and approval, shall be registered, at the place, and within the time, required by the laws of the State, in which the land may be situated; otherwise to be void. And where such certificate is not obtained; upon the recommendation of a majority of the Delegation, and the approval of the agent, at the discretion of the President of the United States, the same may be sold; but the consideration thereof, shall remain as part of the general Chickasaw fund in the hands of the Government, until such time as the chiefs in council shall think it advisable to pay it to the claimant or to those, who may rightfully claim under said claimant, and shall so recommend it. And as the King, Levi Colbert, and the Delegation, who have signed this agreement, and to whom certain important and interesting duties purtaining to the nation, are assigned, may die, resign, or remove, so that their people may be without the benefit of their services, it is stipulated, that as often as any vacancy happens, by death, resignation, or otherwise, the chiefs shall select some discrete person of their nation to fill the occurring vacancy, who, upon a certificate of qualification, discretion and capability, by the agent, shall be appointed by the Secretary of War; whereupon, he shall possess all the authority granted to those who are here named, and the nation will make to the person so appointed such reasonable compensation, as they with the assent of the agent and the Secretary of War, may think right, proper and reasonable to be allowed.

ART. V. It is agreed that the fourth article of the "Treaty of Pontitock," be so changed, that the following reservations be granted in fee: — To heads of families, being Indians, or having Indian families, consisting of ten persons, and upwards, four sections of land are reserved. To those who have five and less than ten persons, three sections. Those who have less than five, two sections. Also those who own more than ten slaves, shall be entitled to one additional section; and those owning ten and less than ten to half a section. These reservations shall be confined, to the sections or fractional sections on which the party claiming lives, or to such as are contiguous or adjoining to the sections resided upon, subject to the following restrictions and conditions: —

Firstly. In cases where there are interferences arising, the oldest occupant or settler, shall have the preference, or,

Secondly. Where the land is adjudged unfit for cultivation, by the Agent, and three of the seven persons, named in the fourth article above, the party entitled, shall be, and is, hereby authorized to locate his claim upon other lands, which may be unappropriated, and not subject to any other claim; and where two or more persons, insist upon the entry of the same unappropriated section or fractional section, the priority of right shall be determined by lot; and where a fractional section is taken, leaving a balance greater or less than the surveyed subdivision of a section, then the deficiency shall be made up by connecting all the deficiencies so arising: and the Register and Receiver thereupon, shall locate full or fractional sections, fit for cultivation, in the names respectively of the different persons claiming which shall be held by them as tenants in common, according to the respective interests of those who are concerned; and the proceeds when sold by the parties claiming, shall be divided according to the interest, which each may have in said section or fractional section, so located, or the same may be divided agreeably to quality or quantity.

ART. VI. Also reservations of a section to each, shall be granted to persons male and female, not being heads of families, who are of the age of twenty-one years, and upwards, a list of whom, within a reasonable time shall be made out by the seven persons herein before mentioned, and filed with the Agent, upon whose certificate of its believed accuracy, the Register and Receiver, shall cause said reservations to be located upon lands fit for cultivation, but not to interfere with the settlement rights of others. The persons thus entitled, are to be excluded from the estimated numbers contained in any family enumeration, as is provided for in the fifth article preceding: and as to the sale, lease, or disposition of their reserves, they are to be subject to the conditions and restrictions, set forth in the fourth article. In these and in all other reserves where the party owning or entitled, shall die, the interest in the same shall belong to his wife, or the wife and children, or to the husband, or to the husband and children, if there be any; and in the cases of death, where there is neither husband, wife, nor children left, the same shall be disposed of for the general benefit; and the proceeds go into the general Chickasaw fund. But where the estate as is prescribed in this article, comes to the children, and having so come, either of them die, the survivor or survivors of them, shall be entitled to the same. But this rule shall not endure longer than for five years, nor beyond the period when the Chickasaws may leave their present for a new home.

ART VII. Where any white man, before the date hereof has married an Indian woman, the reservation he may be entitled to under this treaty, she being alive, shall be in her name, and no right or alienation of the same shall purtain to the husband unless he divest her of the title, after the mode and manner that feme coverts, usually divest themselves of the title to real estate, that is, by the acknowledgment of the wife which may be taken before the Agent, and certified by him, that she consents to the sale freely, and without compulsion from her husband, who shall at the same time certify that the head of such family is prudent, and competent to care of and manage his affairs; otherwise the proceeds of said sale shall be subject to the provisions and restrictions contained in the fourth article of this agreement. Rights to reservations as are herein, and in other articles of this agreement secured, will purtain to those who have heretofore intermarried with the Chickasaws and are residents of the nation.

ART. VIII. Males and females below the age of twenty-one years, whose father being dead, the mother again married, or who have neither father nor mother, shall each be entitled to half a section of land, but shall not be computed as parts of families under the fifth article, the same to be located under the direction of the Agent, and under the supervision of the Secretary of War, so as not to interfere with any settlement right. These lands may be sold upon a recommendation of a majority of the seven persons, heretofore named in this agreement, setting forth that it will prove advantageous to the parties interested; subject however, to the approval of the President, or such other person as he shall designate. If sold, the funds arising shall be retained, in the possession of the Government, or if the President deem it advisable they shall be invested in stocks for the benefit of the parties interested, if there be a sufficient sum to be invested, (and it can be invested,) until said persons marry or come of age, when the amount shall be paid over to those who are entitled to receive it, provided a majority of the seven persons, with the Agent, shall certify, that in their opinion, it will be to their interest and advantage, then, and in that case, the proceeds shall be paid over to the party or parties entitled to receive them.

ART. IX. But, in running the sectional lines, in some cases it will happen, that the spring and the dwelling house, or the spring and the cleared land, or the cleared land and the dwelling house of settlers, may be separated by sectional lines, whereby manifest inconvenience and injury will be occasioned; it is agreed, that when any of these occurrences arise, the party shall be entitled as parts and portions of his reservations, to the adjoining section or fraction, as the case may be, unless there be some older occupant, claiming a preference; and in that event, the right of the party shall extend no farther than to give to the person, thus affected and injured, so much of his separated property, as will secure the spring; also, where a sectional line shall separate any improvement, dwelling house, kitchen or stable, so much of the section, which contains them, shall be added into the occupied section, as will secure them to their original owner; and then and in that case, the older occupant being deprived of preference, shall have his deficiency thus occasioned, made up to him by some fractional section, or after the mode pointed out in the latter part of the fifth article of this treaty.

ART. X. Reservations are admitted to the following persons, in addition to those which may be claimed under the fifth article of this Treaty to wit: — Four sections to their beloved and faithful old Chief Levi Colbert; To George Colbert, Martin Colbert, Isaac Alberson, Henry Love and Benj. Love, in consideration of the trouble they have had in coming to Washington, and of the farther trouble hereafter to be encountered in taking care of the interests of their people, under the provisions of this treaty, one section of land to each. Also there is a fractional section, between the residence of George Colbert, and the Tennessee river, upon which he has a ferry, it is therefore consented, that said George Colbert, shall own and have so much of said fraction, as may be contained in the following lines, to wit. — beginning near Smith's ferry at the point where the base meridian line and the Tennessee river come in contact, — thence south so far as to pass the dwelling-house, (and sixty yards beyond it,) within which is interred the body of his wife, — thence east of the river and down the same to the point of beginning. Also there shall be reserved to him an island, in said river, nearly opposite to this fraction, commonly called Colberts Island. A reservation also of two sections is admitted to Ish-ta-ho-ta-pa the King of the Chickasaw nation. And to Min-ta-ho-yea the mother of Charles Colbert one section of land. Also one section, each, to the following persons: -Im-mub-bee, Ish-tim-o-lut-ka, Ah-to-ho-woh, Pis-tah-lah-tubbe, Capt. Samuel Seley and William McGilvery. To Col. Benj. Reynolds their long tried and faithful Agent, who has guarded their interests and twice travelled with their people far west, beyond the Mississippi, to aid them in seeking and finding a home, there is granted two sections of land. Jointly to William Cooper and John Davis, lawyers of Mississippi who have been faithful to the Indians, in giving them professional advice, and legal assistance, and who are to continue to do so, within the States of Tennessee, Alabama and Mississippi, while the Chickasaw people remain in said States, one section is granted. To Mrs. Margt. Allen wife of the sub-agent in her own right, half a section. These reservations to Benj. Reynolds, William Cooper, James Davis and Margt. Allen, are to be located so as not to interfere with the Indian reservations.

ART. XI. After the reservations are taken and located, which shall be the case as speedily as may be after the surveys are completed, of which the Register and Receiver shall give notice, the residue of the Chickasaw country shall be sold, as public lands of the United States are sold, with this difference; The lands as surveyed shall be offered at public sale at a price not less than one dollar and a quarter per acre; and thereafter for one year those which are unsold, and which shall have been previously offered at public sale, shall be liable to private entry and sale at that price; Thereafter, and for one year longer they shall be subject to entry and private sale, at one dollar per acre; Thereafter and during the third year, they shall be subject to sale and entry, at fifty cents per acre; Thereafter, and during the fourth year, at twenty-five cents per acre; and afterwards at twelve and a half cents per acre. But as it may happen, in the fourth and after years, that the expenses may prove greater than the receipts, it is agreed, that at any time after the third year, the Chickasaws may declare the residue of their lands abandoned to the United States, and if so, they shall be thenceforth acquitted of all and every expense on account of the sale of them same.

And that they may be advised of these matters it is stipulated, that the Government of the United States, within six months after any public sale takes place, shall advise them of the receipts and expenditures, and of balances in their favor; and also at regular intervals of six months, after the first report is made, will afford them information of the proceeds of all entries and sales. The funds thence resulting, after the necessary expenses of surveying and selling, and other advances which may be made, are repaid to the United States, shall from time to time be invested in some secure stocks, redeemable within a period of not more than twenty years; and the United States will cause the interest arising therefrom, annually to be paid to the Chickasaws.

ART. XII. When any portion of the country is fully surveyed, the President may order the same to be sold, but will allow six months, from the date of the first notice to the first sale; and three months' notice of any subsequent intended public sale, within which periods of time, those who can claim reservations, in the offered ranges of country, shall file their applications and entries with the Register and Receiver; that the name of the owner or claimant of the same, may be entered and marked on the general plat, at the office, whereby mistakes in the sales may be avoided, and injuries be prevented.

ART. XIII. If the Chickasaws shall be so fortunate as to procure a home, within the limits of the United States, it is agreed, that with the consent of the President and Senate so much of their invested stocks, as may be necessary to the purchase of a country for them to settle in, shall be permitted to them to be sold, or the United States will advance the necessary amount, upon a guarantee and pledge of an equal amount of their stocks; also, as much of them may be sold, with the consent of the President and Senate, as shall be adjudged necessary for establishing schools, mills, blacksmiths shops; and for the education of their children; and for any other needful purpose, which their situation and condition, may make, and by the President and Senate be considered, necessary; and on the happening of such a contingency, and information thereof being given of an intention of the whole or any portion of the nation to remove; the United States will furnish competent persons, safely to conduct them to their future destination, and also supplies necessary to the same, and for one year after their arrival at the west, provided the Indians shall desire supplies, to be furnished for so long a period; the supplies so afforded, to be chargeable to the general Chickasaw account, provided the funds of said nation shall be found adequate to the expenses which under this and other articles of this agreement may be required.

ART. XIV. It is understood and agreed, that articles twelve and thirteen of the "Treaty of Pontitock," of the twentieth day of October, one thousand, eight hundred and thirty-two, and which was concluded, with Genl. John Coffee shall be retained; all the other articles of said treaty, inconsistent in any respect with the provisions of this, are declared to be revoked. Also so much of the supplemental treaty as relates to Colbert Moore; to the bond of James Colbert transferred to Robert Gordon; to the central position of the Land Office; to the establishment of mail routes through the Chickasaw country; and as it respects the privilege given to John Donely; be, and the same are declared to be in full force.

ART. XV. By the sixth article of a treaty made with the Chickasaw nation, by Andrew Jackson and Isaac Shelby, on the nineteenth day of October, one thousand eight hundred and eighteen, it was provided that a Commissioner should be appointed, to mark the southern boundary of said cession; now it is agreed that the line which was run and marked by the Commissioner on the part of the United States, in pursuance of said treaty, shall be considered the true line to the extent that the rights and interests of the Chickasaws are conserned, and no farther.

ART. XVI. The United States agree that the appropriation made by
Congress, in the year one thousand eight hundred and thirty-three, for carrying into effect "the treaty with the Chickasaws," shall be applicable to this;
to be reimbursed by them; and their agent may receive and be charged with
the same, from time to time, as in the opinion of the Secretary of War, any
portion may be wanted for national purposes, by the Chickasaws; of which
nature and character, shall be considered their present visit to Washington
City.

Done at the city of Washington, on the 24th day of May, one thousand
eight hundred and thirty-four.

>   Jn. H. Eaton,
>   commissioner on the part of the United States.
>   George Colbert, his x mark,
>   Isaac Albertson, his x mark,
>   Martin Colbert,   L.S.
>   Henry Love,   L.S.
>   Benjamin Love,   L.S.

Witnesses —

>   Charles F. Little, secretary to the commissioner,
>   Ben Reynolds, Indian agent,
>   G.W. Long,
>   James Standefer,
>   Thomas S. Smith,
>   Saml. Swartwout,
>   Wm. Gordon,
>   F.W. Armstrong, c. agent,
>   John M. Millard.

The undersigned, appointed by the Chickasaw nation of Indians in the
two-fold capacity of a delegate and interpreter, hereby declares that in all
that is set forth in the above articles of convention and agreement, have been
by him fully and accurately interpreted and explained, and that the same
has been approved by the entire delegation.

May 24, 1834.

>   Benjamin Love, delegate and interpreter.
>   Charles F. Little, secretary to commissioner.
>   Ben. Reynolds, Indian agent.

TREATY WITH
THE CHICKASAW, 1834 [Second]

Articles supplementary to those concluded and signed, by the United States Commissioner, and the Chickasaw delegation on the 24th day of May, one thousand eight hundred and thirty-four; which being agreed to by the President and Senate of the United States, are to stand as part of said treaty.

ART. I. It is represented that the old chiefs Levi Colbert and Isaac Alberson, who have rendered many and valuable services to their nation, desire on account of their health, to visit some watering place, during the present year, for recovery and restoration; it is agreed that there be paid to the agent for these purposes, and to discharge some debts which are due and owing from the nation, the sum of three thousand dollars, out of the appropriation of one thousand eight hundred and thirty-three, for carrying into effect the "treaty of Pontitock," which said sum so far as used is to be hereafter reimbursed to the nation, by said Levi Colbert and Isaac Alberson, and by the nation to the United States, as other advances are to be reimbursed, from the sale of their lands.

ART. II. The Chickasaw people express a desire that the Government shall at the expense of the United States, educate some of their children, and they urge the justice of their application, on the ground, that they have ever been faithful and friendly to the people of this country, — that they have never raised the tomahawk, to shed the blood of an American, and have given up heretofore to their white brothers, extensive and valuable portions of their country, at a price wholly inconsiderable and inadequate; and from which the United States have derived great wealth and important advantages; therefore, with the advice and consent of the President and Senate of the United States, it is consented, that three thousand dollars for fifteen years, be appropriated and applied under the direction of the Secretary of War, for the education and instruction within the United States, of such children male and female or either, as the seven persons named in the treaty to which this is a supplement, and their successors, with the approval of the agent, from time to time may select and recommend.

ART. III. The Chickasaw nation desire to close finally, all the business they have on the east side of the Mississippi, that their Great Father, may be no more troubled with their complaints, and to this end, they ask the Government to receive from them a tract of land, of four miles square, heretofore reserved under the 4th article of their "Treaty of 1818," and to pay them within three months, from the date of this arrangement, the Government price of one dollar and a quarter per acre, for said reserve; and accordingly the same is agreed to, provided a satisfactory relinquishment of title from the parties interested, be filed with the Secretary of War, previous to said payment being made.

ART. IV. Benj. Reynolds, agent at the time of paying their last annuity, had stolen from him by a negro slave of the Chickasaws, a box containing one thousand dollars; the chiefs of the Chickasaw people satisfied of the fact, and hence unwilling to receive the lost amount from the agent, ask, and it is agreed, that the sum so stolen and lost, shall be passed to the credit of their nation by the United States, to be drawn on hereafter for their national purposes.

ART. V. The Chickasaw people are aware that one clerk is insufficient to the bringing of their lands early into market; and rather than encounter the delay which must ensue, they prefer the increased expense of an additional one. It is therefore stipulated that the President shall appoint another clerk, at the same annual compensation, agreed upon by the "Treaty of Pontitock;" who shall be paid after the manner prescribed therein. But whenever the President shall be of that opinion that the services of any officer employed under this treaty, for the sale of lands can be dispensed with; he will in justice to the Chickasaws, and to save them from unnecessary expenses, discontinue the whole, or such as can be dispensed with.

Signed the 24th of May, 1834.

Jn. H. Eaton, commissioner on the part	Martin Colbert,	L.S.
of the United States.	Henry Love,	L.S.
George Colbert, his x mark,	Benjamin Love,	L.S.
Isaac Albertson, his x mark,		

Witnesses:

Charles F. Little, secretary to	Thomas S. Smith,
commissioner,	Saml. Swartwout,
Ben. Reynolds, Indian agent,	Wm. Gordon,
G.E. Long,	F.E. Armstrong, C. agent,
James Standefer,	John M. Millard.

TREATY WITH THE CHEROKEE, 1835

Articles of a treaty, concluded at New Echota in the State of Georgia on the 29th day of Decr. 1835 by General William Carroll and John F. Schermerhorn commissioners on the part of the United States and the Chiefs Head Men and People of the Cherokee tribe of Indians.

Whereas the Cherokees are anxious to make some arrangements with the Government of the United States whereby the difficulties they have experienced by a residence within the settled parts of the United States under the jurisdiction and laws of the State Governments may be terminated and adjusted; and with a view to reuniting their people in one body and securing a permanent home for themselves and their posterity in the country selected by their forefathers without the territorial limits of the State sovereignties, and where they can establish and enjoy a government of their choice and perpetuate such a state of society as may be most consonant with their views, habits and condition; and as may tend to their individual comfort and their advancement in civilization.

And whereas a delegation of the Cherokee nation composed of Messrs. John Ross Richard Taylor Danl. McCoy Samuel Gunter and William Rogers with full power and authority to conclude a treaty with the United States did on the 28th day of February 1835 stipulate and agree with the Government of the United States to submit to the Senate to fix the amount which should be allowed the Cherokees for their claims and for a cession of their lands east of the Mississippi river, and did agree to abide by the award of the Senate of the United States themselves and to recommend the same to their people for their final determination.

And whereas on such submission the Senate advised "that a sum not exceeding five millions of dollars be paid to the Cherokee Indians for all their lands and possessions east of the Mississippi river."

And whereas this delegation after said award of the Senate had been made, were called upon to submit propositions as to its disposition to be arranged in a treaty which they refused to do, but insisted that the same "should be referred to their nation and there in general council to deliberate and determine on the subject in order to ensure harmony and good feeling among themselves."

And whereas a certain other delegation composed of John Ridge Elias Boudinot Archilla Smith S.W. Bell John West Wm. A. Davis and Ezekiel West, who represented that portion of the nation in favor of emigration to the Cherokee country west of the Mississippi entered into propositions for a treaty with John F. Schermerhorn commissioner on the part of the United States which were to be submitted to their nation for their final action and determination:

And whereas the Cherokee people, at their last October council at Red Clay, fully authorized and empowered a delegation or committee of twenty persons of their nation to enter into and conclude a treaty with the United States commissioner then present, *at that place or elsewhere* and as the people had good reason to believe that a treaty would then and there be made or at a subsequent council at New Echota which the commissioners it was well known and understood, were authorized and instructed to convene for said purpose; and since the said delegation have gone on to Washington city, with a view to close negotiations there, as stated by them notwithstanding they were officially informed by the United States commissioner that they would not be received by the President of the United States; and that the Government would transact no business of this nature with them, and that if a treaty was made it must be done here in the nation, where the delegation at Washington last winter *urged that it should be done for the purpose of promoting peace and harmony among the people*; and since these facts have also been corroborated to us by a communication recently received by the commissioner from the Government of the United States and read and explained to the people in open council and therefore believing said delegation can effect nothing and since our difficulties are daily increasing and our situation is rendered more and more precarious uncertain and insecure in consequence of the legislation of the States; and seeing no effectual way of relief, but in accepting the liberal overtures of the United States.

And whereas Genl. William Carroll and John F. Schermerhorn were appointed commissioners on the part of the United States, with full power and authority to conclude a treaty with the Cherokees east and were directed by the President to convene the people of the nation in general council at New Echota and to submit said propositions to them with power and authority to vary the same so as to meet the views of the Cherokees in reference to its details.

And whereas the said commissioners did appoint and notify a general council of the nation to convene at New Echota on the 21st day of December 1835; and informed them that the commissioners would be prepared to make a treaty with the Cherokee people who should assemble there and those who did not come they should conclude gave their assent and sanction to whatever should be transacted at this council and the people having met in council according to said notice.

Therefore the following articles of a treaty are agreed upon and concluded between William Carroll and John F. Schermerhorn commissioners on the part of the United States and the chiefs and head men and people of the Cherokee nation in general council assembled this 29th day of Decr 1835.

ARTICLE 1. The Cherokee nation hereby cede relinquish and convey to the United States all the lands owned claimed or possessed by them east of the Mississippi river, and hereby release all their claims upon the United States for spoliations of every kind for and in consideration of the sum of five millions of dollars to be expended paid and invested in the manner stipulated and agreed upon in the following articles. But as a question has arisen between the commissioners and the Cherokees whether the Senate in their resolution by which they advised "that a sum not exceeding five millions of dollars be paid to the Cherokee Indians for all their lands and possessions east of the Mississippi river" have included and made any allowance or consideration for claims for spoliations it is therefore agreed on the part of the United States that this question shall be again submitted to the Senate for their consideration and decision and if no allowance was made for spoliations that then an additional sum of three hundred thousand dollars be allowed for the same.

ARTICLE 2. Whereas by the treaty of May 6th 1828 and the supplementary treaty thereto of Feb. 14th 1833 with the Cherokees west of the Mississippi the United States guarantied and secured to be conveyed by patient, to the Cherokee nation of Indians the following tract of country "Beginning at a point on the old western territorial line of Arkansas Territory being twenty-five miles north from the point where the territorial line crosses Arkansas river, thence running from said north point south on the said territorial line where the said territorial line crosses Verdigris river; thence down said Verdigris river to the Arkansas river; thence down said Arkansas to a point where a stone is placed opposite the east or lower bank of Grand river at its junction with the Arkansas; thence running south forty-four degrees west one mile; thence in a straight line to a point four miles northerly, from the mouth of the north fork of the Canadian; thence along the said four mile line to the Canadian; thence down the Canadian to the Arkansas; thence down the Arkansas to that point on the Arkansas where the eastern Choctaw boundary strikes said river and running thence with the western line of Arkansas Territory as now defined, to the southwest corner of the Missouri; thence along the western Missouri line to the land assigned the Senecas; thence on the south line of the Senecas to Grand river;

thence up said Grand river as far as the south line of the Osage reservation, extended if necessary; thence up and between said south Osage line extended west if necessary, and a line drawn due west from the point of beginning to a certain distance west, at which a line running north and south from said Osage line to said due west line will make seven milions of acres within the whole described boundaries. In addition to the seven millions of acres of land thus provided for and bounded, the United States further guaranty to the Cherokee nation a perpetual outlet west, and a free and unmolested use of all the country west of the western boundary of said seven millions of acres, as far west as the sovereignty of the United States and their right of soil extend;

Provided however That if the saline or salt plain on the western prairie shall fall within said limits prescribed for said outlet, the right is reserved to the United States to permit other tribes of red men to get salt on said plain in common with the Cherokees; And letters patent shall be issued by the United States as soon as practicable for the land hereby guarantied."

And whereas it is apprehended by the Cherokees that in the above cession there is not contained a sufficient quantity of land for the accommodation of the whole nation on their removal west of the Mississippi the United States in consideration of the sum of five hundred thousand dollars therefore hereby covenant and agree to convey to the said Indians, and their descendants by patent, in fee simple the following additional tract of land situated between the west line of the State of Missouri and the Osage reservation beginning at the southeast corner of the same and runs north along the east line of the Osage lands fifty miles to the northeast corner thereof; and thence east to the west line of the State of Missouri; thence with said line south fifty miles; thence west to the place of beginning; estimated to contain eight hundred thousand acres of land; but it is expressly understood that if any of the lands assigned the Quapaws shall fall within the aforesaid bounds the same shall be reserved and excepted out of the lands above granted and a pro rata reduction shall be made in the price to be allowed to the United States for the same by the Cherokees.

ARTICLE 3. The United States also agree that the lands above ceded by the treaty of Feb. 14 1833, including the outlet, and those ceded by this treaty shall all be included in one patent executed to the Cherokee nation of Indians by the President of the United States according to the provisions of the act of May 28 1830. It is, however, agreed that the military reservation at Fort Gibson shall be held by the United States. But should the United States abandon said post and have no further use for the same it shall revert to the Cherokee nation. The United States shall always have the right to make and establish such post and military roads and forts in any part of the Cherokee country, as they may deem proper for the interest and protection of the same and the free use of as much land, timber, fuel and materials of all kinds for the construction and support of the same as may be necessary; provided that if the private rights of individuals are interfered with, a just compensation therfor shall be made.

ARTICLE 4. The United States also stipulate and agree to extinguish for the benefit of the Cherokees the titles to the reservations within their country made in the Osage treaty of 1825 to certain half-breeds and for this purpose they hereby agree to pay to the persons to whom the same belong or have been assigned or to their agents or guardians whenever they shall execute after the ratification of this treaty a satisfactory conveyance for the same, to the United States, the sum of fifteen thousand dollars according to a schedule accompanying this treaty of the relative value of the several reservations.

And whereas by the several treaties between the United States and the Osage Indians the Union and Harmony Missionary reservations which were established for their benefit are now situated within the country ceded by them to the United States; the former being situated in the Cherokee country and the latter in the State of Missouri. It is therefore agreed that the United States shall pay the American Board of Commissioners for Foreign Missions for the improvements on the same what they shall be appraised at by Capt. Geo. Vashon Cherokee sub-agent Abraham Redfield and A.P. Chouteau or such persons as the President of the United States shall appoint and the money allowed for the same shall be expended in schools among the Osages and improving their condition. It is understood that the United States are to pay the amount allowed for the reservations in this article and not the Cherokees.

ARTICLE 5. The United States hereby covenant and agree that the lands ceded to the Cherokee nation in the forgoing article shall, in no future time without their consent, be included within the territorial limits or jurisdiction of any State or Territory. But they shall secure to the Cherokee nation the right by their national councils to make and carry into effect all such laws as they may deem necessary for the government and protection of the persons and property within their own country belonging to their people or such persons as have connected themselves with them: provided always that they shall not be inconsistent with the constitution of the United States and such acts of Congress as have been or may be passed regulating trade and intercourse with the Indians; and also, that they shall not be considered as extending to such citizens and army of the United States as may travel or reside in the Indian country by permission according to the laws and regulations established by the Government of the same.

ARTICLE 6. Perpetual peace and friendship shall exist between the citizens of the United States and the Cherokee Indians. The United States agree to protect the Cherokee nation from domestic strife and foreign enemies and against intestine wars between the several tribes. The Cherokees shall endeavor to preserve and maintain the peace of the country and not make war upon their neighbors they shall also be protected against interruption and intrusion from citizens of the United States, who may attempt to settle in the country without their consent; and all such persons shall be removed from the same by order of the President of the United States. But this is not intended to prevent the residence among them of useful farmers mechanics and teachers for the instruction of Indians according to treaty stipulations.

ARTICLE 7. The Cherokee nation having already made great progress in civilization and deeming it important that every proper and laudable inducement should be offered to their people to improve their condition as well as to guard and secure in the most effectual manner the rights guarantied to them in this treaty, and with a view to illustrate the liberal and enlarged policy of the Government of the United States towards the Indians in their removal beyond the territorial limits of the States, it is stipulated that they shall be entitled to a delegate in the House of Representatives of the United States whenever Congress shall make provision for the same.

ARTICLE 8. The United States also agree and stipulate to remove the Cherokees to their new homes and to subsist them one year after their arrival there and that a sufficient number of steamboats and baggage-wagons shall be furnished to remove them comfortably, and so as not to endanger their health, and that a physician well supplied with medicines shall accompany each detachment of emigrants removed by the Government. Such persons and families as in the opinion of the emigrating agent are capable of subsisting and removing themselves shall be permitted to do so; and they shall be allowed in full for all claims for the same twenty dollars for each member of their family; and in lieu of their one year's rations they shall be paid the sum of thirty-three dollars and thirty-three cents if they prefer it.

Such Cherokees also as reside at present out of the nation and shall remove with them in two years west of the Mississippi shall be entitled to allowance for removal and subsistence as above provided.

ARTICLE 9. The United States agree to appoint suitable agents who shall make a just and fair valuation of all such improvements now in the possession of the Cherokees as add any value to the lands; and also of the ferries owned by them, according to their net income; and such improvements and ferries from which they have been dispossessed in a lawless manner or under any existing laws of the State where the same may be situated.

The just debts of the Indians shall be paid out of any monies due them for their improvements and claims; and they shall also be furnished at the discretion of the President of the United States with a sufficient sum to enable them to obtain the necessary means to remove themselves to their new homes, and the balance of their dues shall be paid them at the Cherokee agency west of the Mississippi. The missionary establishments shall also be valued and appraised in a like manner and the amount of them paid over by the United States to the treasurers of the respective missionary societies by whom they have been established and improved in order to enable them to erect such buildings and make such improvements among the Cherokees west of the Mississippi as they may deem necessary for their benefit. Such teachers at present among the Cherokees as this council shall select and designate shall be removed west of the Mississippi with the Cherokee nation and on the same terms allowed to them.

ARTICLE 10. The President of the United States shall invest in some safe and most productive public stocks of the country for the benefit of the whole Cherokee nation who have removed or shall remove to the lands assigned by this treaty to the Cherokee nation west of the Mississippi the following sums as a permanent fund for the purposes hereinafter specified and pay over the net income of the same annually to such person or persons as shall be authorized or appointed by the Cherokee nation to receive the same and their receipt shall be a full discharge for the amount paid to them viz: the sum of two hundred thousand dollars in addition to the present annuities of the nation to constitute a general fund the interest of which shall be applied annually by the council of the nation to such purposes as they may deem best for the general interest of their people. The sum of fifty thousand dollars to constitute an orphans' fund the annual income of which shall be expended towards the support and education of such orphan children as are destitute of the means of subsistence. The sum of one hundred and fifty thousand dollars in addition to the present school fund of the nation shall constitute a permanent school fund, the interest of which shall be applied annually by the council of the nation for the support of common schools and such a literary institution of a higher order as may be established in the Indian country. And in order to secure as far as possible the true and beneficial application of the orphans' and school fund the council of the Cherokee nation when required by the President of the United States shall make a report of the application of those funds and he shall at all times have the right if the funds have been misapplied to correct any abuses of them and direct the manner of their application for the purposes for which they were intended. The council of the nation may be giving two years' notice of their intention withdraw their funds by and with the consent of the President and Senate of the United States, and invest them in such manner as they may deem most proper for their interest. The United States also agree and stipulate to pay the just debts and claims against the Cherokee nation held by the citizens of the same and also the just claims of citizens of the United States for services rendered to the nation and the sum of sixty thousand dollars is appropriated for this purpose but no claims against individual persons of the nation shall be allowed and paid by the nation. The sum of three hundred thousand dollars is hereby set apart to pay and liquidate the just claims of the Cherokees upon the United States for spoliations of every kind, that have not been already satisfied under former treaties.

ARTICLE 11. The Cherokee nation of Indians believing it will be for the interest of their people to have all their funds and annuities under their own direction and future disposition hereby agree to commute their permanent annuity of ten thousand dollars for the sum of two hundred and fourteen thousand dollars, the same to be invested by the President of the United States as a part of the general fund of the nation; and their present school fund amounting to about fifty thousand dollars shall constitute a part of the permanent school fund of the nation.

ARTICLE 12. Those individuals and families of the Cherokee nation that are averse to a removal to the Cherokee country west of the Mississippi and are desirous to become citizens of the States where they reside and such as are qualified to take care of themselves and their property shall be entitled to receive their due portion of all the personal benefits accruing under this treaty for their claims, improvements and *per capita*; as soon as an appropriation is made for this treaty.

Such heads of Cherokee families as are desirous to reside within the States of No. Carolina Tennessee and Alabama subject to the laws of the same; and who are qualified or calculated to become useful citizens shall be entitled, on the certificate of the commissioners to a pre-emption right to one hundred and sixty acres of land or one quarter section at the minimum Congress price; so as to include the present buildings or improvements of those who now reside there and such as do not live there at present shall be permitted to locate within two years any lands not already occupied by persons entitled to pre-emption privilege under this treaty and if two or more families live on the same quarter section and they desire to continue their residence in these States and are qualified as above specified they shall, on receiving their pre-emption certificate be entitled to the right of pre-emption to such lands as they may select not already taken by any person entitled to them under this treaty.

It is stipulated and agreed between the United States and the Cherokee people that John Ross James Starr George Hicks John Gunter George Chambers John Ridge Elias Boudinot George Sanders John Martin William Rogers Roman Nose Situwake and John Timpson shall be a committee on the part of the Cherokees to recommend such persons for the privilege of pre-emption rights as may be deemed entitled to the same under the above articles and to select the missionaries who shall be removed with the nation; and that they be hereby fully empowered and authorized to transact all business on the part of the Indians which may arise in carrying into effect the provisions of this treaty and settling the same with the United States. If any of the persons above mentioned should decline acting or be removed by death; the vacancies shall be filled by the committee themselves.

It is also understood and agreed that the sum of one hundred thousand dollars shall be expended by the commissioners in such manner as the committee deem best for the benefit of the poorer class of Cherokees as shall remove west or have removed west and are entitled to the benefits of this treaty. The same to be delivered at the Cherokee agency west as soon after the removal of the nation as possible.

ARTICLE 13. In order to make a final settlement of all the claims of the Cherokees for reservations granted under former treaties to any individuals belonging to the nation by the United States it is therefore hereby stipulated and agreed and expressly understood by the parties to this treaty — that all the Cherokees and their heirs and descendants to whom any reservations have been made under any former treaties with the United States, and who have not sold or conveyed the same by deed or otherwise and who in the opinion of the commissioners have complied with the terms on which the reservations were granted as far as practicable in the several cases; and which reservations have since been sold by the United States shall constitute a just claim against the United States and the original reservee or their heirs or descendants shall be entitled to receive the present value thereof from the United States as unimproved lands. And all such reservations as have not been sold by the United States and where the terms on which the reservations were made in the opinion of the commissioners have been complied with as far as practicable, they or their heirs or descendants shall be entitled to the same. They are hereby granted and confirmed to them — and also all persons who were entitled to reservations under the treaty of 1817 and who are far as practicable in the opinion of the commissioners, have complied with the stipulations of said treaty, although by the treaty of 1819 such reservations were included in the unceded lands belonging to the Cherokee nation are hereby confirmed to them and they shall be entitled to receive a grant for the same. And all such reservees as were obliged by the laws of the States in which their reservations were situated, to abandon the same or purchase them from the States shall be deemed to have a just claim against the United States for the amount by them paid to the States with interest thereon for such reservations and if obliged to abandon the same, to the present value of such reservations as unimproved lands but in all cases where the reservees have sold their reservations or any part thereof and conveyed the same by deed or otherwise and have been paid for the same, they their heirs or descendants or their assigns shall not be considered as having any claims upon the United States under this article of the treaty nor be entitled to receive any compensation for the lands thus disposed of. It is expressly understood by the parties to this treaty that the amount to be allowed for reservations under this article shall not be deducted out of the consideration money allowed to the Cherokees for their claims for spoliations and the cession of their lands; but the same is to be paid for independently by the United States as it is only a just fulfillment of former treaty stipulations.

ARTICLE 14. It is also agreed on the part of the United States that such warriors of the Cherokee nation as were engaged on the side of the United States in the late war with Great Britain and the southern tribes of Indians, and who were wounded in such service shall be entitled to such pensions as shall be allowed them by the Congress of the United States to commence from the period of their disability.

ARTICLE 15. It is expressly understood and agreed between the parties to this treaty that after deducting the amount which shall be actually expended for the payment for improvements, ferries, claims, for spoliations, removal subsistence and debts and claims upon the Cherokee nation and for the additional quantity of lands and goods for the poorer class of Cherokees and the several sums to be invested for the general national funds; provided for in the several articles of this treaty the balance whatever the same may be shall be equally divided between all the people belonging to the Cherokee nation east according to the census just completed; and such Cherokees as have removed west since June 1833 who are entitled by the terms of their enrolment and removal to all the benefits resulting from the final treaty between the United States and the Cherokees east they shall also be paid for their improvements according to their approved value before their removal where fraud has not already been shown in their valuation.

ARTICLE 16. It is hereby stipulated and agreed by the Cherokees that they shall remove to their new homes within two years from the ratification of this treaty and that during such time the United States shall protect and defend them in their possessions and property and free use and occupation of the same and such persons as have been dispossessed of their improvements and houses; and for which no grant has actually issued previously to the enactment of the law of the State of Georgia, of December 1835 to regulate Indian occupancy shall be again put in possession and placed in the same situation and condition, in reference to the laws of the State of Georgia, as the Indians that have not been dispossessed; and if this is not done, and the people are left unprotected, then the United States shall pay the several Cherokees for their losses and damages sustained by them in consequence thereof. And it is also stipulated and agreed that the public buildings and improvements on which they are situated at New Echota for which no grant has been actually made previous to the passage of the above recited act if not occupied by the Cherokee people shall be reserved for the public and free use of the United States and the Cherokee Indians for the purpose of settling and closing all the Indian business arising under this treaty between the commissioners of claims and the Indians.

The United States, and the several States interested in the Cherokee lands, shall immediately proceed to survey the lands ceded by this treaty; but it is expressly agreed and understood between the parties that the agency buildings and that tract of land surveyed and laid off for the use of Colonel R.J. Meigs Indian agent or heretofore enjoyed and occupied by his successors in office shall continue subject to the use and occupancy of the United States, or such agent as may be engaged specially superintending the removal of the tribe.

ARTICLE 17. All the claims arising under or provided for in the several articles of this treaty, shall be examined and adjudicated by such commissioners as shall be appointed by the President of the United States for that purpose and their decision shall be final and on their certificate of the amount due the several claimants they shall be paid by the United States. All stipulations in former treaties which have not been superseded or annulled by this shall continue in full force and virtue.

ARTICLE 18. Whereas in consequence of the unsettled affairs of the Cherokee people and the early frosts, their crops are insufficient to support their families and great distress is likely to ensue and whereas the nation will not, until after their removal be able advantageously to expend the income of the permanent funds of the nation it is therefore agreed that the annuities of the nation which may accrue under this treaty for two years, the time fixed for their removal shall be expended in provision and clothing for the benefit of the poorer class of the nation; and the United States hereby agree to advance the same for that purpose as soon after the ratification of this treay as an appropriation for the same shall be made. It is however not intended in this article to interfere with that part of the annuities due the Cherokees west by the treaty of 1819.

ARTICLE 19. This treaty after the same shall be ratified by the President and Senate of the United States shall be obligatory on the contracting parties.

ARTICLE 20. [Supplemental article. Stricken out by Senate.]

In testimony whereof, the commissioners and the chiefs, head men, and people whose names are hereunto annexed, being duly authorized by the people in general council assembled, have affixed their hands and seals for themselves, and in behalf of the Cherokee nation.

I have examined the foregoing treaty, and although not present when it was made, I approve its provisions generally, and therefore sign it.

Wm. Carroll,
J.F. Schermerhorn.

Major Ridge, his x mark,	L.S.	Te-gah-e-ske, his x mark,	L.S.
James Foster, his x mark,	L.S.	Robert Rogers,	L.S.
Tesa-ta-esky, his x mark,	L.S.	John Gunter,	L.S.
Charles Moore, his x mark,	L.S.	John A. Bell,	L.S.
George Chambers, his x mark,	L.S.	Charles F. Foreman,	L.S.
Tah-yeske, his x mark,	L.S.	William Rogers,	L.S.
Archilla Smith, his x mark,	L.S.	George W. Adair,	L.S.
Andrew Ross,	L.S.	Elias Boudinot,	L.S.
William Lassley,	L.S.	James Starr, his x mark,	L.S.
Cae-te-hee, his x mark,	L.S.	Jesse Half-breed, his x mark,	L.S.

Signed and sealed in presence of—

Western B. Thomas, secretary.
Ben. F. Currey, special agent.
M. Wolfe Batman, first lietenant,
  sixth U.S. Infantry, disbursing
  agent.
Jon. L. Hooper, lieutenant,
  fourth Infantry.

C.M. Hitchcock, M.D., assistant
  surgeon, U.S.A.
G.W. Currey,
Wm. H. Underwood,
Cornelius D. Terhune,
John W.H. Underwood.

In compliance with instructions of the council at New Echota, we sign this treaty.

Stand Watie,
John Ridge.

March 1, 1836.
Witnesses:

Elbert Herring,
Alexander H. Everett,
John Robb,
D. Kurtz,

Wm. Y. Hansell,
Samuel J. Potts,
Jno. Litle,
S. Rockwell.

Whereas the western Cherokees have appointed a delegation to visit the eastern Cherokees to assure them of the friendly disposition of their people and their desire that the nation should again be united as one people and to urge upon them the expediency of accepting the overtures of the Government; and that, on their removal they may be assured of a hearty welcome and an equal participation with them in all the benefits and privileges of the

Cherokee country west and the undersigned two of said delegation being the only delegates in the eastern nation from the west at the signing and sealing of the treaty lately concluded at New Echota between their eastern brethren and the United States; and having fully understood the provisions of the same they agree to it in behalf of the western Cherokees. But it is expressly understood that nothing in this treaty shall affect any claims of the western Cherokees on the United States.

In testimony whereof, we have, this 31st day of December, 1835, hereunto set our hands and seals.

James Rogers,
John Smith,
Delegates from the western Cherokees.

Test:

    Ben. F. Currey, special agent.
    M.W. Batman, first lieutenant, Sixth Infantry,
    Jno. F. Hooper, lieutenant, Fourth Infantry,
    Elias Boudinot.

* * * *

Schedule and estimated value of the Osage half-breed reservations within the territory ceded to the Cherokees west of the Mississippi, (referred to in article 5 on the foregoing treaty,) viz:

Augustus Clamont one section	$6,000
James " " "	1,000
Paul " " "	1,300
Henry " " "	800
Anthony " " "	1,800
Rosalie " " "	1,800
Emilia D, of Mihanga	1,000
Emilia D, of Shemianga	1,300
	$15,000

I hereby certify that the above schedule is the estimated value of the Osage reservations; as made out and agreed upon with Col. A.P. Choteau who represented himself as the agent or guardian of the above reservees.

March 14, 1835.   J.F. Schermerhorn.

* * * *

Supplementary articles to a treaty concluded at New Echota, Georgia, December 29, 1835, between the United States and Cherokee people.

Whereas the undersigned were authorized at the general meeting of the Cherokee people held at New Echota as above stated, to make and assent to such alterations in the preceding treaty as might be thought necessary, and whereas the President of the United States has expressed his determination not to allow any pre-emptions or reservations his desire being that the whole Cherokee people should remove together and establish themselves in the country provided for them west of the Mississippi river.

ARTICLE 1. It is therefore agreed that all the pre-emption rights and reservations provided for in articles 12 and 13 shall be and are hereby relinquished and declared void.

ARTICLE 2. Whereas the Cherokee people have supposed that the sum of five million dollars fixed by the Senate in their resolution of _____ day of March, 1835, as the value of the Cherokee lands and possessions east of the Mississippi river was not intended to include the amount which may be required to remove them, nor the value of certain claims which many of their people had against citizens of the United States, which suggestion has been confirmed by the opinion expressed to the War Department by some of the Senators who voted upon the question and whereas the President is willing that this subject should be referred to the Senate for their consideration and if it was not intended by the Senate that the above-mentioned sum of five millions of dollars should include the objects herein specified that in that case such further provision should be made therefor as might appear to the Senate to be just.

ARTICLE 3. It is therefore agreed that the sum of six hundred thousand dollars shall be and the same is hereby allowed to the Cherokee people to include the expense of their removal, and all claims of every nature and description against the Government of the United States not herein otherwise expressly provided for, and to be in lieu of the said reservations and pre-emptions and of the sum of three hundred thousand dollars for spoliations described in the 1st article of the above-mentioned treaty. This sum of six hundred thousand dollars shall be applied and distributed agreeably to the provisions of the said treaty, and any surplus which may remain after removal and payment of the claims so ascertained shall be turned over and belong to the education fund.

But it is expressly understood that the subject of this article is merely referred hereby to the consideration of the Senate and if they shall approve the same then this supplement shall remain part of the treaty.

ARTICLE 4. It is also understood that the provisions in article 16, for the agency reservation is not intended to interfere with the occupant right of any Cherokees should their improvement fall within the same.

It is also understood and agreed, that the one hundred thousand dollars appropriated in article 12 for the poorer class of Cherokees and intended as a set-off to the pre-emption rights shall now be transferred from the funds of the nation and added to the general national fund of four hundred thousand dollars so as to make said fund equal to five hundred thousand dollars.

ARTICLE 5. The necessary expenses attending the negotiations of the aforesaid treaty and supplement and also of such persons of the delegation as may sign the same shall be defrayed by the United States.

* * * *

In testimony whereof, John F. Schermerhorn, commissioner on the part of the United States, and the undersigned delegation have hereunto set their hands and seals, this first day of March, in the year one thousand eight hundred and thirty-six.

J.F. Schermerhorn.

Major Ridge, his x mark,	L.S.	John A. Bell,	L.S.
James Foster, his x mark,	L.S.	Jos. A. Foreman,	
Tah-ye-ske, his x mark,	L.S.	Robert Sanders,	L.S.
Long Shell Turtle, his x mark,	L.S.	Elias Boudinot,	L.S.
John Fields, his x mark,	L.S.	Johnson Rogers,	L.S.
James Fields, his x mark,	L.S.	James Starr, his x mark,	L.S.
George Welch, his x mark,	L.S.	Stand Watie,	L.S.
Andrew Ross,	L.S.	John Ridge,	L.S.
William Rogers,	L.S.	James Rogers,	L.S.
John Gunter,	L.S.	John Smith, his x mark,	L.S.

Witnesses:

Elbert Herring,	John Robb,
Thos. Glascock,	Wm. Y. Hansell,
Alexander H. Everett,	Saml. J. Potts,
Jno. Garland, Major, U.S. Army,	Jno. Litle,
C.A. Harris,	S. Rockwell.

TREATY WITH THE CHOCTAW
AND THE CHICKASAW, 1837

Articles of convention and agreement made on the seventeenth day of January, 1837, between the undersigned chiefs and commissioners duly appointed and empowered by the Choctaw tribe of red people, and John McLish, Pitman Colbert, James Brown, and James Perry, delegates of the Chickasaw tribe of Indians, duly authorized by the chiefs and head-men of said people for that purpose, at Doaksville, near Fort Towson, in the Choctaw country.

ARTICLE 1. It is agreed by the Choctaws that the Chickasaws shall have the privilege of forming a district within the limits of their country, to be held on the same terms that the Choctaws now hold it, except the right of disposing of it, (which is held in common with the Choctaws and Chickasaws,) to be called the Chickasaw district of the Choctaw Nation; to have an equal representation in their general council, and to be placed on an equal footing in every other respect with any of the other districts of said nation, except a voice in the management of the consideration which is given for these rights and privileges; and the Chickasaw people to be entitled to all the rights and privileges of Choctaws, with the exception of participating in the Choctaw annuities and the consideration to be paid for these rights and privileges, and to be subject to the same laws to which the Choctaws are; but the Chickasaws reserve to themselves the sole right and privilege of controlling and managing the residue of their funds as far as is consistent with the late treaty between the said people and the Government of the United States, and of making such regulations and electing such officers for that purpose as they may think proper.

ARTICLE 2. The Chickasaw district shall be bounded as follows, viz: beginning on the north bank of Red River, at the mouth of Island Bayou, about eight or ten miles below the mouth of False Wachitta; thence running north along the main channel of said bayou to its source; thence along the dividing ridge between the Wachitta and Low Blue Rivers to the road leading from Fort Gibson to Fort Wachitta; thence along said road to the line dividing Musha-la-tubbee and Push-metahaw districts; thence eastwardly along said district line to the source of Brushy Creek; thence down said creek to where it flows into the Canadian River, ten or twelve miles above the mouth of the south fork of the Canadian; thence west along the main Canadian River to its source, if in the limits of the United States, or to those limits; and thence due south to Red River, and down Red River to the beginning.

ARTICLE 3. The Chickasaws agree to pay the Choctaws, as a consideration for these rights and privileges, the sum of five hundred and thirty thousand dollars-thirty thousand of which shall be paid at the time and in the manner that the Choctaw annuity of 1837 is paid, and the remaining five hundred thousand dollars to be invested in some safe and secure stocks, under the direction of the Government of the United States, redeemable within a period of not less than twenty years- and the Government of the United States shall cause the interest arising therefrom to be paid annually to the Choctaws in the following manner: twenty thousand dollars of which to be paid as the present Choctaw annuity is paid, for four years, and the residue to be subject to the control of the general council of the Choctaws; and after the expiration of the four years the whole of said interest to be subject to the entire control of the said council.

ARTICLE 4. To provide for the future adjustment of all complaints or dissatisfaction which may arise to interrupt the peace and harmony which have so long and so happily existed between the Choctaws and Chickasaws, it is hereby agreed by the parties that all questions relative to the construction of this agreement shall be referred to the Choctaw agent to be by him decided; reserving, however, to either party, should it feel itself aggrieved thereby, the rights of appealing to the President of the United States, whose decision shall be final and binding. But as considerable time might elapse before the decision of the President could be had, *in the mean time* the decision of the said agent shall be binding.

ARTICLE 5. It is hereby declared to be the intention of the parties hereto, that equal rights and privileges shall pertain to both Choctaws and Chickasaws to settle in whatever district they may think proper, and to be eligible to all the different offices of the Choctaw Nation, and to vote on the same terms in whatever district they may settle, except that the Choctaws are not to vote *in anywise* for officers in relation to the residue of the Chickasaw fund.

In testimony whereof, the parties hereto have hereunto subscribed their names and affixed their seals, at Doaksville, near fort Towson in the Choctaw country, on the day and year first above written.

In the presence of—

Wm. Armstrong, Acting Superintendent Western Territory,
Henry R. Carter, Conductor of the Chickasaw Delegation,
Josiah S. Doak,
Vincent B. Tims,
Daniel McCurtain, United States Interpreter,
P.J. Humphreys,
J.T. Sprague, Lieutenant U.S. Marine Corps,
Thomas Lafloor, his x mark, Chief Oaklafalaya district,
Nituchachue, his x mark, Chief of Pushmatahaw district,
Joseph Kincaid, his x mark, Chief of Mushalatubbee district.

Commissioners of the Choctaw
  Nation:

Commissioners of the Choctaw Nation:		Captains:
P.P. Pitchlynn,	L.S.	Oak-chi-a, his x mark.
George W. Haskins,	L.S.	Thomas Hays, his x mark,
Israel Folsom,	L.S.	Pis-tam-bee, his x mark,
R.M. Jones,	L.S.	Ho-lah-ta-ho-ma, his x mark,
Silas D. Fisher,	L.S.	E-yo-tah, his x mark,
Samuel Wowster,	L.S.	Isaac Perry, his x mark,
John McKenney, his x mark,		No-wah-ham-bee, his x mark.
Eyachahofaa, his x mark,		Chickasaw delegation:
Nathaniel Folsom, his x mark,		J. McLish,
Lewis Breashears, his x mark,		Pitman Colbert,
James Fletcher, his x mark,		James Brown, his x mark,
George Pusley, his x mark.		Jerry Perry, his x mark.

TREATY WITH THE UTAH, 1849

The following articles have been duly considered and solemnly adopted by the undersigned, that is to say, James S. Calhoun, Indian agent, residing at Santa Fé, acting as commissioner on the part of the United States of America, and Quixiachigiate, Nanito, Nincocunachi, Abaganixe, Ramahi, Subleta, Rupallachi, Saguasoxego, Paguisachi, Cobaxanor, Amuche, Puigniachi, Panachi, Sichuga, Uvicaxinape, Cuchuticay, Nachitope, Pueguate, Guano Juas, Pacachi, Saguanchi, Acaguate nochi, Puibuquiacte, Quixache tuate, Saxiabe, Pichiute, Nochichigue, Uvive, principal and subordinate chiefs, representing the Utah tribe of Indians.

I. The Utah tribe of Indians do hereby acknowledge and declare they are lawfully and exclusively under the jurisdiction of the government of said States: and to its power and authority they now unconditionally submit.

II. From and after the signing of this treaty, hostilities between the contracting parties shall cease, and perpetual peace and amity shall exist, the said tribe hereby binding themselves most solemnly never to associate with, or give countenance or aid to, any tribe or band of Indians, or other persons or powers, who may be, at any time, at enmity with the people or Government of said States; and that they will, in all future time, treat honestly and humanely every citizen of the United States, and all persons and powers at peace with the said States, and all cases of aggression against the said Utahs shall be referred to the aforesaid Government for adjustment and settlement.

III. All American and Mexican captives, and others, taken from persons or powers at peace with the said States shall be restored and delivered by said Utahs to an authorized officer or agent of said States, at Abiquin, on or before the first day of March, in the year of our Lord one thousand eight hundred and fifty. And, in like manner, all stolen property, of every description, shall be restored by or before the aforesaid first day of March, 1850. In the event such stolen property shall have been consumed or destroyed, the said Utah Indians do agree and are hereby bound to make such restitution and under such circumstances as the Government of the United States may order and prescribe. But this article is not to be so construed or understood, as to create a claim against said States, for any losses or depredations committed by said Utahs.

IV. The contracting parties agree that the laws now in force, and such others as may be passed, regulating the trade and intercourse, and for the preservation of peace with the various tribes of Indians under the protection and guardianship of the Government of the United States, shall be as binding and obligatory upon the said Utahs as if said laws had been enacted for their sole benefit and protection. And that said laws may be duly executed, and for all other useful purposes, the territory occupied by the Utahs is hereby annexed to New Mexico as now organized or as it may be organized or until the Government of the United States shall otherwise order.

V. The people of the United States, and all others in amity with the United States, shall have free passage through the territory of said Utahs, under such rules and regulations as may be adopted by authority of said States.

VI. In order to preserve tranquility, and to afford protection to all the people and interests of the contracting parties, the Government of the United States will establish such military posts and agencies, and authorize such trading-houses, at such time and in such places as the said Government may designate.

VII. Relying confidently upon the justice and liberality of the United States, and anxious to remove every possible cause that might disturb their peace and quiet, it is agreed by the Utahs that the aforesaid Government shall, at its earliest convenience, designate, settle, and adjust their territorial boundaries, and pass and execute such laws, in their territory, as the Government of said States may deem conducive to the happiness and prosperity of said Indians. And the said Utahs, further, bind themselves not to depart from their accustomed homes or localities unless specially permitted by an agent of the aforesaid Government; and so soon as their boundaries are distinctly defined, the said Utahs are further bound to confine themselves to said limits, under such rules as the said Government may prescribe, and to build up pueblos, or to settle in such other manner as will enable them most successfully to cultivate the soil, and pursue such other industrial pursuits as will best promote their happiness and prosperity: and they now deliberately and considerately, pledge their existence as a distinct tribe, to abstain, for all time to come, from all depredations; to cease the roving and rambling habits which have hitherto marked them as a people; to confine themselves strictly to the limits which may be assigned them; and to support themselves by their own industry, aided and directed as it may be by the wisdom, justice, and humanity of the America people.

VIII. For, and in consideration of the faithful performance of all the stipulations contained in this treaty by the said Utahs, the Government of the United States will grant to said Indians such donations, presents, and implements, and adopt such other liberal and humane measures, as said Government may deem meet and proper.

IX. This treaty shall be binding upon the contracting parties from and after the signing of the same, subject, in the first place, to the approval of the civil and military governor of New Mexico, and to such other modifications, amendments, and orders as may be adopted by the Government of the United States.

In faith whereof, the undersigned have signed this treaty, and affixed thereunto their seals, at Abiquin, in New Mexico, this the thirtieth day of December, in the year of our Lord one thousand eight hundred and forty-nine.

James S. Calhoun,	L.S.
Indian Agent, Commissioner,	U.S.
Quixiachigiate, his x mark,	L.S.
Principal Chief.	

Nanito, his x mark,	L.S.	Cuchuticay, his x mark,	L.S.
Nincocunachi, his x mark,	L.S.	Nachitope, his x mark,	L.S.
Abaganixe, his x mark,	L.S.	Pueguate, his x mark,	L.S.
Ramahi, his x mark,	L.S.	Guano Juas, his x mark,	L.S.
Subleta, his x mark,	L.S.	Pacachi, his x mark,	L.S.
Rupallachi, his x mark,	L.S.	Saguanchi, his x mark,	L.S.
Saguasoxego, his x mark,	L.S.	Acaguate nochi, his x mark,	L.S.
Paguishachi, his x mark,	L.S.	Puibuquiacte, his x mark,	L.S.
Cobaxanor, his x mark,	L.S.	Quixache tuate, his x mark,	L.S.
Amuche, his x mark,	L.S.	Saxiabe, his x mark,	L.S.
Puigniachi, his x mark,	L.S.	Pichiute, his x mark,	L.S.
Panachi, his x mark,	L.S.	Nochichigue, his x mark,	L.S.
Sichuga, his x mark,	L.S.	Uvive, his x mark,	L.S.
Uvicaxinape, his x mark,	L.S.	Subordinates.	

TREATY OF FORT LARAMIE
WITH SIOUX, ETC., 1851

Articles of a treaty made and concluded at Fort Laramie, in the Indian Territory, between D.D. Mitchell, superintendent of Indian affairs, and Thomas Fitzpatrick, Indian agent, commissioners specially appointed and authorized by the President of the United States, of the first part, and the chiefs, headmen, and braves of the following Indian nations, residing south of the Missouri River, east of the Rocky Mountains, and north of the lines of Texas and New Mexico, viz, the Sioux or Dahcotahs, Cheyennes, Arrapahoes, Crows, Assinaboines, Gros-Ventre, Mandans, and Arrickaras, parties of the second part, on the seventeenth day of September, A.D. one thousand eight hundred and fifty-one.

ARTICLE 1. The aforesaid nations, parties to this treaty, having assembled for the purpose of establishing and confirming peaceful relations amongst themselves, do hereby covenant and agree to abstain in future from all hostilities whatever against each other, to maintain good faith and friendship in all their mutual intercourse, and to make an effective and lasting peace.

ARTICLE 2. The aforesaid nations do hereby recognize the right of the United States Government to establish roads, military and other posts, within their respective territories.

ARTICLE 3. In consideration of the rights and privileges acknowledged in the preceding article, the United States bind themselves to protect the aforesaid Indian nations against the commission of all depredations by the people of the said United States, after the ratification of this treaty.

ARTICLE 4. The aforesaid Indian nations do hereby agree and bind themselves to make restitution or satisfaction for any wrongs committed, after the ratification of this treaty, by any band or individual of their people, on the people of the United States, whilst lawfully residing in or passing through their respective territories.

ARTICLE 5. The aforesaid Indian nations do hereby recognize and acknowledge the following tracts of country, included within the metes and boundaries hereinafter designated, as their respective territories, viz:

The territory of the Sioux or Dahcotah Nation, commencing the mouth of the White Earth River, on the Missouri River; thence in a southwesterly direction to the forks of the Platte River; thence up the north fork of the Platte River to a point known as the Red Bute, or where the road leaves the river; thence along the range of mountains known as the Black Hills, to the head-waters of Heart River; thence down Heart River to its mouth; and thence down the Missouri River to the place of beginning.

The territory of the Gros Ventre, Mandans, and Arrickaras Nations, commencing at the mouth of Heart River; thence up the Missouri River to the mouth of the Yellowstone River; thence up the Yellowstone River to the mouth of Powder River in a southeasterly direction, to the head-waters of the Little Missouri River; thence along the Black Hills to the head of Heart River, and thence down Heart River to the place of beginning.

The territory of the Assinaboin Nation, commencing at the mouth of the Yellowstone River; thence up the Missouri River to the mouth of the Muscle-shell River; thence from the mouth of the Muscle-shell River in a southeasterly direction until it strikes the head-waters of Big Dry Creek; thence down that creek to where it empties into the Yellowstone River, nearly opposite the mouth of Powder River, and thence down the Yellowstone River to the place of beginning.

The territory of the Blackfoot Nation, commencing at the mouth of Muscle-shell River; thence up the Missouri River to its source; thence along the main range of the Rocky Mountains, in a southerly direction, to the head-waters of the northern source of the Yellowstone River; thence down the Yellowstone River to the mouth of Twenty-five Yard Creek; thence across to the head-waters of the Muscle-shell River, and thence down the Muscle-shell River to the place of beginning.

The territory of the Crow Nation, commencing at the mouth of Powder River on the Yellowstone; thence up Powder River to its source; thence along the main range of the Black Hills and Wind River Mountains to the head-waters of the Yellowstone River; thence down the Yellowstone River to the mouth of Twenty-five Yard Creek; thence to the head-waters of the Muscle-shell River; thence down the Muscle-shell River to its mouth; thence to the head-waters of Big Dry Creek, and thence to its mouth.

The territory of the Cheyennes and Arrapahoes, commencing at the Red Bute, or the place where the road leaves the north fork of the Platte River; thence up the north fork of the Platte River to its source; thence along the main range of the Rocky Mountains to the head-waters of the Arkansas River; thence down the Arkansas River to the crossing of the Santa Fé road; thence in a northwesterly direction to the forks of the Platte River, and thence up the Platte River to the place of beginning.

It is, however, understood that, in making this recognition and acknowlegement, the aforesaid Indian nations do not hereby abandon or prejudice any rights or claims they may have to other lands; and further, that they do not surrender the privilege of hunting, fishing, or passing over any of the tracts of country heretofore described.

ARTICLE 6. The parties to the second part of this treaty having selected principals or head-chiefs for their respective nations, through whom all national business will hereafter be conducted, do hereby bind themselves to sustain said chiefs and their successors during good behavior.

ARTICLE 7. In consideration of the treaty stipulations, and for the damages which have or may occur by reason thereof to the Indian nations, parties hereto, and for their maintenance and the improvement of their moral and social customs, the United States bind themselves to deliver to the said Indian nations the sum of fifty thousand dollars per annum for the term of ten years, with the right to continue the same at the discretion of the President of the United States for a period not exceeding five years thereafter, in provisions, merchandise, domestic animals, and agricultural implements, in such proportions as may be deemed best adapted to their condition by the President of the United States, to be distributed in proportion to the population of the aforesaid Indian nations.

ARTICLE 8. It is understood and agreed that should any of the Indian nations, parties to this treaty, violate any of the provisions thereof, the United States may withhold the whole or a portion of the annuities mentioned in the preceding article from the nation so offending, until, in the opinion of the President of the United States, proper satisfaction shall have been made.

In testimony whereof the said D.D. Mitchell and Thomas Fitzpatrick commissioners as aforesaid, and the chiefs, headmen, and braves, parties hereto, have set their hands and affixed their marks, on the day and at the place first above written.

                                                            D.C. Mitchell
                                                            Thomas Fitzpatrick
                                                            Commissioners.

Sioux: Crows:
Mah-toe-wha-you-whey, his x mark.   Arra-tu-ri-sash, his x mark.
Mah-kah-toe-zah-zah, his x mark.   Doh-chepit-seh-chi-es, his x mark.
Bel-o-ton-kah-tan-ga, his x mark.   Assinaboines:
Nah-ka-pah-gi-gi, his x mark.   Mah-toe-wit-ko, his x mark.
Mak-toe-sah-bi-chis, his x mark.   Toe-tah-ki-eh-nan, his x mark.
Meh-wha-tah-ni-hans-kah-, his x mark.   Mandans and Gros Ventres:
  Cheyennes: Nochk-pit-shi-toe-pish, his x mark.
Wah-ha-nis-satta, his x mark.   She-oh-mant-ho, his x mark.
Voist-ti-toe-vetz, his x mark.   Arickarees:

Nahk-ko-me-ien, his x mark.
Koh-kah-y-wh-cum-est, his x mark.
  Arrapahoes:
Bè-ah-té-a-qui-sah, his x mark.
Neb-ni-bah-seh-it, his x mark.
Beh-kah-jay-beth-sah-es, his x mark.

Koun-hei-ti-shan, his x mark.
Bi-atch-tah-wetch, his x mark.

In the presence of—

A.B. Chambers, secretary.
S. Cooper, colonel, U.S. Army.
R.H. Chilton, captain, First Drags.
Thomas Duncan, captain,
  Mounted Riflemen.
Thos. G. Rhett, brevet captain R.M.R.
W.L. Elliott, first lieutenant R.M.R.
C. Campbell, interpreter for Sioux.
John S. Smith, interpreter for Cheyennes.
Robert Meldrum, interpreter for the Crows.

H. Culbertson, interpreter for
  Assiniboines and Gros Ventres.
Francois L'Etalie, interpretor for
  Arickarees.
John Pizelle, interpreter for the
  Arrapahoes.
B. Gratz Brown.
Robert Campbell.
Edmond F. Chouteau.

TREATY WITH THE NISQUALLI,
PUYALLUP, ETC., 1854

Articles of agreement and convention made and concluded on the She-nah-nam, or Medicine Creek, in the Territory of Washington, this twenty-sixth day of December, in the year one thousand eight hundred and fifty-four, by Isaac I. Stevens, governor and superintendent of Indian affairs of the said Territory, on the part of the United States, and the undersigned chiefs, head-men, and delegates of the Nisqually, Puyallup, Steilacoom, Squawskin, S'Homamish, Stehchass, T'Peeksin, Squi-aitl, and Sa-heh-wamish tribes and bands of Indians, occupying the lands lying round the head of Puget's Sound and the adjacent inlets, who, for the purpose of this treaty, are to be regarded as one nation, on behalf of said tribes and bands, and duly authorized by them.

ARTICLE 1. The said tribes and bands of Indians hereby cede, relinquish, and convey to the United States, all their right, title, and interest in and to the lands and country occupied by them, bounded and described as follows, to wit: Commencing at the point on the eastern side of Admiralty Inlet, known as Point Pully, about midway between Commencement and Elliott Bays; thence running in a southeasterly direction, following the divide between the waters of the Puyallup and Dwamish, or White Rivers, to the summit of the Cascade Mountains; thence southerly, along the summit of said range, to a point opposite the main source of the Skookum Chuck Creek; thence to and down said creek, to the coal mine; thence northwesterly, to the summit of the Black Hills; thence northerly, to the upper forks of the Satsop River; thence northeasterly, through the portage known as Wilkes's Portage, to Point Southworth, on the western side of Admiralty Inlet; thence round the foot of Vashon's Island, easterly and southeasterly, to the place of beginning.

ARTICLE 2. There is, however, reserved for the present use and occupation of the said tribes and bands, the following tracts of land, viz: The small island called Klah-che-min, situated opposite the mouths of Hammersley's and Totten's Inlets, and separated from Hartstene Island by Peale's

Passage, containing about two sections of land by estimation: a square tract containing two sections, or twelve hundred and eighty acres, on Puget's Sound, near the mouth of the She-nah-nam Creek, one mile west of the meridian line of the United States land survey, and a square tract containing two sections, or twelve hundred and eighty acres, lying on the south side of Commencement Bay; all which tracts shall be set apart, and, so far as necessary, surveyed and marked out for their exclusive use; nor shall any white man be permitted to reside upon the same without permission of the tribe and the superintendent or agent. And the said tribes and bands agree to remove to and settle upon the same within one year after the ratification of this treaty, or sooner if the means are furnished them. In the mean time, it shall be lawful for them to reside upon any ground not in the actual claim and occupation of citizens of the United States, and upon any ground claimed or occupied, if with the permission of the owner or claimant. If necessary for the public convenience, roads may be run through their reserves, and, on the other hand, the right of way with free access from the same to the nearest public highway is secured to them.

ARTICLE 3. The right of taking fish, at all usual and accustomed grounds and stations, is further secured to said Indians in common with all citizens of the Territory, and of erecting temporary houses for the purpose of curing, together with the privilege of hunting, gathering roots and berries, and pasturing their horses on open and unclaimed lands: *Provided, however*, That they shall not take shellfish from any beds staked or cultivated by citizens, and that they shall alter all stallions not intended for breeding-horses, and shall keep up and confine the latter.

ARTICLE 4. In consideration of the above session, the United States agree to pay to the said tribes and bands the sum of thirty-two thousand five hundred dollars, in the following manner, that is to say: For the first year after the ratification hereof, three thousand two hundred and fifty dollars; for the next two years, three thousand dollars each year; for the next three years, two thousand dollars each year; for the next four years fifteen hundred dollars each year; for the next five years twelve hundred dollars each year; and for the next five years one thousand dollars each year; all which said sums of money shall be applied to the use and benefit of the said Indians, under the direction of the President of the United States, who may from time to time determine, at his discretion, upon what beneficial objects to expend the same. And the superintendent of Indian affairs, or other proper officer, shall each year inform the President of the wishes of said Indians in respect thereto.

ARTICLE 5. To enable the said Indians to remove to and settle upon their aforesaid reservations, and to clear, fence, and break up a sufficient quantity of land for cultivaton, the United States further agree to pay the sum of three thousand two hundred and fifty dollars, to be laid out and expended under the direction of the President, and in such manner as he shall approve.

ARTICLE 6. The President may hereafter, when in his opinion the interests of the Territory may require, and the welfare of the said Indians be promoted, remove them from either or all of said reservations to such other suitable place or places within said Territory as he may deem fit, on remunerating them for their improvements and the expenses of their removal, or may consolidate them with other friendly tribes or bands. And he may further, at his discretion, cause the whole or any portion of the lands hereby reserved, or of such other land as may be selected in lieu thereof, to be surveyed into lots, and assign the same to such individuals or families as are willing to avail themselves of the privilege, and will locate on the same as a permanent home, on the same terms and subject to the same regulations as are provided in the sixth article of the treaty with the Omahas, so far as the same may be applicable. Any substantial improvements heretofore made by any Indian, and which he shall be compelled to abandon in consequence of this treaty, shall be valued under the direction of the President, and payment be made accordingly therefor.

ARTICLE 7. The annuities of the aforesaid tribes and bands shall not be taken to pay the debts of individuals.

ARTICLE 8. The aforesaid tribes and bands acknowledge their dependence on the Government of the United States, and promise to be friendly with all citizens thereof, and pledge themselves to commit no depredations on the property of such citizens. And should any one or more of them violate this pledge, and the fact be satisfactorily proved before the agent, the property taken shall be returned, or in default thereof, or if injured or destroyed, compensation may be made by the Government out of their annuities. Nor will they make war on any other tribe except in self-defence, but will submit all matters of difference between them and other Indians to the Government of the United States, or its agent, for decision, and abide thereby. And if any of the said Indians commit any depredations on any other Indians within the Territory, the same rule shall prevail as that prescribed in this article, in cases of depredations against citizens. And the said tribes agree not to shelter or conceal offenders against the laws of the United States, but to deliver them up to the authorities for trial.

ARTICLE 9. The above tribes and bands are desirous to exclude from their reservations the use of ardent spirits, and to prevent their people from drinking the same; and therefore it is provided, that any Indian belonging to said tribes, who is guilty of bringing liquor into said reservations, or who drinks liquor, may have his or her proportion of the annuities witheld from him or her for such time as the President may determine.

ARTICLE 10. The United States further agree to establish at the general agency for the district of Puget's Sound, within one year from the ratification hereof, and to support, for a period of twenty years, an agricultural and industrial school, to be free to children of the said tribes and bands, in common with those of the other tribes of said district, and to provide the said school with a suitable instructor or instructors, and also to provide a smithy and carpenter's shop, and furnish them with the necessary tools, and employ a blacksmith, carpenter, and farmer, for the term of twenty years, to instruct the Indians in their respective occupations. And the United States further agree to employ a physician to reside at the said central agency, who shall furnish medicine and advice to their sick, and shall vaccinate them; the expenses of the said school, shops, employées, and medical attendance, to be defrayed by the United States, and not deducted from the annuities.

ARTICLE 11. The said tribes and bands agree to free all slaves now held by them, and not to purchase or acquire others hereafter.

ARTICLE 12. The said tribes and bands finally agree not to trade at Vancouver's Island, or elsewhere out of the dominions of the United States; nor shall foreign Indians be permitted to reside in their reservations without consent of the superintendent or agent.

ARTICLE 13. This treaty shall be obligatory on the contracting parties as soon as the same shall be ratified by the President and Senate of the United States.

In testimony whereof, the said Isaac I. Stevens, governor and superintendent of Indian Affairs, and the undersigned chiefs, headmen, and delegates of the aforesaid tribes and bands, have hereunto set their hands and seals at the place and on the day and year hereinbefore written.

Isaac I. Stevens   L.S.

Governor and Superintendent Territory of Washington.

Qui-ee-metl, his x mark.	L.S.	Klo-out, his x mark.	L.S.
Sno-ho-dumset, his x mark.	L.S.	Se-uch-ka-nam, his x mark.	L.S.
Lesh-high, his x mark.	L.S.	Ske-mah-han, his x mark.	L.S.
Slip-o-elm, his x mark.	L.S.	Wuts-un-a-pum, his x mark.	L.S.
Kwi-ats, his x mark.	L.S.	Quuts-a-tadm, his x mark.	L.S.
Stee-high, his x mark.	L.S.	Quuts-a-heh-mtsn, his x mark.	L.S.
Di-a-keh, his x mark.	L.S.	Yah-leh-chn, his x mark.	L.S.
Hi-ten, his x mark.	L.S.	To-lahl-kut, his x mark.	L.S.
Squa-ta-hun, his x mark.	L.S.	Yul-lout, his x mark.	L.S.
Kahk-tse-min, his x mark.	L.S.	See-ahts-oot-soot, his x mark.	L.S.
Sonan-o-yutl, his x mark.	L.S.	Ye-takho, his x mark.	L.S.
Kl-tehp, his x mark.	L.S.	We-po-it-ee, his x mark.	L.S.
Sahl-ko-min, his x mark.	L.S.	Kah-sld, his x mark.	L.S.
T'bet-ste-heh-bit, his x mark.	L.S.	La'h-hom-kan, his x mark.	L.S.

Tcha-hoos-tan, his x mark.	L.S.	Pah-how-at-ish, his x mark.	L.S.
Ke-cha-hat, his x mark.	L.S.	Swe-yehm, his x mark.	L.S.
Spee-peh, his x mark.	L.S.	Sah-hwill, his x mark.	L.S.
Swe-yah-tum, his x mark.	L.S.	Se-kwaht, his x mark.	L.S.
Cha-achsh, his x mark.	L.S.	Kah-hum-klt, his x mark.	L.S.
Pich-kehd, his x mark.	L.S.	Yah-kwo-bah, his x mark.	L.S.
S'Klah-o-sum, his x mark.	L.S.	Wut-sah-le-wun, his x mark.	L.S.
Sah-le-tatl, his x mark.	L.S.	Sah-ba-hat, his x mark.	L.S.
See-lup, his x mark.	L.S.	Tel-e-kish, his x mark.	L.S.
E-la-kah-ka, his x mark.	L.S.	Swe-keh-nam, his x mark.	L.S.
Slug-yeh, his x mark.	L.S.	Sit-oo-ah, his x mark.	L.S.
Hi-nuk, his x mark.	L.S.	Ko-quel-a-cut, his x mark.	L.S.
Ma-mo-nish, his x mark.	L.S.	Jack, his x mark.	L.S.
Cheels, his x mark.	L.S.	Keh-kise-bel-lo, his x mark.	L.S.
Knutcanu, his x mark.	L.S.	Go-yeh-hn, his x mark.	L.S.
Bats-ta-kobe, his x mark.	L.S.	Sah-putsh, his x mark.	L.S.
Win-ne-ya, his x mark.	L.S.	William, his x mark.	L.S.

Executed in the presence of us —

M.T. Simmons, Indian agent.
James Doty, secretary of the
  commission.
C.H. Mason, secretary Wash-
  ington Territory.
W.A. Slaughter, first lieutenant,
  Fourth Infantry.
James McAlister,
E. Giddings, jr.
George Shazer,
Henry D. Cock,

S.S. Ford, jr.,
John W. McAlister,
Clovington Cushman,
Peter Anderson,
Samuel Klady,
W.H. Pullen,
P.O. Hough,
E.R. Tyerall,
George Gibbs,
Benj. F. Shaw, interpreter,
Hazard Stevens.

TREATY WITH THE BLACKFEET, 1855

Articles of agreement and convention made and concluded at the council-ground on the Upper Missouri, near the mouth of the Judith River, in the Territory of Nebraska, this seventeenth day of October, in the year one thousand eight hundred and fifty-five, by and between A. Cumming and Isaac I. Stevens, commissioners duly appointed and authorized, on the part of the United States, and the undersigned chiefs, headmen, and delegates of the following nations and tribes of Indians, who occupy, for the purposes of hunting, the territory on the Upper Missouri and Yellowstone Rivers, and who have permanent homes as follows: East of the Rocky Mountains, the Blackfoot Nation, consisting of the Piegan, Blood, Blackfoot, Gros Ventres tribes of Indians. West of the Rocky Mountains, the Flathead Nation, consisting of the Flathead, Upper Pend d'Oreille, and Kootenay tribes of Indians, and the Nez Percé tribe of Indians, the said chiefs, headmen and delegates, in behalf of and acting for said nations and tribes, and being duly authorized thereto by them.

ARTICLE 1. Peace, friendship and amity shall hereafter exist between the United States and the aforesaid nations and tribes of Indians, parties to this treaty, and the same shall be perpetual.

ARTICLE 2. The aforesaid nations and tribes of Indians, parties to this treaty, do hereby jointly and severally covenant that peaceful relations shall likewise be maintained among themselves in future; and that they will abstain from all hostilities whatsoever against each other, and cultivate mutual good-will and friendship. And the nations and tribes aforesaid do furthermore jointly and severally covenant, that peaceful relations shall be maintained with and that they will abstain from all hostilities whatsoever, excepting in self-defense, against the following-named nations and tribes of Indians, to wit: the Crows, Assineboins, Crees, Snakes, Blackfeet, Sans Arcs, and Aunce-pa-pas bands of Sioux, and all other neighboring nations and tribes of Indians.

ARTICLE 3. The Blackfoot Nation consent and agree that all that portion of the country recognized and defined by the treaty of Laramie as Blackfoot territory, lying within lines drawn from the Hell Gate or Medicine Rock Passes in the main range of the Rocky Mountains, in an easterly

tion to the nearest source of the Muscle Shell River, thence to the mouth of Twenty-five Yard Creek, thence up the Yellowstone River to its northern source, and thence along the main range of the Rocky Mountains, in a northerly direction, to the point of beginning, shall be a common hunting-ground for ninety-nine years, where all the nations, tribes and bands of Indians, parties to this treaty, may enjoy equal and uninterrupted privileges of hunting, fishing and gathering fruit, grazing animals, curing meat and dressing robes. They further agree that they will not establish villages, or in any way exercise exclusive rights within ten miles of the northern line of the common hunting-ground, and that the parties to this treaty may hunt on said northern boundary line and within ten miles thereof.

Provided, That the western Indians, parties to this treaty, may hunt on the trail leading down the Muscle Shell to the Yellowstone; the Muscle Shell River being the boundary separating the Blackfoot from the Crow territory.

And provided, That no nation, band, or tribe of Indians, parties to this treaty, nor any other Indians, shall be permitted to establish permanent settlements, or in any other way exercise, during the period above mentioned, exclusive rights or privileges within the limits of the above-described hunting-ground.

And provided further, That the rights of the western Indians to a whole or part of the common hunting-ground, derived from occupancy and possession, shall not be affected by this article, except so far as said rights may be determined by the treaty of Laramie.

ARTICLE 4. The parties to this treaty agree and consent, that the tract of country lying within lines drawn from the Hell Gate or Medicine Rock Passes, in an easterly direction, to the nearest source of the Muscle Shell River, thence down said river to its mouth, thence down the channel of the Missouri River to the mouth of Milk River, thence due north to the forty-ninth parallel, thence due west on said parallel to the main range of the Rocky Mountains, and thence southerly along said range to the place of beginning, shall be the territory of the Blackfoot Nation, over which said nation shall exercise exclusive control, excepting as may be otherwise provided in this treaty. Subject, however, to the provisions of the third article of this treaty, giving the right to hunt, and prohibiting the establishment of permanent villages and the exercise of any exclusive rights within ten miles of the northern line of the common hunting-ground, drawn from the nearest source of the Muscle Shell River to the Medicine Rock Passes, for the period of ninety-nine years.

Provided also, That the Assiniboins shall have the right of hunting, in common with the Blackfeet, in the country lying between the aforesaid eastern boundary line, running from the mouth of Milk River to the forty-ninth parallel, and a line drawn from the left bank of the Missouri River, opposite the Round Butte north, to the forty-ninth parallel.

ARTICLE 5. The parties to this treaty, residing west of the main range of the Rocky Mountains, agree and consent that they will not enter the common hunting ground, nor any part of the Blackfoot territory, or return home, by any pass in the main range of the Rocky Mountains to the north of the Hell Gate or Medicine Rock Passes. And they further agree that they will not hunt or otherwise disturb the game, when visiting the Blackfoot territory for trade or social intercourse.

ARTICLE 6. The aforesaid nations and tribes of Indians, parties to this treaty, agree and consent to remain within their own respective countries, except when going to or from, or whilst hunting upon, the "common hunting ground," or when visiting each other for the purpose of trade or social intercourse.

ARTICLE 7. The aforesaid nations and tribes of Indians agree that citizens of the United States may live in and pass unmolested through the countries respectively occupied and claimed by them. And the United States is hereby bound to protect said Indians against depredations and other unlawful acts which white men residing in or passing through their country commit.

ARTICLE 8. For the purpose of establishing travelling thoroughfares through their country, and the better to enable the President to execute the provisions of this treaty, the aforesaid nations and tribes do hereby consent and agree, that the United States may, within the countries respectively occupied and claimed by them, construct roads of every description; establish lines of telegraph and military posts; use materials of every description found in the Indian country; build houses for agencies, missions, schools, farms, shops, mills, stations, and for any other purpose for which they may be required, and permanently occupy as much land as may be necessary for the various purposes above enumerated, including the use of wood for fuel and land for grazing, and that the navigation of all lakes and streams shall be forever free to citizens of the United States.

ARTICLE 9. In consideration of the foregoing agreements, stipulations, and cessions, and on condition of their faithful observance, the United States agree to expend, annually, for the Piegan, Blood, Blackfoot, and Gros Ventres tribes of Indians, constituting the Blackfoot Nation, in addition to the goods and provisions distributed at the time of signing the treaty, twenty thousand dollars, annually, for ten years, to be expended in such useful goods and provisions, and other articles, as the President, at his discretion, may from time to time determine; and the superintendent, or other proper officer, shall each year inform the President of the wishes of the Indians in relation thereto: *Provided, however,* That if, in the judgment of the

President and Senate, this amount be deemed insufficient, it may be increased not to exceed the sum of thirty-five thousand dollars per year.

ARTICLE 10. The United States further agree to expend annually, for the benefit of the aforesaid tribes of the Blackfoot Nation, a sum not exceeding fifteen thousand dollars annually, for ten years, in establishing and instructing them in agricultural and mechanical pursuits, and in educating their children, and in any other respect promoting their civilization and Christianization: *Provided, however,* That to accomplish the objects of this article, the President may, at his discretion, apply any or all the annuities provided for in this treaty: *And provided, also,* That the President may, at his discretion, determine in what proportions the said annuities shall be divided among the several tribes.

ARTICLE 11. The aforesaid tribes acknowledge their dependence on the Government of the United States, and promise to be friendly with all citizens thereof, and to commit no depredations or other violence upon such citizens. And should any one or more violate this pledge, and the fact to be proved to the satisfaction of the President, the property taken shall be returned, or, in default thereof, or if injured or destroyed, compensation may be made by the Government out of the annuities. The aforesaid tribes are hereby bound to deliver such offenders to the proper authorities for trial and punishment, and are held responsible, in their tribal capacity, to make reparation for depredations so committed.

Nor will they make war upon any other tribes, except in self-defense, but will submit all matter of difference, between themselves and other Indians, to the Government of the United States, through its agents, for adjustment, and will abide thereby. And if any of the said Indians, parties to this treaty, commit depredations on any other Indians within the jurisdiction of the United States, the same rule shall prevail as that prescribed in this article in case of depredations against citizens. And the said tribes agree not to shelter or conceal offenders against the laws of the United States, but to deliver them up to the authorities for trial.

ARTICLE 12. It is agreed and understood, by and between the parties to this treaty, that if any nation or tribe of Indians aforesaid, shall violate any of the agreements, obligations, or stipulations, herein contained, the United States may withhold, for such length of time as the President and Congress may determine, any portion or all of the annuities agreed to be paid to said nation or tribe under the ninth and tenth articles of this treaty.

ARTICLE 13. The nations and tribes of Indians, parties to this treaty, desire to exclude from their country the use of ardent spirits or other intoxicating liquor, and to prevent their people from drinking the same. Therefore, it is provided, that any Indian belonging to said tribes who is guilty of bringing such liquor into the Indian country, or who drinks liquor, may have his or her proportion of the annuities withheld from him or her, for such time as the President may determine.

ARTICLE 14. The aforesaid nations and tribes of Indians, west of the Rocky Mountains, parties to this treaty, do agree, in consideration of the provisions already made for them in existing treaties, to accept the guarantees of the peaceful occupation of their hunting-grounds, east of the Rocky Mountains, and of remunerations for depredations made by the other tribes, pledged to be secured to them in this treaty out of the annuities of said tribes, in full compensation for the concessions which they, in common with the said tribes, have made in this treaty.

The Indians east of the mountains, parties to this treaty, likewise recognize and accept the guarantees of this treaty, in full compensation for the injuries or depredations which have been, or may be committed by the aforesaid tribes, west of the Rocky Mountains.

ARTICLE 15. The annuities of the aforesaid tribes shall not be taken to pay the debts of individuals.

ARTICLE 16. This treaty shall be obligatory upon the aforesaid nations and tribes of Indians, parties hereto, from the date hereof, and upon the United States as soon as the same shall be ratified by the President and Senate.

In testimony whereof the said A. Cumming and Isaac I. Stevens, commissioners on the part of the United States, and the undersigned chiefs, headmen, and delegates of the aforesaid nations and tribes of Indians, parties to this treaty, have hereunto set their hands and seals at the place and on the day and year hereinbefore written.

A. Cumming.	L.S.
Isaac I. Stevens.	L.S.

Piegans:		The Father of All Children,
Nee-ti-nee, or "the only chief"		his x mark.	L.S.
now called the Lame Bull,		The Bull's Back Fat, his x
his x mark.	L.S.	mark.	L.S.
Mountain Chief, his x mark.	L.S.	Heavy Shield, his x mark.	L.S.
Low Horn, his x mark.	L.S.	Nah-tose-onistah, his x mark.	L.S.
Little Gray Head, his x mark.	L.S.	The Calf Shirt, his x mark.	L.S.
Little Dog, his x mark.	L.S.	Nez Percés:
Big Snake, his x mark.	L.S.	Spotted Eagle, his x mark.	L.S.
The Skunk, his x mark.	L.S.	Looking Glass, his x mark.	L.S.
The Bad Head, his x mark.	L.S.	The Three Feathers, his x mark.	L.S.
Kitch-eepone-istah, his x		Eagle from the Light, his x
mark.	L.S.	mark.	L.S.
Middle Sitter, his x mark.	L.S.	Lone Bird, his x mark.	L.S.
Bloods:		Ip-shun-nee-wus, his x mark.	L.S.
Onis-tay-say-nah-que-im, his		Wat-ti-wat-ti-we-hinck, his x
x mark.	L.S.	mark.	L.S.

White Bird, his x mark.	L.S.	The Big Straw, his x mark.	L.S.
Stabbing Man, his x mark.	L.S.	Flathead:	
Jesse, his x mark.	L.S.	Bear Track, his x mark.	L.S.
Plenty Bears, his x mark.	L.S.	Little Michelle,	L.S.
Flathead Nation:		Palchinah, his x mark.	L.S.
Victor, his x mark.	L.S.	Gros Ventres:	
Alexander, his x mark..	L.S.	Bear's Shirt, his x mark.	L.S.
Moses, his x mark.	L.S.	Little Soldier, his x mark.	L.S.
Big Canoe, his x mark.	L.S.	Star Robe, his x mark.	L.S.
Ambrose, his x mark.	L.S.	Sitting Squaw, his x mark.	L.S.
Kootle-cha, his x mark.	L.S.	Weasel Horse, his x mark.	L.S.
Michelle, his x mark.	L.S.	The Rider, his x mark.	L.S.
Francis, his x mark.	L.S.	Eagle Chief, his x mark.	L.S.
Vincent, his x mark.	L.S.	Heap of Bears, his x mark.	L.S.
Andrew, his x mark.	L.S.	Blackfeet:	
Adolphe, his x mark.	L.S.	The Three Bulls, his x mark.	L.S.
Thunder, his x mark.	L.S.	The Old Kootomais, his x mark.	L.S.
Piegans:		Pow-ah-que, his x mark.	L.S.
Running Rabbit, his x mark.	L.S.	Chief Rabbit Runner, his x mark.	L.S.
Chief Bear, his x mark.	L.S.	Bloods:	
The Little White Buffalo, his		The Feather, his x mark.	L.S.
x mark.	L.S.	The white Eagle, his x mark.	L.S.

Executed in presence of—

James Doty, secretary.
Alfred J. Vaughan, jr.
E. Alw. Hatch, agent for Blackfeet.
Thomas Adams, special agent Flathead Nation.
R.H. Lansdale, Indian agent Flathead Nation.
W.H. Tappan, sub-agent for the Nez Percés.
James Bird,
A. Culbertson, } Blackfoot interpreters.
Benj. Deroche,
Benj. Kiser, his x mark,
    Witness, James Doty, } Flat Head interpreters.
Gustavus Sohon,
W. Craig,
Delaware Jim, his x mark, } Nez Percé interpreters.
    Witness, James Doty,
A Cree Chief (Broken Arm,) his mark.
    Witness, James Doty.
A.J. Hoeekeorsg,
James Croke,
E.S. Wilson,
A.C. Jackson,
Charles Shucette, his x mark.
Christ. P. Higgins,
A.H. Robie,
S.S. Ford, jr.

TREATY WITH THE
WESTERN SHOSHONI, 1863

Treaty of Peace and Friendship made at Ruby Valley, in the Territory of Nevada, this first day of October, A.D. one thousand eight hundred and sixty-three, between the United States of America, represented by the undersigned commissioners, and the Western Bands of the Shoshonee Nation of Indians, represented by their Chiefs and Principal Men and Warriors, as follows:

ARTICLE 1.

Peace and friendship shall be hereafter established and maintained between the Western Bands of the Shoshonee nation and the people and Government of the United States; and the said bands stipulate and agree that hostilities and all depredations upon the emigrant trains, the mail and telegraph lines, and upon the citizens of the United States within their country, shall cease.

ARTICLE 2.

The several routes of travel through the Shoshonee country, now or hereafter used by white men, shall be forever free, and unobstructed by the said bands, for the use of the government of the United States, and of all emigrants and travellers under its authority and protection, without molestation or injury from them. And if depredations are at any time committed by bad men of their nation, the offenders shall be immediately taken and delivered up to the proper officers of the United States, to be punished as their offences shall deserve; and the safety of all travellers passing peaceably over either of said routes is hereby guarantied by said bands.

Military posts may be established by the President of the United States along said routes or elsewhere in their country; and station houses may be erected and occupied at such points as may be necessary for the comfort and convenience of travellers or for mail or telegraph companies.

ARTICLE 3.

The telegraph and overland stage lines having been established and operated by companies under the authority of the United States through a part of the Shoshonee country, it is expressly agreed that the same may be continued without hindrance, molestation, or injury from the people of said bands, and that their property and the lives and property of passengers in the stages and of the employes of the respective campanies, shall be protected by them. And further, it being understood that provision has been made by the government of the United States for the construction of a railway from the plains west to the Pacific ocean, it is stipulated by the said bands that the said railway or its branches may be located, constructed, and operated, and without molestation from them, through any portion of country claimed or occupied by them.

ARTICLE 4.

It is further agreed by the parties hereto, that the Shoshonee country may be explored and prospected for gold and silver, or other minerals; and when mines are discovered, they may be worked, and mining and agricultural settlements formed, and ranches established whenever they may be required. Mills may be erected and timber taken for their use, as also for building and other purposes in any part of the country claimed by said bands.

ARTICLE 5.

It is understood that the boundaries of the country claimed and occupied by said bands are defined and described by them as follows:

On the north by Wong-goga-da Mountains and Shoshonee River Valley; on the west by Su-non-to-yah Mountains or Smith Creek Mountains; on the south by Wi-co-bah and the Colorado Desert; on the east by Po-ho-no-be Valley or Steptoe Valley and Great Salt Lake Valley.

ARTICLE 6.

The said bands agree that whenever the President of the United States shall deem it expedient for them to abandon the roaming life, which, they now lead, and become herdsmen or agriculturalists, he is hereby authorized to make such reservations for their use as he may deem necessary within the country above described; and they do also hereby agree to remove their camps to such reservations as he may indicate, and to reside and remain therein.

ARTICLE 7.

The United States, being aware of the inconvenience resulting to the Indians in consequence of the driving away and destruction of game along the routes travelled by white men, and by the formation of agricultural and mining settlements, are willing to fairly compensate them for the same; therefore, and in consideration of the preceding stipulations, and of their faithful observance by the said bands, the United States promise and agree to pay to the said bands of the Shoshonee nation parties hereto, annually for the term of twenty years, the sum of five thousand dollars in such articles, including cattle for herding or other purposes, as the President of the United States shall deem suitable for their wants and condition, either as hunters or herdsmen. And the said bands hereby acknowledge the reception of the said stipulated annuities as a full compensation and equivalent for the loss of game and the rights and privileges hereby conceded.

ARTICLE 8.

The said bands hereby acknowledge that they have received from said commissioners provisions and clothing amounting to five thousand dollars as presents at the conclusion of this treaty.

Done at Ruby Valley the day and year above written.

James W. Nye.
James Duane Doty.

Te-moak, his x mark.
Mo-ho-a.
Kirk-weedgwa, his x mark.
To-nag, his x mark.
To-so-wee-so-op, his x mark.
Sow-er-e-gah, his x mark.

Po-on-go-sah, his x mark.
Par-a-woat-ze, his x mark.
Ga-ha-dier, his x mark.
Ko-ro-kout-ze, his x mark.
Pon-ge-mah, his x mark.
Buck, his x mark.

Witnesses:

J.B. Moore, lieutenant-colonel Third Infantry California Volunteers.
Jacob T. Lockhart, Indian agent Nevada Territory.
Henry Butterfield, interpreter.

TREATY WITH THE CREEKS, 1866

Treaty of cession and indemnity concluded at the city of Washington on the fourteenth day of June, in the year of our Lord one thousand eight hundred and sixty-six, by and between the United States, represented by Dennis N. Cooley, Commissioner of Indian Affairs, Elija Sells, superintendent of Indian affairs for the southern superintendency, and Col. Ely S. Parker, special commissioner, and the Creek Nation of Indians, represented by Ok-tars-sars-harjo, or Sands; Cow-e-to-me-co and Che-chu-chee, delegates at large, and D.N. McIntosh and James Smith, special delegates of the Southern Creeks.

PREAMBLE

Whereas existing treaties between the United States and the Creek Nation have become insufficient to meet their mutual necessities; and whereas the Creeks made a treaty with the so-called Confederate States, on the tenth of July, one thousand eight hundred and sixty-one, whereby they ignored their allegiance to the United States, and unsettled the treaty relations existing between the Creeks and the United States, and did so render themselves liable to forfeit to the United States all benefits and advantages enjoyed by them in lands, annuities, protection, and immunities, including their lands and other property held by grant or gift from the United States; and whereas in view of said liabilities the United States require of the Creeks a portion of their land whereon to settle other Indians; and whereas a treaty of peace and amity was entered into between the United States and the Creeks and other tribes at Fort Smith, September *thirteenth* (tenth.) eighteen hundred and sixty-five, whereby the Creeks revoked, cancelled, and repudiated the aforesaid treaty made with the so-called Confederate States; and whereas the United States, through its commissioners, in said treaty of peace and amity, promised to enter into treaty with the Creeks to arrange and settle all questions relating to and growing out of said treaty with the so-called Confederate States: Now, therefore, the United States, by its commissioners, and the above-named delegates of the Creek Nation, the day and year above mentioned, mutually stipulate and agree, on behalf of the respective parties, as follows, to wit:

108

ARTICLE 1. There shall be perpetual peace and friendship between the parties to this treaty, and the Creeks bind themselves to remain firm allies and friends of the United States, and never to take up arms against the United States, but always faithfully to aid in putting down its enemies. They also agree to remain at peace with all other Indian tribes; and, in return, the United States guarantees them quiet possession of their country, and protection against hostilities on the part of other tribes. In the event of hostilities, the United States agree that the tribe, commencing and prosecuting the same shall, as far as may be practicable, make just reparation therefor. To insure this protection, the Creeks agree to a military occupation of their country, at any time, by the United States, and the United States agree to station and continue in said country from time to time, at its own expense, such force as may be necessary for that purpose. A general amnesty of all past offenses against the laws of the United States, committed by any member of the Creek Nation, is hereby declared. And the Creeks, anxious for the restoration of kind and friendly feelings among themselves, do hereby declare an amnesty for all past offenses against their government, and no Indian or Indians shall be proscribed, or any act of forfeiture or confiscation passed against those who have remained friendly to, or taken up arms against, the United States, but they shall enjoy equal privileges with other members of said tribe, and all laws heretofore passed inconsistent herewith are hereby declared inoperative.

ARTICLE 2. The Creeks hereby covenant and agree that henceforth neither slavery nor involuntary servitude, otherwise than in the punishment of crimes, whereof the parties shall have been duly convicted in accordance with laws applicable to all members of said tribe, shall ever exist in said nation; and inasmuch as there are among the Creeks many persons of African descent, who have no interest in the soil, it is stipulated that hereafter these persons lawfully residing in said Creek country under their laws and usages, or who have been thus residing in said country, and may return within one year from the ratification of this treaty, and their descendants and such others of the same race as may be permitted by the laws of the said nation to settle within the limits of the jurisdiction of the Creek Nation as citizens (thereof,) shall have and enjoy all the rights and privileges of native citizens, including an equal interest in the soil and national funds, and the laws of the said nation shall be equally binding upon and give equal protection to all such persons, and all others, of whatsoever race or color, who may be adopted as citizens or members of said tribe.

ARTICLE 3. In compliance with the desire of the United States to locate other Indians and freedmen thereon, the Creeks hereby cede and convey to the United States, to be sold to and used as homes for such other civilized Indians as the United States may choose to settle thereon, the west half of

their entire domain, to be divided by a line running north and south; the
eastern half of said Creek lands, being retained by them, shall, except as
herein otherwise stipulated, be forever set apart as a home for said Creek
Nation; and in consideration of said cession of the west half of their lands,
estimated to contain three millions two hundred and fifty thousand five hundred and sixty acres, the United States agree to pay the sum of thirty (30)
cents per acre, amounting to nine hundred and seventy-five thousand one
hundred and sixty-eight dollars, in the manner hereinafter provided, to wit:
two hundred thousand dollars shall be paid per capita in money, unless
otherwise directed by the President of the United States, upon the ratification of this treaty, to enable the Creeks to occupy, restore, and improve their
farms, and to make their nation independent and self-sustaining, and to pay
the damages sustained by the mission schools on the North Fork and the
Arkansas Rivers, not to exceed two thousand dollars, and to pay the
delegates such per diem as the agent and Creek council may agree upon,
as a just and fair compensation, all of which shall be distributed for that purpose by the agent, with the advice of the Creek council, under the direction
of the Secretary of the Interior. One hundred thousand dollars shall be paid
in money and divided to soldiers that enlisted in the Federal Army and the
loyal refugee Indians and freedmen who were driven from their homes by
the rebel forces, to reimburse them in proportion to their respective losses;
four hundred thousand dollars be paid in money and divided per capita to
said Creek Nation, unless otherwise directed by the President of the United
States, under the direction of the Secretary of the Interior, as the same may
accrue from the sale of land to other Indians. The United States agree to
pay to said Indians, in such manner and for such purposes as the Secretary
of the Interior may direct, interest at the rate of five per cent per annum
from the date of the ratification of this treaty, on the amount hereinbefore
agreed upon for said ceded lands, after deducting the said two hundred
thousand dollars; the residue, two hundred and seventy-five thousand one
hundred and sixty-eight dollars, shall remain in the Treasury of the United
States, and the interest thereon, at the rate of five per centum per annum,
be annually paid to said Creeks as above stipulated.

ARTICLE 4. Immediately after the ratification of this treaty the United
States agree to ascertain the amount due the respective soldiers who enlisted
in the Federal Army, loyal refugee Indians and freedmen, in proportion to
their several losses, and to pay the amount awarded each, in the following
manner, to wit: A census of the Creeks shall be taken by the agent of the
United States for said nation, under the direction of the Secretary of the Interior, and a roll of the names of all soldiers that enlisted in the Federal Army, loyal refugee Indians, and freedmen, be made by him. The superintendent of Indian affairs for the Southern superintendency and the agent of the

United States for the Creek Nation shall proceed to investigate and determine from said roll the amounts due the respective refugee Indians, and shall transmit to the Commissioner of Indian affairs for his approval, and that of the Secretary of the Interior, their awards, together with the reasons therefor. In case the awards so made shall be duly approved, said awards shall be paid from the proceeds of the sale of said lands within one year from the ratification of this treaty, or so soon as said amount of one hundred thousand ($100,000) dollars can be raised from the sale of said land to other Indians.

ARTICLE 5. The Creek Nation hereby grant a right of way through their lands, to the Choctaw and Chickasaw country, to any company which shall be duly authorized by Congress, and shall, with the express consent and approbation of the Secretary of the Interior, undertake to construct a railroad from any point north of to any point in or south of the Creek country, and likewise from any point on their eastern to their western or southern boundary, but said railroad company, together with all its agents and employés, shall be subject to the laws of the United States relating to intercourse with Indian tribes, and also to such rules and regulations as may be prescribed by the Secretary of the Interior for that purpose, and the Creeks agree to sell to the United States, or any company duly authorized as aforesaid, such lands not legally owned or occupied by a member or members of the Creek Nation, lying along the line of said contemplated railroad, not exceeding on each side thereof a belt or strip of land three miles in width, at such price per acre as may be eventually agreed upon between said Creek Nation and the party or parties building said road, subject to the approval of the President of the United States: *Provided, however,* That said land thus sold shall not be reconveyed, leased, or rented to, or be occupied by any one not a citizen of the Creek Nation, according to its laws and recognized usages: *Provided, also,* That officers, servants, and employés of said railroad necessary to its construction and management, shall not be excluded from such necessary occupancy, they being subject to the provisions of the Indian intercourse law and such rules and regulations as may be established by the Secretary of the Interior, nor shall any conveyance of any of said lands be made to the party building and managing said road until its completion as a first-class railroad, and its acceptance as such by the Secretary of the Interior.

ARTICLE 6. (Stricken out.)

ARTICLE 7. The Creeks hereby agree that the Seminole tribe of Indians may sell and convey to the United States all or any portion of the Seminole lands, upon such terms as may be mutually agreed upon by and between the Seminoles and the United States.

ARTICLE 8. It is agreed that the Secretary of the Interior forthwith cause the line dividing the Creek country, as provided for by the terms of the sale of Creek lands to the United States in article third of this treaty, to be accurately surveyed under the direction of the Commissioner of Indian Affairs, the expenses of which survey shall be paid by the United States.

ARTICLE 9. Inasmuch as the agency buildings of the Creek tribe have been destroyed during the late war, it is further agreed that the United States shall at their own expense, not exceeding ten thousand dollars, cause to be erected suitable agency buildings, the sites whereof shall be selected by the agent of said tribe, in the reduced Creek reservation, under the direction of the superintendent of Indian affairs.

In consideration whereof, the Creeks hereby cede and relinquish to the United States one section of their lands, to be designated and selected by their agent, under the direction of the superintendent of Indian affairs, upon which said agency buildings shall be erected, which section of land shall revert to the Creek nation when said agency buildings are no longer used by the United States, upon said nation paying a fair and reasonable value for said buildings at the time vacated.

ARTICLE 10. The Creeks agree to such legislation as Congress and the President of the United States may deem necessary for the better administration of justice and the protection of the rights of persons and property within the Indian territory: *Provided, however,* (That) said legislation shall not in any manner interfere with or annul their present tribal organization, rights, laws, privileges, and customs. The Creeks also agree that a general council, consisting of delegates elected by each nation or tribe lawfully resident within the Indian territory, may be annually convened in said territory, which council shall be organized in such manner and possess such powers as are hereinafter described.

First. After the ratification of this treaty, and as soon as may be deemed practicable by the Secretary of the Interior, and prior to the first session of said council, a census, or enumeration of each tribe lawfully resident in said territory, shall be taken under the direction of the superintendent of Indian affairs, who for that purpose is hereby authorized to designate and appoint competent persons, whose compensation shall be fixed by the Secretary of the Interior, and paid by the United States.

Second. The first general council shall consist of one member from each tribe, and an additional member from each one thousand Indians, or each fraction of a thousand greater than five hundred, being members of any tribe lawfully resident in said territory, and shall be selected by said tribes respectively, who may assent to the establishment of said general council, and if none should be thus formerly selected by any nation or tribe, the said nation or tribe shall be represented in said general council by the chief or chiefs and head men of said tribe, to be taken in the order of their rank as recognized in tribal usage, in the same number and proportion as above indicated. After the said census shall have been taken and completed, the superintendent of Indian affairs shall publish and declare to each tribe the number of members of said council to which they shall be entitled under the provisions of this article, and the persons entitled to so represent said tribes shall meet at such time and place as he shall appoint, but thereafter the time and place of the sessions of said council shall be determined by its action: *Provided*, That no sessions in any one year shall exceed the term of thirty days, and provided that special sessions of said council may be called whenever, in the judgement of the Secretary of the Interior, the interest of said tribe shall require.

Third. Said general council shall have power to legislate upon all rightful subjects and matters pertaining to the intercourse and relations of the Indian tribes and nations resident in said territory, the arrest and extradition of criminals and offenders escaping from one tribe to another, the administration of justice between members of the several tribes of said territory, and persons other than Indians and members of said tribes or nations, the construction of works of internal improvement, and the common defence and safety of the nations of said territory. All laws enacted by said general council shall take effect at such time as may therein be provided, unless suspended by direction of the Secretary of the Interior or the President of the United States. No law shall be enacted inconsistent with the Constitution of the United States, or the laws of Congress, or existing treaty stipulations with the United States, nor shall said council legislate upon matters pertaining to the organization, laws, or customs of the several tribes, except as herein provided for.

Fourth. Said council shall be presided over by the superintendent of Indian affairs, or, in case of his absence from any cause, the duties of said superintendent enumerated in this article shall be performed by such person as the Secretary of the Interior may direct.

Fifth. The Secretary of the Interior shall appoint a secretary of said council, whose duty it shall be to keep an accurate record of all the proceedings of said council, and who shall transmit a true copy of all such proceedings, duly certified by the superintendent of Indian affairs, to the Secretary of the Interior immediately after the sessions of said council shall terminate. He shall be paid out of the Treasury of the United States an annual*ly* salary of five hundred dollars.

Sixth. The members of said council shall be paid by the United States the sum of four dollars per diem during the time actually in attendance on the sessions of said council, and at the rate of four dollars for every twenty miles necessar(il)ly traveled by them in going to and returning to their homes respectively, from said council, to be certified by the secretary of said council and the superintendent of Indian affairs.

Seventh. The Creeks also agree that a court or courts may be established in said territory, with such jurisdiction and organized in such manner as Congress may by law provide.

ARTICLE 11. The stipulations of this treaty are to be a full settlement of all claims of said Creek Nation for damages and losses of every kind growing out of the late rebellion and all expenditures by the United States of annuities in clothing and feeding refugee and destitute Indians since the diversion of annuities for that purpose consequent upon the late war with the so-called Confederate States; and the Creeks hereby ratify and confirm all such diversions of annuities heretofore made from the funds of the Creek Nation by the United States, and the United States agree that no annuities shall be diverted from the objects for which they were originally devoted by treaty stipulations with the Creeks, to the use of refugee and destitute Indians other than the Creeks or members of the Creek Nation after the close of the present fiscal year, June thirtieth, eighteen hundred and sixty-six.

ARTICLE 12. The United States re-affirms and re-assumes all obligations of treaty stipulations with the Creek Nation entered into before the treaty of said Creek Nation with the so-called Confederate States. July tenth, eighteen hundred and sixty-one, not inconsistent herewith: and further agrees to renew all payments accruing by force of said treaty stipulations from and after the close of the present fiscal year, June thirtieth, eighteen hundred and sixty-six, except as is provided in article eleventh.

ARTICLE 13. A quantity of land not exceeding one hundred and sixty acres, to be selected according to legal subdivision, in one body, and to include their improvements, is hereby granted to every religious society or denomination, which has erected, or which, with the consent of the Indians, may hereafter erect, buildings within the Creek country for missionary or educational purposes; but no land thus granted, nor the buildings which have been or may be erected thereon, shall ever be sold or otherwise disposed of, except with the consent and approval of the Secretary of the Interior; and whenever any such lands or buildings shall be so sold or disposed of, the proceeds thereof shall be applied, under the direction of the Secretary of the Interior, to the support and maintenance of other similar establishments for the benefit of the Creeks and such other persons as may be or may hereafter become members of the tribe according to its laws, customs, and usages; and if at any time said improvements shall be abandoned for one year for missionary or educational purposes, all the rights herein granted for missionary and educational purposes shall revert to the said Creek Nation.

ARTICLE 14. It is further agreed that all treaties heretofore entered into between the United States and the Creek Nation which are inconsistent with any of the articles or provisions of this treaty shall be, and are hereby, rescinded and annulled; and it is further agreed that ten thousand dollars shall be paid by the United States, or so much thereof as may be necessary, to pay the expenses incurred in negotiating the foregoing treaty.

In testimony whereof, we, the commissioners representing the United States and the delegates representing the Creek nation, have hereunto set our hands and seals at the place and on the day and year above written.

D.N. Cooley, Commissioner Indian Affairs.	SEAL
Elijah Sells, Superintendent Indian Affairs.	SEAL
Ok-ta-has Harjo, his x mark.	SEAL
Cow Mikko, his x mark.	SEAL
Coteh-cho-chee, his x mark.	SEAL
D.N. McIntosh.	SEAL
James M.C. Smith.	SEAL

In the presence of—

J.W. Dunn, United States Indian agent.
J. Harlan, United States Indian agent.
Charles E. Mix.
J.M. Tebbetts.
Geo. A. Reynolds, United States Indian agent.
John B. Sanborn.
John F. Brown, Seminole delegate.
John Chupco, his x mark.
Fos-har-jo, his x mark.
Cho-cote-huga, his x mark.
R. Fields, Cherokee delegate.
Douglas H. Cooper.
Wm. Penn Adair.
Harry Island, his x mark, United States interpreter, Creek Nation
Suludin Watie.

TREATY WITH THE NAVAHO, 1868

Articles of a treaty and agreement made and entered into at Fort Sumner, New Mexico, on the first day of June, one thousand eight hundred and sixty-eight, by and between the United States, represented by its commissioners, Lieutenant-General W.T. Sherman and Colonel Samuel F. Tappan, of the one part, and the Navajo Nation or tribe of Indians, represented by their chiefs and head-men, duly authorized and empowered to act for the whole people of said nation or tribe, (the names of said chiefs and head-men being hereto subscribed,) of the other part, witness:

ARTICLE 1. From this day forward all war between the parties to this agreement shall forever cease. The Government of the United States desires peace, and its honor is hereby pledged to keep it. The Indians desire peace, and they now pledge their honor to keep it.

If bad men among the whites, or among other people subject to the authority of the United States, shall commit any wrong upon the person or property of the Indians, the United States will, upon proof made to the agent and forwarded to the commissioner of Indian Affairs at Washington City, proceed at once to cause the offender to be arrested and punished according to the laws of the United States, and also to reimburse the injured for the loss sustained.

If the bad men among the Indians shall commit a wrong or depredation upon the person or property of any one, white, black, or Indian, subject to the authority of the United States and at peace therewith, the Navajo tribe agree that they will, on proof made to their agent, and on notice by him, deliver up the wrongdoer to the United States, to be tried and punished according to its laws; and in case they wilfully refuse so to do, the person injured shall be reimbursed for his loss from the annuities or other moneys due or to become due to them under this treaty, or any others that may be made with the United States. And the President may prescribe such rules and regulations for ascertaining damages under this article as in his judgement may be proper; but no such damage shall be adjusted and paid until examined and passed upon by the Commissioner of Indian Affairs, and no one sustaining loss whilst violating, or because of his violating, the provisions of this treaty or the laws of the United States, shall be reimbursed therefor.

ARTICLE 2. The United States agrees that the following district of country, to wit: bounded on the north by the 37th degree of north latitude, south by an east and west line passing through the site of old Fort Defiance, in Cañon Bonito, east by the parallel of longitude which, if prolonged south, would pass through old Fort Lyon, or the Ojo-de-oso, Bear Spring, and west by a parallel of longitude about 109° 30′ west of Greenwich, provided it embraces the outlet of the Cañon-de-Chilly, which cañon is to be all included in this reservation, shall be, and the same is hereby, set apart for the use and occupation of the Navajo tribe of Indians, and for such other friendly tribes or individual Indians as from time to time they may be willing, with the consent of the United States, to admit among them; and the United States agrees that no persons except those herein so authorized to do, and except such officers, soldiers, agents, and employés of the Government, or of the Indians, as may be authorized to enter upon Indian reservations in discharge of duties imposed by law, or the orders of the President, shall ever be permitted to pass over, settle upon, or reside in, the territory described in this article.

ARTICLE 3. The United States agrees to cause to be built, at some point within said reservation, where timber and water may be convenient, the following buildings: a warehouse, to cost not exceeding twenty-five hundred dollars; an agency building for the residence of the agent, not to cost exceeding three thousand dollars; a carpenter-shop and blacksmith-shop, not to cost exceeding one thousand dollars each; and a schoolhouse and chapel, so soon as a sufficient number of children can be induced to attend school, which shall not cost to exceed five thousand dollars.

ARTICLE 4. The United States agrees that the agent for the Navajos shall make his home at the agency building; that he shall reside among them, and shall keep an office open at all times for the purpose of prompt and diligent inquiry into such matters of complaint by or against the Indians as may be presented for investigation, as also for the faithful discharge of other duties enjoined by law. In all cases of depredation on person or property he shall cause the evidence to be taken in writing and forwarded, together with his findings, to the Commissioner of Indian Affairs, whose decision shall be binding on the parties to this treaty.

ARTICLE 5. If any individual belonging to said tribe, or legally incorporated with it, being the head of a family, shall desire to commence farming, he shall have the privilege to select, in the presence and with the assistance of the agent then in charge, a tract of land within said reservation, not exceeding one hundred and sixty acres in extent, which tract, when so selected, certified, and recorded in the "land-book" as herein described, shall cease to be held in common, but the same may be occupied and held in the exclusive possession of the person selecting it, and of his family, so long as he or they may continue to cultivate it.

Any person over eighteen years of age, not being the head of a family, may in like manner select, and cause to be certified to him or her for purposes of cultivation, a quantity of land, not exceeding eighty acres in extent, and thereupon be entitled to the exclusive possession of the same as above directed.

For each tract of land so selected a certificate containing a description thereof, and the name of the person selecting it, with a certificate endorsed thereon, that the same has been recorded, shall be delivered to the party entitled to it by the agent, after the same shall have been recorded by him in a book to be kept in his office, subject to inspection, which said book shall be known as the "Navajo land-book."

The President may at any time order a survey of the reservation, and when so surveyed, Congress shall provide for protecting the rights of said settlers in their improvements, and may fix the character of the title held by each.

The United States may pass such laws on the subject of alienation and descent of property between the Indians and their descendants as may be thought proper.

ARTICLE 6. In order to insure the civilization of the Indians entering into this treaty, the necessity of education is admitted, especially of such of them as may be settled on said agricultural parts of this reservation, and they therefore pledge themselves to compel their children, male and female, between the ages of six and sixteen years, to attend school; and it is hereby made the duty of the agent for said Indians to see that this stipulation is strictly complied with; and the United States agrees that, for every thirty children between said ages who can be induced or compelled to attend school, a house shall be provided, and a teacher competent to teach the elementary branches of an English education shall be furnished, who will reside among said Indians, and faithfully discharge his or her duties as a teacher.

The provisions of this article to continue for not less than ten years.

ARTICLE 7. When the head of a family shall have selected lands and received his certificate as above directed, and the agent shall be satisfied that he intends in good faith to commence cultivating the soil for a living, he shall be entitled to receive seeds and agricultural implements for the first year, not exceeding in value one hundred dollars, and for each succeeding year he shall continue to farm, for a period of two years, he shall be entitled to receive seeds and implements to the value of twenty-five dollars.

ARTICLE 8. In lieu of all sums of money or other annuities provided to be paid to the Indians herein named under any treaty or treaties heretofore made, the United States agrees to deliver at the agency-house on the reservation herein named, on the first day of September of each year for ten years, the following articles, to wit:

Such articles of clothing, goods, or raw materials in lieu thereof, as the agent may make his estimate for, not exceeding in value five dollars per Indian-each Indian being encouraged to manufacture their own clothing, blankets, &c.; to be furnished with no article which they can manufacture themselves. And, in order that the Commissioner of Indian Affairs may be able to estimate properly for the articles herein named, it shall be the duty of the agent each year to forward to him a full and exact census of the Indians, on which the estimate from year to year can be based.

And in addition to the articles herein named, the sum of ten dollars for each person entitled to the beneficial effects of this treaty shall be annually appropriated for a period of ten years, for each person who engages in farming or mechanical pursuits, to be used by the Commissioner of Indian Affairs in the purchase of such articles as from time to time the condition and necessities of the Indians may indicate to be proper; and if within the ten years at any time it shall appear that the amount of money needed for clothing, under the article, can be appropriated to better uses for the Indians named herein, the Commissioner of Indian Affairs may change the appropriation to other purposes, but in no event shall the amount of this appropriation be withdrawn or discontinued for the period named, provided they remain at peace. And the President shall annually detail an officer of the Army to be present and attest the delivery of all the goods herein named to the Indians, and he shall inspect and report on the quantity and quality of the goods and the manner of their delivery.

ARTICLE 9. In consideration of the advantages and benefits conferred by this treaty, and the many pledges of friendship by the United States, the tribes who are parties to this agreement hereby stipulate that they will relinquish all right to occupy any territory outside their reservation, as herein defined, but retain the right to hunt on any unoccupied lands contiguous to their reservation, so long as the large game may range thereon in such numbers as to justify the chase; and they, the said Indians, further expressly agree:

1st. That they will make no opposition to the construction of railroads now being built or hereafter to be built across the continent.

2nd. That they will not interfere with the peaceful construction of any railroad not passing over their reservation as herein defined.

3d. That they will not attack any persons at home or travelling, nor molest or disturb any wagon-trains, coaches, mules, or cattle belonging to the people of the United States, or to persons friendly therewith.

4th. That they will never capture or carry off from the settlements women or children.

5th. They will never kill or scalp white men, nor attempt to do them harm.

6th. They will not in the future oppose the construction of railroads, wagon-roads, mail stations, or other works of utility or necessity which may be ordered or permitted by the laws of the United States; but should such roads or other works be constructed on the lands of their reservation, the Government will pay the tribe whatever amount of damage may be assessed by three disinterested commissioners to be appointed by the President for that purpose, one of said commissioners to be a chief or head-man of the tribe.

7th. They will make no opposition to the military posts or roads now established, or that they may be established, not in violation of treaties heretofore made or hereafter to be made with any of the Indian tribes.

ARTICLE 10. No future treaty for the cession of any portion or part of the reservation herein described, which may be held in common, shall be of any validity or force against said Indians unless agreed to and executed by at least three-fourths of all the adult male Indians occupying or interested in the same; and no cession by the tribe shall be understood or construed in such manner as to deprive, without his consent, any individual member of the tribe of his rights to any tract of land selected by him as provided in article (5) of this treaty.

ARTICLE 11. The Navajos also hereby agree that at any time after the signing of these presents they will proceed in such manner as may be required of them by the agent, or by the officer charged with their removal, to the reservation herein provided for, the United States paying for their subsistence en route, and providing a reasonable amount of transportation for the sick and feeble.

ARTICLE 12. It is further agreed by and between the parties to this agreement that the sum of one hundred and fifty thousand dollars appropriated or to be appropriated shall be disbursed as follows, subject to any condition provided in the law, to wit:

1st. The actual cost of the removal of the tribe from the Bosque Redondo reservation to the reservation, say fifty thousand dollars.

2d. The purchase of fifteen thousand sheep and goats, at a cost not to exceed thirty thousand dollars.

3d. The purchase of five hundred beef cattle and a million pounds of corn, to be collected and held at the military post nearest the reservation, subject to the orders of the agent, for the relief of the needy during the coming winter.

4th. The balance, if any, of the appropriation to be invested for the maintenance of the Indians pending their removal, in such manner as the agent who is with them may determine.

5th. The removal of this tribe to be made under the supreme control and direction of the military commander of the Territory of New Mexico, and when completed, the management of the tribe to revert to the proper agent.

ARTICLE 13. The tribe herein named, by their representatives, parties to this treaty, agree to make the reservation herein described their permanent home, and they will not as a tribe make any permanent settlement elsewhere, reserving the right to hunt on the lands adjoining the said reservation formerly called theirs, subject to the modifications named in this treaty and the orders of the commander of the department in which said reservation may be for the time being; and it is further agreed and understood by the parties to this treaty, that if any Navajo Indian or Indians shall leave the reservation herein described to settle elsewhere, he or they shall forfeit all the rights, privileges, and annuities conferred by the terms of this treaty; and it is further agreed by the parties to this treaty, that they will do all they can to induce Indians now away from reservations set apart for the exclusive use and occupation of the Indians, leading a nomadic life, or engaged in war against the people of the United States, to abandon such life and settle permanently in one of the territorial reservations set apart for the exclusive use and occupation of the Indians.

In testimony of all which the said parties have hereunto, on this the first day of June, one thousand eight hundred and sixty-eight, at Fort Sumner, in the Territory of New Mexico, set their hands and seals.

W.T. Sherman,
Lieutenant-General, Indian Peace Commissioner.
S.F. Tappan,
Indian Peace Commissioner.

Barboncito, chief, his x mark.
Armijo, his x mark.
Delgado.
Manuelito, his x mark.
Largo, his x mark.
Herrero, his x mark.
Chiqueto, his x mark.
Muerto de Hombre, his x mark.
Hombro, his x mark.
Narbono, his x mark.
Narbono Segundo, his x mark.
Ganado Mucho, his x mark.
  Council:

Serginto, his x mark.
Grande, his x mark.
Inoetenito, his x mark.
Muchachos Mucho, his x mark.
Chiqueto Segundo, his x mark.
Cabello Amarillo, his x mark.
Francisco, his x mark.
Torivio, his x mark.
Desdendado, his x mark.
Juan, his x mark.
Guero, his x mark.
Gugadore, his x mark.
Cabason, his x mark.

Riquo, his x mark.   Barbon Segundo, his x mark.
Juan Martin, his x mark.   Cabares Colorados, his x mark.

Attest:
Geo. W.G. Getty, colonel Thirty-seventh Infantry, brevet major-general U.S. Army.
B.S. Roberts, brevet brigadier-general U.S. Army, lieutenant-colonel Third Cavalry.
J. Cooper McKee, brevet lieutenant-colonel, surgeon U.S. Army.
Theo. H. Dodd, United States Indian agent for Navajos.
Chas. McClure, brevet major and commissary of subsistence, U.S. Army.
James F. Weeds, brevet major and assistant surgeon, U.S. Army.
J.C. Sutherland, interpreter.
William Vaux, chaplain U.S. Army.

TREATY WITH THE SIOUX — BRULÉ, OGLALA, MINICONJOU, YANKTONAI, HUNKPAPA, BLACKFEET, CUTHEAD, TWO KETTLE, SANS ARCS, AND SANTEE — AND ARAPAHO, 1868

Articles of a treaty made and concluded by and between Lieutenant-General William T. Sherman, General William S. Harney, General Alfred H. Terry, General C.C. Augur, J.B. Henderson, Nathaniel G. Taylor, John B. Sanborn, and Samuel F. Tappan, duly appointed commissioners on the part of the United States, and the different bands of the Sioux Nation of Indians, by their chiefs and head-men, whose names are hereto subscribed, they being duly authorized to act in the premises.

ARTICLE 1. From this day forward all war between the parties to this agreement shall forever cease. The Government of the United States desires peace, and its honor is hereby pledged to keep it. The Indians desire peace, and they now pledge their honor to maintain it.

If bad men among the whites, or among other people subject to the authority of the United States, shall commit any wrong upon the person or property of the Indians, the United States will, upon proof made to the agent and forwarded to the Commissioner of Indian Affairs at Washington City, proceed at once to cause the offender to be arrested and punished according to the laws of the United States, and also re-imburse the injured person for the loss sustained.

If bad men among the Indians shall commit a wrong or depredation upon the person or property of any one, white, black, or Indian, subject to the authority of the United States, and at peace therewith, the Indians herein named solemnly agree that they will, upon proof made to their agent and notice by him, deliver up the wrong-doer to the United States, to be tried and punished according to its laws; and in case they wilfully refuse so to do, the person injured shall be re-imbursed for his loss from the annuities or other moneys due or to become due to them under this or other treaties made with the United States. And the President, on advising with the Commissioner of Indian Affairs, shall prescribe such rules and regulations for ascertaining damages under the provisions of this article as in his judgment may be proper. But no one sustaining loss while violating the provisions of this treaty or the laws of the United States shall be re-imbursed therefor.

ARTICLE 2. The United States agrees that the following district of country, to wit, viz: Commencing on the east bank of the Missouri River where the forty-sixth parallel of north latitude crosses the same, thence along low-water mark down said east bank to a point opposite where the northern line of the State of Nebraska strikes the river, thence west across said river, and along the northern line of Nebraska to the one hundred and fourth degree of longitude west from Greenwich, thence north on said meridian to a point where the forty-sixth parallel of north latitude intercepts the same, thence due east along said parallel to the place of beginning; and in addition thereto, all existing reservations on the east bank of said river shall be, and the same is, set apart for the absolute and undisturbed use and occupation of the Indians herein named, and for such other friendly tribes or individual Indians as from time to time they may be willing, with the consent of the United States, to admit amongst them; and the United States now solemnly agrees that no persons except those herein designated and authorized so to do, and except such officers, agents, and employés of the Government as may be authorized to enter upon Indian reservations in discharge of duties enjoined by law, shall ever be permitted to pass over, settle upon, or reside in the territory described in this article, or in such territory as may be added to this reservation for the use of said Indians, and henceforth they will and do hereby relinquish all claims or right in and to any portion of the United States or Territories, except such as is embraced within the limits aforesaid, and except as hereinafter provided.

ARTICLE 3. If it should appear from actual survey or other satisfactory examination of said tract of land that it contains less than one hundred and sixty acres of tillable land for each person who, at the time, may be authorized to reside on it under the provisions of this treaty, and a very considerable number of such persons shall be disposed to commence cultivating the soil as farmers, the United States agrees to set apart, for the use of said Indians, as herein provided, such additional quantity of arable land, adjoining to said reservation, or as near to the same as it can be obtained, as may be required to provide the necessary amount.

ARTICLE 4. The United States agrees, at its own proper expense, to construct at some place on the Missouri River, near the center of said reservation, where timber and water may be convenient, the following buildings, to wit: a warehouse, a store-room for the use of the agent in storing goods belonging to the Indians, to cost not less than twenty-five hundred dollars;

an agency-building for the residence of the agent, to cost not exceeding three thousand dollars; a residence for the physician, to cost not more than three thousand dollars; and five other buildings, for a carpenter, farmer, blacksmith, miller, and engineer, each to cost not exceeding two thousand dollars; also a school-house or mission-building, so soon as a sufficient number of children can be induced by the agent to attend school, which shall not cost exceeding five thousand dollars.

The United States agrees further to cause to be erected on said reservation, near the other buildings herein authorized, a good steam circular-saw mill, with a grist-mill and shingle-machine attached to the same, to cost not exceeding eight thousand dollars.

ARTICLE 5. The United States agrees that the agent for said Indians shall in the future make his home at the agency-building; that he shall reside among them, and keep an office open at all times for the purpose of prompt and diligent inquiry into such matters of complaint by and against the Indians as may be presented for investigation under the provisions of their treaty stipulations, as also for the faithful discharge of other duties enjoined on him by law. In all cases of depredation on person or property he shall cause the evidence to be taken in writing and forwarded, together with his findings, to the Commissioner of Indian Affairs, whose decision, subject to the revision of the Secretary of the Interior, shall be binding on the parties to this treaty.

ARTICLE 6. If any individual belonging to said tribes of Indians, or legally incorporated with them, being the head of a family, shall desire to commence farming, he shall have the privilege to select, in the presence and with the assistance of the agent then in charge, a tract of land within said reservation, not exceeding three hundred and twenty acres in extent, which tract, when so selected, certified, and recorded in the "land-book," as herein directed, shall cease to be held in common, but the same may be occupied and held in the exclusive possession of the person selecting it, and of his family, so long as he or they may continue to cultivate it.

Any person over eighteen years of age, not being the head of a family, may in like manner select and cause to be certified to him or her, for purposes of cultivation, a quantity of land not exceeding eighty acres in extent, and thereupon be entitled to the exclusive possession of the same as above directed.

For each tract of land so selected a certificate, containing a description thereof and the name of the person selecting it, with a certificate endorsed thereon that the same has been recorded, shall be delivered to the party entitled to it, by the agent, after the same shall have been recorded by him in a book to be kept in his office, subject to inspection, which said book shall be known as the "Sioux Land-Book."

The President may, at any time, order a survey of the reservation, and, when so surveyed, Congress shall provide for protecting the rights of said settlers in their improvements, and may fix the character of the title held by each. The United States may pass such laws on the subject of alienation and descent of property between the Indians and their descendants as may be thought proper. And it is further stipulated that any male Indians, over eighteen years of age, of any band or tribe that is or shall hereafter become a party to this treaty, who now is or who shall hereafter become a resident or occupant of any reservation or Territory not included in the tract of country designated and described in this treaty for the permanent home of the Indians, which is not mineral land, nor reserved by the United States for special purposes other than Indian occupation, and who shall have made improvements thereon of the value of two hundred dollars or more, and continuously occupied the same as a homestead for the term of three years, shall be entitled to receive from the United States a patent for one hundred and sixty acres of land including his said improvements, the same to be in the form of the legal subdivisions of the surveys of the public lands. Upon application in writing, sustained by the proof of two disinterested witnesses, made to the register of the local land-office when the land sought to be entered is within a land district, and when the tract sought to be entered is not in any land district, then upon said application and proof being made to the Commissioner of the General Land-Office, and the right of such Indian or Indians to enter such tract or tracts of land shall accrue and be perfect from the date of his first improvements thereon, and shall continue as long as he continues his residence and improvements, and no longer. And any Indian or Indians receiving a patent for land under the foregoing provisions, shall thereby and from thenceforth become and be a citizen of the United States, and be entitled to all the privileges and immunities of such citizens, and shall, at the same time, retain all his rights to benefits accruing to Indians under this treaty.

ARTICLE 7. In order to insure the civilization of the Indians entering into this treaty, the necessity of education is admitted, especially of such of them as are or may be settled on said agricultural reservations, and they therefore pledge themselves to compel their children, male and female, between the ages of six and sixteen years, to attend school; and it is hereby made the duty of the agent for said Indians to see that this stipulation is strictly complied with; and the United States agrees that for every thirty children between said ages who can be induced or compelled to attend school, a house shall be provided and a teacher competent to teach the elementary branches of an English education shall be furnished, who will reside among said Indians, and faithfully discharge his or her duties as a teacher. The provisions of this article to continue for not less than twenty years.

ARTICLE 8. When the head of a family or lodge shall have selected lands and received his certificate as above directed, and the agent shall be satisfied that he intends in good faith to commence cultivating the soil for a living, he shall be entitled to receive seeds and agricultural implements for the first year, not exceeding in value one hundred dollars, and for each succeeding year he shall continue to farm, for a period of three years more, he shall be entitled to receive seeds and implements as aforesaid, not exceeding in value twenty-five dollars.

And it is further stipulated that such persons as commence farming shall receive instruction from the farmer herein provided for, and whenever more than one hundred persons shall enter upon the cultivation of the soil, a second blacksmith shall be provided, with such iron, steel, and other material as may be needed.

ARTICLE 9. At any time after ten years from the making of thist treaty, the United States shall have the privilege of withdrawing the physician, farmer, blacksmith, carpenter, engineer, and miller herein provided for, but in case of such withdrawal, an additional sum thereafter of ten thousand dollars per annum shall be devoted to the education of said Indians, and the Commissioner of Indian Affairs shall, upon careful inquiry into their condition, make such rules and regulations for the expenditure of said sum as will best promote the educational and moral improvement of said tribes.

ARTICLE 10. In lieu of all sums of money or other annuities provided to be paid to the Indians herein named, under any treaty or treaties heretofore made, the United States agrees to deliver at the agency-house on the reservation herein named, on or before the first day of August of each year, for thirty years, the following articles, to wit:

For each male person over fourteen years of age, a suit of good substantial woolen clothing, consisting of coat, pantaloons, flannel shirt, hat, and a pair of home-made socks.

For each female over twelve years of age, a flannel skirt, or the goods necessary to make it, a pair of woolen hose, twelve yards of calico, and twelve yards of cotton domestics.

For the boys and girls under the ages named, such flannel and cotton goods as may be needed to make each a suit as aforesaid, together with a pair of woolen hose for each.

And in order that the Commissioner of Indian Affairs may be able to estimate properly for the articles herein named, it shall be the duty of the agent each year to forward to him a full and exact census of the Indians, on which the estimate from year to year can be based.

And in addition to the clothing herein named, the sum of ten dollars for each person entitled to the beneficial effects of this treaty shall be annually appropriated for a period of thirty years, while such persons roam and hunt, and twenty dollars for each person who engages in farming, to be used by the Secretary of the Interior in the purchase of such articles as from time to time the condition and necessities of the Indians may indicate to be proper. And if within the thirty years, at any time, it shall appear that the amount of money needed for clothing under this article can be appropriated to better uses for the Indians named herein, Congress may, by law, change the appropriation to other purposes; but in no event shall the amount of this appropriation be withdrawn or discontinued for the period named. And the President shall annually detail an officer of the Army to be present and attest the delivery of all the goods herein named to the Indians, and he shall inspect and report on the quantity and quality of the goods and the manner of their delivery. And it is hereby expressly stipulated that each Indian over the age of four years, who shall have removed to and settled permanently upon said reservation and complied with the stipulations of this treaty, shall be entitled to receive from the United States, for the period of four years after he shall have settled upon said reservation, one pound of meat and one pound of flour per day, provided the Indians cannot furnish their own subsistence at an earlier date. And it is further stipulated that the United States will furnish and deliver to each lodge of Indians or family of persons legally incorporated with them, who shall remove to the reservation herein described and commence farming, one good American cow, and one good well-broken pair of American oxen within sixty days after such lodge or family shall have so settled upon said reservation.

ARTICLE 11. In consideration of the advantages and benefits conferred by this treaty, and the many pledges of friendship by the United States, the tribes who are parties to this agreement hereby stipulate that they will relinquish all right to occupy permanently the territory outside their reservation as herein defined, but yet reserve the right to hunt on any lands north of North Platte, and on the Republican Fork of the Smoky Hill River, so long as the buffalo may range thereon in such numbers as to justify the chase. And they, the said Indians, further expressly agree:

1st. That they will withdraw all opposition to the construction of the railroads now being built on the plains.

2d. That they will permit the peaceful construction of any railroad not passing over their reservation as herein defined.

3d. That they will not attack any persons at home, or travelling, nor molest or disturb any wagon-trains, coaches, mules, or cattle belonging to the people of the United States, or to persons friendly therewith.

4th. They will never capture, or carry off from the settlements, white women or children.

5th. They will never kill or scalp white men, nor attempt to do them harm.

6th. They withdraw all pretence of opposition to the construction of the railroad now being built along the Platte River and westward to the Pacific Ocean, and they will not in future object to the construction of railroads, wagon-roads, mail-stations, or other works of utility or necessity, which may be ordered or permitted by the laws of the United States. But should such roads or other works be constructed on the lands of their reservation, the Government will pay the tribe whatever amount of damage may be assessed by three disinterested commissioners to be appointed by the President for that purpose, one of said commissioners to be a chief or head-man of the tribe.

7th. They agree to withdraw all opposition to the military posts or roads now established south of the North Platte River, or that may be established, not in violation of treaties heretofore made or hereafter to be made with any of the Indian tribes.

ARTICLE 12. No treaty for the cession of any portion or part of the reservation herein described which may be held in common shall be of any validity or force as against the said Indians, unless executed and signed by at least three-fourths of all the adult male Indians, occupying or interested in the same; and no cession by the tribe shall be understood or construed in such manner as to deprive, without his consent, any individual member of the tribe of his rights to any tract of land selected by him, as provided in article 6 of this treaty.

ARTICLE 13. The United States hereby agrees to furnish annually to the Indians the physician, teachers, carpenter, miller, engineer, farmer, and blacksmiths as herein contemplated, and that such appropriations shall be made from time to time, on the estimates of the Secretary of the Interior, as will be sufficient to employ such persons.

ARTICLE 14. It is agreed that the sum of five hundred dollars annually, for three years from date, shall be expended in presents to the ten persons of said tribe who in the judgement of the agent may grow the most valuable crops for the respective year.

ARTICLE 15. The Indians herein named agree that when the agency-house or other buildings shall be constructed on the reservation named, they will regard said reservation their permanent home, and they will make no permanent settlement elsewhere; but they shall have the right, subject to the conditions and modifications of this treaty, to hunt, as stipulated in Article 11 hereof.

ARTICLE 16. The United States hereby agrees and stipulates that the country north of the North Platte River and east of the summits of the Big Horn Mountains shall be held and considered to be unceded Indian territory, and also stipulates and agrees that no white person or persons shall be permitted to settle upon or occupy any portion of the same; or without the consent of the Indians first had and obtained, to pass through the same; and it is further agreed by the United States that within ninety days after the conclusion of peace with all the bands of the Sioux Nation, the military posts now established in the territory in this article named shall be abandoned, and that the road leading to them and by them to the settlements in the Territory of Montana shall be closed.

ARTICLE 17. It is hereby expressly understood and agreed by and between the respective parties to this treaty that the execution of this treaty and its ratification by the United States Senate shall have the effect, and shall be construed as abrogating and annulling all treaties and agreements heretofore entered into between the respective parties hereto, so far as such treaties and agreements obligate the United States to furnish and provide money, clothing, or other articles of property to such Indians and bands of Indians as become parties to this treaty, but no further.

In testimony of all which, we, the said commissioners, and we, the chiefs and headmen of the Brulé band of the Sioux nation, have hereunto set our hands and seals at Fort Laramie, Dakota Territory, this twenty-ninth day of April, in the year one thousand eight hundred and sixty-eight.

N.G. Taylor,	SEAL
W.T. Sherman,	SEAL
Lieutenant-General.	
Wm. S. Harney,	SEAL
Brevet Major-General U.S. Army.	
John B. Sanborn,	SEAL
S.F. Tappan,	SEAL
C.C. Augur,	SEAL
Brevet Major-General.	
Alfred H. Terry	SEAL
Brevet Major-General U.S. Army.	

Attest:
A.S.H. White, Secretary.

Executed on the part of the Brulé band of Sioux by the chiefs and headmen whose names are hereto annexed, they being thereunto duly authorized, at Fort Laramie, D.T., the twenty-ninth day of April, in the year A.D. 1868.

Ma-za-pon-kaska, his x mark,		Bella-tonka-tonka, his x mark,	
Iron Shell.	SEAL	Big Partisan.	SEAL
Wah-pat-shah, his x mark,		Mah-to-ho-honka, his x mark,	
Red Leaf.	SEAL	Swift Bear.	SEAL
Hah-sah-pah, his x mark,		To-wis-ne, his x mark,	
Black Horn.	SEAL	Cold Place.	SEAL

Zin-tah-gah-lat-skah, his
  x mark, Spotted Tail.   SEAL

Zin-tah-skah, his x mark,
  White Tail.   SEAL

Me-wah-tah-ne-ho-skah, his
  x mark, Tall Mandas.   SEAL

She-cha-chat-kah, his x mark,
  Bad Left Hand.   SEAL

No-mah-no-pah, his x mark,
  Two and Two.   SEAL

Tah-tonka-skah, his x mark,
  White Bull.   SEAL

Con-ra-washta, his x mark,
  Pretty Coon.   SEAL

Ha-cah-cah-she-chah, his x
  mark, Bad Elk.   SEAL

Wa-ha-ka-zah-ish-tah, his x
  mark, Eye Lance.   SEAL

Ma-to-ha-ke-tah, his x mark,
  Bear that looks behind.   SEAL

Ish-tah-skah, his x mark,
  White Eyes.   SEAL

Ma-ta-loo-zah, his x mark,
  Fast Bear.   SEAL

As-hah-kah-nah-zhe, his x
  mark, Standing Elk.   SEAL

Can-te-te-ki-ya, his x mark,
  The Brave Heart.   SEAL

Shunka-shaton, his x mark,
  Day Hawk.   SEAL

Tatanka-wakon, his x mark,
  Sacred Bull.   SEAL

Mapia shaton, his x mark,
  Hawk Cloud.   SEAL

Ma-sha-a-ow, his x mark,
  Stands and Comes.   SEAL

Shon-ka-ton-ka, his x mark,
  Big Dog.   SEAL

Attest:

Ashton S.H. White, secretary of
  commission.

George B. Withs, phonographer
  to commission.

Geo. H. Holtzman.

John D. Howland.

James D. O'Connor.

Chas. E. Guern, interpreter.

Leon F. Pallardy, interpreter.

Nicholas Janis, interpreter.

Executed on the part of the Ogallalah band of Sioux by the chiefs and headmen whose names are hereto subscribed, they being thereunto duly authorized, at Fort Laramie, the twenty-fifth day of May, in the year A.D. 1868.

Tah-skun-ka-co-qui-tah, his
  x mark, Man-afraid-of-his-
  horses.   SEAL

Sha-ton-skah, his x mark,
  White Hawk.   SEAL

Sha-ton-sapah, his x mark,
  Black Hawk.   SEAL

E-ga-mon-ton-ka-sapah, his x
  mark, Black Tiger.   SEAL

Oh-wah-she-cha, his x mark,
  Bad Wound.   SEAL

Pah-gee, his x mark. Grass.   SEAL

Wah-non-reh-che-geh, his x
  mark, Ghost Heart.   SEAL

Con-reeh, his x mark. Crow.   SEAL

Oh-huns-ee-ga-non-sken, his x
  mark, Mad Shade.   SEAL

Sha-ton-oh-nah-om-minne-ne-
  oh-minne, his x mark, Whirling
  Hawk.   SEAL

Mah-to-chun-ka-oh, his x mark,
  Bear's Back.   SEAL

Che-ton-wee-koh, his x mark,
  Fool Hawk.   SEAL

Wah-hoh-ke-za-ah-hah, his x
  mark. One that has the lance. SEAL

Shon-gah-manni-toh-tan-ka-seh,
  his x mark, Big Wolf Foot.   SEAL

Eh-ton-kah, his x mark,
  Big Mouth.   SEAL

Oh-he-te-kah, his x mark,
The Brave.   SEAL
Tah-ton-kah-he-yo-ta-kah, his x
x mark, Sitting Bull.   SEAL
Shon-ka-oh-wah-mon-ye, his x
mark, Whirlwind Dog.   SEAL
Ha-hah-kah-tah-miech, his x
mark, Poor Elk.   SEAL
Wam-bu-lee-wah-kon, his x
mark, Medicine Eagle.   SEAL
Chon-gah-ma-he-to-hans-ka,
his x mark, High Wolf.   SEAL
Wah-se-chun-ta-shun-kah, his
x mark, American Horse.   SEAL
Mah-hah-mah-ha-mak-near, his
x mark, Man that walks
under the ground.   SEAL
Mah-to-tow-pah, his x mark,
Four Bears.   SEAL
Ma-to-wee-sha-kta-, his x mark,
One that kills the bear.   SEAL
Oh-tah-kee-toka-wee-chakta, his
x mark, One that kills in a
hard place.   SEAL
Tah-ton-kah-ta-miech, his x
mark, The poor Bull.   SEAL

Ma-pah-che-tah, his x mark,
Bad Hand.   SEAL
Wah-ke-yun-shah, his x mark,
Red Thunder.   SEAL
Wak-sah, his x mark, One that
Cuts Off.   SEAL
Cham-nom-qui-yah, his x mark,
One that Presents the Pipe.   SEAL
Wah-ke-ke-yan-puh-tah, his x
mark, Fire Thunder.   SEAL
Mah-to-nonk-pah-ze, his x mark,
Bear with Yellow Ears.   SEAL
Con-ree-teh-ka, his x mark,
The Little Crow.   SEAL
He-hup-pah-toh, his x mark,
The Blue War Club.   SEAL
Shon-kee-toh, his x mark,
The Blue Horse.   SEAL
Wam-Balla-oh-con-quo, his x
mark, Quick Eagle.   SEAL
Ta-tonka-suppa, his x mark,
Black Bull.   SEAL
Moh-to-ha-she-na, his x mark,
The Bear Hide.   SEAL

Attest:
S.E. Ward.
Jas. C. O'Connor.
J.M. Sherwood.
W.C. Slicer.
Sam Deon.

H.M. Matthews.
Joseph Bissonette, interpreter.
Nicholas Janis, interpreter.
Lefroy Jott, interpreter.
Antoine Janis, interpreter.

Executed on the part of the Minneconjon band of Sioux by the chiefs and
headmen whose names are hereto subscribed, they being thereunto duly
authorized.

At Fort Laramie, D.T.,   May 26, '68, 13 names.   SEAL
                            Heh-won-ge-chat, his x mark, One Horn.
                            Oh-pon-ah-tah-e-manne, his x mark,   SEAL
                            The Elk that bellows Walking.
At Fort Laramie, D.T.,   May 25, '68, 2 names.
                            Heh-ho-lah-reh-cha-skah, his x mark,   SEAL
                            Young White Bull.

Wah-chah-chum-kah-coh-kee-
pah, his x mark, One that is
afraid of Shield.   SEAL

Wom-beh-le-ton-kah, his x
mark, The Big Eagle.   SEAL
Ma-toh-eh-schne-lah, his x

He-hon-ne-shakta, his x mark,
   The Old Owl.   SEAL
Moc-pe-a-toh, his x mark,
   Blue Cloud.   SEAL
Oh-pong-ge-le-skah, his x mark,
   Spotted Elk.   SEAL
Tah-tonk-ka-hon-ke-schne, his
   x mark, Slow Bull.   SEAL
Shonk-a-nee-shah-shah-a-tah-pe,
   his x mark, The Dog Chief.   SEAL
Ma-to-tah-ta-tonk-ka, his x
   mark, Bull Bear.   SEAL

   mark, The Lone Bear.   SEAL
Mah-toh-ke-su-yah, his x
   mark, The One who Remembers
   the Bear.   SEAL
Ma-toh-oh-he-to-keh, his x
   mark, The Brave Bear.   SEAL
Eh-che-ma-heh, his x mark,
   The Runner.   SEAL
Ti-ki-ya, his x mark,
   The Hard.   SEAL
He-ma-za, his x mark,
   Iron Horn.   SEAL

Attest:
Jas. C. O'Connor.
Wm. H. Brown.

Nicholas Janis, interpreter.
Antoine Janis, interpreter.

Executed on the part of the Yanctonais band of Sioux by the chiefs and headmen whose names are hereto subscribed, they being thereunto duly authorized.

Mah-to-non-pah, his x mark,   SEAL
   Two Bears.
Ma-to-hna-skin-ya, his x mark,
   Mad Bear.   SEAL
He-o-pu-za, his x mark, Louzy. SEAL
Ah-ke-che-tah-che-ca-dan, his
   x mark, Little Soldier.   SEAL
Mah-to-e-tan-chan, his x mark,
   Chief Bear.   SEAL
Cu-wi-h-win, his x mark,
   Rotten Stomach.   SEAL
Skun-ka-we-tko, his x mark,
   Fool Dog.   SEAL
Ish-ta-sap-pah, his x mark,
   Black Eye.   SEAL
Ih-tan-chan, his x mark,
   The Chief.   SEAL
I-a-wi-ca-ka, his x mark, The
   one who Tells the Truth.   SEAL
Ah-ke-che-tah, his x mark,
   The Soldier.   SEAL
Ta-shi-na-gi, his x mark,
   Yellow Robe.   SEAL
Nah-pe-ton-ka, his x mark,
   Big Hand.   SEAL
Chan-tee-we-kto, his x mark,
   Fool Heart.   SEAL

Cha-ton-che-ca, his x mark,
   Small Hawk, or Long Fare.   SEAL
Shu-ter-mon-e-too-ha-ska, his
   x mark, Tall Wolf.   SEAL
Ma-to-u-tah-kah, his x mark,
   Sitting Bear.   SEAL
Hi-ha-cah-ge-na-skene, his
   x mark, Mad Elk.   SEAL
   Arapahoes:
Little Chief, his x mark.   SEAL
Tall Bear, his x mark.   SEAL
Top Man, his x mark.   SEAL
Neva, his x mark.   SEAL
The Wounded Bear, his x mark. SEAL
Thirlwind, his x mark.   SEAL
The Fox, his x mark.   SEAL
The Dog Big Mouth,
   his x mark.   SEAL
Spotted Wolf, his x mark.   SEAL
Sorrel Horse, his x mark.   SEAL
Black Coal, his x mark.   SEAL
Big Wolf, his x mark.   SEAL
Knock-knee, his x mark.   SEAL
Black Crow, his x mark.   SEAL
The Lone Old Man,
   his x mark.   SEAL
Paul, his x mark.   SEAL

Hoh-gan-sah-pa, his x mark,
 Black Catfish.   SEAL
Mah-to-wah-kan, his x mark,
 Medicine Bear.   SEAL
Shun-ka-kan-sha, his x mark,
 Red Horse.   SEAL
Wan-rode, his x mark,
 The Eagle.   SEAL
Can-hpi-sa-pa, his x mark,
 Black Tomahawk.   SEAL
War-he-le-re, his x mark,
 Yellow Eagle.   SEAL

Black Bull, his x mark.   SEAL
Big Track, his x mark.   SEAL
The Foot, his x mark.   SEAL
Black White, his x mark. SEAL
Yellow Hair, his x mark. SEAL
Little Shield, his x mark. SEAL
Black Bear, his x mark. SEAL
Wolf Mocassin, his x mark. SEAL
Big Robe, his x mark.   SEAL
Wolf Chief, his x mark. SEAL

Witnesses:

Robt. P. McKibbin, captain,
 Fourth Infantry, brevet
 lieutenant-colonel, U.S. Army
 commanding Fort Laramie.
Wm. H. Powell, brevet major,
 captain Fourth Infantry.
Henry W. Patterson, captain,
 Fourth Infantry.

Theo. E. True, second lieutenant,
 Fourth Infantry.
W.G. Bullock.
Chas. E. Guern, special Indian
 interpreter for the peace
 commission.

FORT LARAMIE, WG. T., *Nov. 6, 1868.*

Makh-pi-ah-lu-tah, his x mark,
 Red Cloud.   SEAL
Wa-ki-ah-we-cha-shah, his x
 mark, Thunder Man.   SEAL
Ma-zah-zah-geh, his x mark,
 Iron Cane.   SEAL

Wa-umble-why-wa-ka-tuyah, his
 x mark, High Eagle.   SEAL
Ko-ke-pah, his x mark,
 Man Afraid.   SEAL
Wa-ki-ah-wa-kou-ah, his x mark,
 Thunder Flying Running. SEAL

Witnesses:

W. McE. Dye, brevet colonel,
 U.S. Army, commanding.
A.B. Cain, captain, Fourth In-
 fantry, brevet major,
 U.S. Army.
Robt. P. McKibbin, captain,
 Fourth Infantry, brevet lieu-
 tenant-colonel, U.S. Army.
Jno. Miller, captain, Fourth
 Infantry.
G.L. Luhn, first lieutenant,
 Fourth Infantry, brevet
 captain, U.S. Army.

H.C. Sloan, second lieutenant,
 Fourth Infantry.
Whittingham Cox, first lieutenant,
 Fourth Infantry.
A.W. Vogdes, first lieutenant,
 Fourth Infantry.
Butler D. Price, second lieutenant,
 Fourth Infantry.

HEADQRS., FORT LARAMIE, *Novr. 6, '68.*

Executed by the above on this date.

All of the Indians are Ogallalahs excepting Thunder Man and Thunder Flying Running, who are Brulés.

Wm. McE. Dye,
Major Fourth Infantry, and Brevet-Colonel
U.S. Army, Commanding.

Attest:

Jas. C. O'Conner.
Nicholas Janis, interpreter.
Franc. La Framboise, interpreter.
P.J. De Smet, S.J., missionary among the Indians.
Saml. D. Hinman, B.D., missionary.

Executed on the part of the Uncpapa band of Sioux, by the chiefs and headmen whose names are hereto subscribed, they being thereunto duly authorized.

Co-kam-i-ya-ya, his x mark, The Man that Goes in the Middle.	SEAL	Shun-ka-i-na-pin, his x mark, Wolf Necklace.	SEAL
Ma-to-ca-wa-weksa, his x mark, Bear Rib.	SEAL	I-we-hi-yu, his x mark, The Man who Bleeds from the Mouth.	SEAL
Ta-to-ka-in-yan-ke, his x mark, Running Antelope.	SEAL	He-ha-ka-pa, his x mark, Elk Head.	SEAL
Kan-gi-wa-ki-ta, his x mark, Looking Crow.	SEAL	I-zu-za, his x mark, Grind Stone.	SEAL
A-ki-ci-ta-han-ska, his x mark, Long Soldier.	SEAL	Shun-ka-wi-tko, his x mark, Fool Dog.	SEAL
Wa-ku-te-ma-ni, his x mark, The One who Shoots Walking	SEAL	Ma-kpi-ya-po, his x mark, Blue Cloud.	SEAL
Un-kca-ki-ka, his x mark, The Magpie.	SEAL	Wa-mln-pi-lu-ta, his x mark, Red Eagle.	SEAL
Kan-gi-o-ta, his x mark, Plenty Crow.	SEAL	Ma-to-can-te, his x mark, Bear's Heart.	SEAL
He-ma-za, his x mark, Iron Horn.	SEAL	A-ki-ci-ta-i-tau-can, his x mark, Chief Soldier.	SEAL

Attest:

Jas. C. O'Connor.
Nicholas Janis, interpreter.
Franc. La Frambois [e], interpreter.
P.J. De Smet, S.J., missionary among the Indians.
Saml. D. Hinman, missionary.

Executed on the part of the Blackfeet band of Sioux by the chiefs and headmen whose names are hereto subscribed, they being thereunto duly authorized.

Can-te-pe-ta, his x mark, Fire Heart.	SEAL
Wan-mdi-kte, his x mark, The One who Kills Eagle.	SEAL
Sho-ta, his x mark, Smoke.	SEAL
Wan-mdi-ma-ni, his x mark, Walking Eagle.	SEAL
Wa-shi-cun-ya-ta-pi, his x mark, Chief White Man.	SEAL
Kan-gi-i-yo-tan-ke, his x mark, Sitting Crow.	SEAL
Pe-ji, his x mark, The Grass.	SEAL
Kda-ma-ni, his x mark, The One that Rattles as he Walks.	SEAL
Wah-han-ka-sa-pa, his x mark, Black Shield.	SEAL
Can-te-non-pa, his x mark, Two Hearts.	SEAL

Attest:

Jas. C. O'Connor.
Nicholas Janis, interpreter.
Franc. La Framboise, interpreter.
P.J. De Smet, S.J., missionary among the Indians.
Saml. D. Hinman, missionary.

Executed on the part of the Cutheads band of Sioux by the chiefs and headmen whose names are hereto subscribed, they being thereunto duly authorized.

To-ka-in-yan-ka, his x mark, The One who Goes Ahead Running.	SEAL
Ta-tan-ka-wa-kin-yan, his x mark, Thunder Bull.	SEAL
Sin-to-min-sa-pa, his x mark, All over Black.	SEAL
Can-i-ca, his x mark, The One who Took the Stick.	SEAL
Pa-tan-ka, his x mark, Big Head.	SEAL

Attest:

Jas. C. O'Connor.
Nicholas Janis, interpreter.
Franc. La Frambois [e], interpreter.
P.J. De Smet, S.J., missionary among the Indians.
Saml. D. Hinman, missionary.

Executed on the part of the Two Kettle band of Sioux by the chiefs and headmen whose names are hereto subscribed, they being thereunto duly authorized.

Ma-wa-tan-ni-han-ska, his x mark, Long Mandan.	SEAL
Can-kpe-du-ta, his x mark, Red War Club.	SEAL
Can-ka-ga, his x mark, The Log.	SEAL

Attest:

    Jas. C. O'Connor.
    Nicholas Janis, interpreter.
    Franc. La Framboise, interpreter.
    P.J. De Smet, S.J., missionary among the Indians.
    Saml. D. Hinman, missionary to the Dakotas.

Executed on the part of the Sans Arch band of Sioux by the chiefs and headmen whose names are hereto annexed, they being thereunto duly authorized.

He-na-pin-wa-ni-ca, his x mark, The One that has Neither Horn.	SEAL
Wa-inlu-pi-lu-ta, his x mark, Red Plume.	SEAL
Ci-tan-gi, his x mark, Yellow Hawk.	SEAL
He-na-pin-wa-ni-ca, his x mark, No Horn.	SEAL

Attest:

    Jas. C. O'Connor.
    Nicholas Janis, interpreter.
    Franc, La Frambois [e], interpreter.
    P.J. De Smet, S.J., Missionary among the Indians.
    Saml. D. Hinman, missionary.

Executed on the part of the Santee band of Sioux by the Chiefs and headmen whose names are hereto subscribed, they being thereunto duly authorized.

Wa-pah-shaw, his x mark, Red Ensign.	SEAL
Wah-koo-tay, his x mark, Shooter.	SEAL
Hoo-sha-sha, his x mark, Red Legs.	SEAL
O-wan-cha-du-ta, his x mark, Scarlet all over.	SEAL
Wau-mace-tan-ka, his x mark, Big Eagle.	SEAL
Cho-tan-ka-e-na-pe, his x mark, Flute-player.	SEAL
Ta-shun-ke-mo-za, his x mark, His Iron Dog.	SEAL

Attest:

    Saml. D. Hinman, B.D., missionary.
    J.N. Chickering,
        Second lieutenant, Twenty-second Infantry, brevet captain,
        U.S. Army.
    P.J. De Smet, S.J.
    Nicholas Janis, interpreter.
    Franc. La Framboise, interpreter.

TREATY WITH THE NEZ PERCÉS, 1868

Whereas certain amendments are desired by the Nez Percé tribe of Indians to their treaty concluded at the council ground in the valley of the Lapwai, in the Territory of Washington, on the ninth day of June in the year of our Lord one thousand eight hundred and sixty-three; and whereas the United States are willing to assent to said amendments; it is therefore agreed by and between Nathaniel G. Taylor, commissioner, on the part of the United States, thereunto duly authorized, and Lawyer, Timothy, and Jason, chiefs of said tribe, also being thereunto duly authorized, in manner and form following, that is to say:

ARTICLE 1. That all lands embraced within the limits of the tract set apart for the exclusive use and benefit of said Indians by the 2d article of said treaty of June 9th, 1863, which are susceptible of cultivation and suitable for Indian farms, which are not now occupied by the United States for military purposes, or which are not required for agency or other buildings and purposes provided for by existing treaty stipulations, shall be surveyed as provided in the 3d article of said treaty of June 9th, 1863, and as soon as the allotments shall be plowed and fenced, and as soon as schools shall be established as provided by existing treaty stipulations, such Indians now residing outside the reservation as may be decided upon by the agent of the tribe and the Indians themselves, shall be removed to and located upon allotments within the reservation: *Provided, however,* That in case there should not be a sufficient quantity of suitable land within the boundaries of the reservation to provide allotments for those now there and those residing outside the boundaries of the same, then those residing outside, or as many thereof as allotments cannot be provided for, may remain upon the lands now occupied and improved by them, provided, that the land so occupied does not exceed twenty acres for each and every male person who shall have attained the age of twenty-one years or is the head of a family, and the tenure of those remaining upon lands outside the reservation shall be the same as is provided in said 3d article of said treaty of June 9th, 1863, for those receiving allotments within the reservation; and it is further agreed that those now residing outside of the boundaries of the reservation and who may continue to so reside shall be protected by the military authorities in their rights upon the allotments occupied by them, and also in the privilege of grazing their animals upon surrounding unoccupied lands.

ARTICLE 2. It is further agreed between the parties hereto that the stipulations contained in the 8th article of the treaty of June 9th, 1863, relative to timber, and hereby annulled as far as the same provides that the United States shall be permitted to use thereof in the maintaining of forts of garrisons, and that the said Indians shall have the aid of the military authorities to protect the timber upon their reservation, and that none of the same shall be cut or removed without the consent of the head-chief of the tribe, together with the consent of the agent and superintendent of Indian affairs, first being given in writing, which written consent shall state the part of the reservation upon which the timber is to be cut, and also the quantity, and the price to be paid thereof.

ARTICLE 3. It is further hereby stipulated and agreed that the amount due said tribe for school purposes and for the support of teachers that has not been expended for that purpose since the year 1864, but has been used for other purposes, shall be ascertained and the same shall be re-imbursed to said tribe by appropriation by Congress, and shall be set apart and invested in United States bonds and shall be held in trust by the United States, the interest on the same to be paid to said tribe annually for the support of teachers.

In testimony whereof the said Commissioner on the part of the United States and the said chiefs representing said Nez Percé tribe of Indians have hereunto set their hands and seals this 13th day of August, in the year of our Lord one thousand eight hundred and sixty-eight, at the city of Washington, D.C.

N.G. Taylor,	L.S.
Commissioner Indian Affairs.	
Lawyer, Head Chief Nez Percés.	L.S.
Timothy, his x mark, Chief.	L.S.
Jason, his x mark, Chief.	L.S.

In presence of—
    Charles E. Mix.
    Robert Newell, United States Agent.
    W.R. Irwin.

ACT OF FIRST CONGRESS, SECOND SESSION, 1790

CHAP. 33.—An Act to regulate trade and intercourse with the Indian tribes.

SEC. 1. *Be it enacted by the Senate and House of Representatives of the United States of America in Congress assembled*, That no person shall be permitted to carry on any trade or intercourse with the Indian tribes, without a license for that purpose under the hand and seal of the superintendent of the department, or of such other person as the President of the United States shall appoint for that purpose; which superintendent, or other person so appointed, shall, on application, issue such license to any proper person, who shall enter into bond with one or more sureties, approved of by the superintendent, or person issuing such license, or by the President of the United States, in the penal sum of one thousand dollars, payable to the President of the United States for the time being, for the use of the United States, conditioned for the true and faithful observance of such rules, regulations and restrictions, as now are, or hereafter shall be made for the government of trade and intercourse with the Indian tribes. The said superintendents, and persons by them licensed as aforesaid, shall be governed in all things touching the said trade and intercourse, by such rules and regulations as the President shall prescribe. And no other person shall be permitted to carry on any trade or intercourse with the Indians without such license as aforesaid. No license shall be granted for a longer term than two years. *Provided nevertheless*, That the President may make such order respecting the tribes surrounded in their settlements by the citizens of the United States, as to secure an intercourse without license, if he may deem it proper.

SEC. 2. *And be it further enacted*, That the superintendent, or person issuing such license, shall have full power and authority to recall all such licenses as he may have issued, if the person so licensed shall transgress any of the regulations or restrictions provided for the government of trade and intercourse with the Indian tribes, and shall put in suit such bonds as he may have taken, immediately on the breach of any condition in said bond: *Provided always*, That if it shall appear on trial, that the person from whom such license shall have been recalled, has not offended against any of the provisions of this act, or the regulations prescribed for the trade and intercourse with the Indian tribes, he shall be entitled to receive a new license.

SEC. 3. *And be it further enacted*, That every person who shall attempt to trade with the Indian tribes, or be found in the Indian country with such merchandise in his possession as are usually vended to the Indians, without a license first had and obtained, as in this act prescribed, and being thereof convicted in any court proper to try the same, shall forfeit all the merchandise so offered for sale to the Indian tribes, or so found in the Indian country, which forfeiture shall be one half to the benefit of the person prosecuting, and the other half to the benefit of the United States.

SEC. 4. *And be it enacted and declared*, That no sale of lands made by any Indians, or any nation or tribe of Indians within the United States, shall be valid to any person or persons, or to any state, whether having the right of preemption to such lands or not, unless the same shall be made and duly executed at some public treaty, held under the authority of the United States.

SEC. 5. *And be it further enacted*, That if any citizen or inhabitant of the United States, or of either of the territorial districts of the United States, shall go into any town, settlement or territory belonging to any nation or tribe of Indians, and shall there commit any crime upon, or trespass against, the person or property of any peaceable and friendly Indian or Indians, which, if committed within the jurisdiction of any state, or within the jurisdiction of either of the said districts, against a citizen or white inhabitant thereof, would be punishable by the laws of such state or district, such offender or offenders shall be subject to the same punishment, and shall be proceeded against in the same manner as if the offence had been committed within the jurisdiction of the state or district to which he or they may belong, against a citizen or white inhabitant thereof.

SEC. 6. *And be it further enacted*, That for any of the crimes or offences aforesaid, the like proceedings shall be had for apprehending, imprisoning or bailing the offender, as the case may be, and for recognizing the witnesses for their appearance to testify in the case, and where the offender shall be committed, or the witnesses shall be in a district other than that in which the offence is to be tried, for the removal of the offender and the witnesses or either of them, as the case may be, to the district in which the trial is to be had, as by the act to establish the judicial courts of the United States, are directed for any crimes or offences against the United States.

SEC. 7. *And be it further enacted*, That this act shall be in force for the term of two years, and from thence to the end of the next session of Congress, and no longer.   Approved, July 22, 1790.

ACT OF TWENTY-FIRST CONGRESS, FIRST SESSION, 1830

CHAP. 148. — An Act to provide for an exchange of lands with the Indians residing in any of the states or territories, and for their removal west of the river Mississippi.

Be it enacted by the Senate and House of Representatives of the United States of America, in Congress assembled, That it shall and may be lawful for the President of the United States to cause so much of any territory belonging to the United States, west of the river Mississippi, not included in any state or organized territory, and to which the Indian title has been extinguished, as he may judge necessary, to be divided into a suitable number of districts, for the reception of such tribes or nations of Indians as may choose to exchange the lands where they now reside, and remove there; and to cause each of said districts to be so described by natural or artificial marks, as to be easily distinguished from every other.

SEC. 2. *And be it further enacted,* That it shall and may be lawful for the President to exchange any or all of such districts, so to be laid off and described, with any tribe or nation of Indians now residing within the limits of any of the states or territories, and with which the United States have existing treaties, for the whole or any part or portion of the territory claimed and occupied by such tribe or nation, within the bounds of any one or more of the states or territories, where the land claimed and occupied by the Indians, is owned by the United States, or the United States are bound to the state within which it lies to extinguish the Indian claim thereto.

SEC. 3. *And be it further enacted,* That in the making of any such exchange or exchanges, it shall and may be lawful for the President solemnly to assure the tribe or nation with which the exchange is made, that the United States will forever secure and guaranty to them, and their heirs or successors, the country so exchanged with them; and if they prefer it, that the United States will cause a patent or grant to be made and executed to them for the same:

Provided always, That such lands shall revert to the United States, if the Indians become extinct, or abandon the same.

SEC. 4. *And be it further enacted*, That if, upon any of the lands now occupied by the Indians, and to be exchanged for, there should be such improvements as add value to the land claimed by any individual or individuals of such tribes or nations, it shall and may be lawful for the President to cause such value to be ascertained by appraisement or otherwise, and to cause such ascertained value to be paid to the person or persons rightfully claiming such improvements. And upon the payment of such valuation, the improvements so valued and paid for, shall pass to the United States, and possession shall not afterwards be permitted to any of the same tribe.

SEC. 5. *And be it further enacted*, That upon the making of any such exchange as is contemplated by this act, it shall and may be lawful for the President to cause such aid and assistance to be furnished to the emigrants as may be necessary and proper to enable them to remove to, and settle in, the country for which they may have exchanged; and also, to give them aid and assistance as may be necessary for their support and subsistence for the first year after their removal.

SEC. 6. *And be it further enacted*, That it shall and may be lawful for the President to cause such tribe or nation to be protected, at their new residence, against all interruption or disturbance from any other tribe or nation of Indians, or from any other person or persons whatever.

SEC. 7. *And be it further enacted*, That it shall and may be lawful for the President to have the same superintendence and care over any tribe or nation in the country to which they may remove, as contemplated by this act, that he is now authorized to have over them at their present places of residence: *Provided*, That nothing in this act contained shall be construed as authorizing or directing the violation of any existing treaty between the United States and any of the Indian tribes.

SEC. 8. *And be it further enacted*, That for the purpose of giving effect to the provisions of this act, the sum of five hundred thousand dollars is hereby appropriated, to be paid out of any money in the treasury, not otherwise appropriated.

Approved, May 28, 1830.

GENERAL LAWS
REGULATING INDIAN AFFAIRS

Congress formally ends treaty making, March 3, 1871

SEC. 2079. No Indian nation or tribe within the territory of the United States shall be acknowledged or recognized as an independent nation, tribe, or power with whom the United States may contract by treaty; but no obligation of any treaty lawfully made and ratified with any such Indian nation or tribe prior to March third, eighteen hundred and seventy-one, shall be hereby invalidated or impaired.

ACT OF FORTY-FOURTH CONGRESS, SECOND SESSION, 1877

CHAP. 72—An act to ratify an agreement with certain bands of the Sioux Nation of Indians, and also with the Northern Arapaho and Cheyenne Indians.

Be it enacted by the Senate and House of Representatives of the United States of America in Congress assembled, That a certain agreement made by George W. Manypenny, Henry B. Whipple, Jared W. Daniels, Albert G. Boone, Henry C. Bulis, Newton Edmunds, and Augustine S. Gaylord, commissioners on the part of the United States, with the different bands of the Sioux Nation of Indians, and also the Northern Arapaho and Cheyenne Indians, be, and the same is hereby, ratified and confirmed: *Provided*, That nothing in this act shall be construed to authorize the removal of the Sioux Indians to the Indian Territory and the President of the United States is hereby directed to prohibit the removal of any portion of the Sioux Indians to the Indian Territory until the same shall be authorized by an act of Congress hereafter enacted, except article four, except also the following portion of article six: "And if said Indians shall remove to said Indian Territory as hereinbefore provided, the Government shall erect for each of the principal chiefs a good and comfortable dwelling-house" said article not having been agreed to by the Sioux Nation; said agreement is in words and figures following, namely: "Articles of agreement made pursuant to the provisions of an act of Congress entitled "An act making appropriations for the current and contingent expenses of the Indian Department, and for fulfilling treaty stipulations with various Indian tribes, for the year ending June thirtieth, eighteen hundred and seventy-seven, and for other purposes," approved August 15, 1876, by and between George W. Manypenny, Henry B. Whipple, Jared W. Daniels, Albert G. Boone, Henry C. Bulis, Newton Edmunds, and Augustine S. Gaylord, commissioners on the part of the United States, and the different bands of the Sioux Nation of Indians, and also the Northern Araphoes and Cheyennes, by their chiefs and headmen, whose names are hereto subscribed, they being duly authorized to act in the premises.

"ARTICLE 1. The said parties hereby agree that the northern and western boundaries of the reservation defined by article 2 of the treaty between the United States and different tribes of Sioux Indians, concluded April 29, 1868, and proclaimed February 24, 1869, shall be as follows: The western boundaries shall commence at the intersection of the one hundred and third meridian of longitude with the northern boundary of the State of Nebraska; thence north along said meridian to its intersection with the South Fork of the Cheyenne River; thence down said stream to its junction with the North Fork; thence up the North Fork of said Cheyenne River to the said one hundred and third meridian; thence north along said meridian to the South Branch of Cannon Ball River or Cedar Creek; and the northern boundary of their said reservation shall follow the said South Branch to its intersection with the main Cannon Ball River, and thence down the said main Cannon Ball River to the Missouri River; and the said Indians do hereby relinquish and cede to the United States all the territory lying outside the said reservation, as herein modified and described, including all privileges of hunting; and article 16 of said treaty is hereby abrogated.

"ARTICLE 2. The said Indians also agree and consent that wagon and other roads, not exceeding three in number, may be constructed and maintained, from convenient and accessible points on the Missouri River, through said reservation, to the country lying immediately west thereof, upon such routes as shall be designated by the President of the United States; and they also consent and agree to the free navigation of the Missouri River.

"ARTICLE 3. The said Indians also agree that they will hereafter receive all annuities provided by the said treaty of 1868, and all subsistence and supplies which may be provided for them under the present or any future act of Congress, at such points and places on the said reservation, and in the vicinity of the Missouri River, as the President of the United States shall designate.

"ARTICLE 4. [The Government of the United States and the said Indians, being mutually desirous that the latter shall be located in a country where they may eventually become self-supporting and acquire the arts of civilized life, it is therefore agreed that the said Indians shall select a delegation of five or more chiefs and principal men from each band, who shall, without delay, visit the Indian Territory under the guidance and protection of suitable persons, to be appointed for that purpose by the Department of the Interior, with a view to selecting therein a permanent home for the said Indians. If such delegation shall make a selection which shall be satisfactory to themselves, the people whom they represent, and to the United States, then the said Indians agree that they will remove to the country so selected within one year from this date. And the said Indians do further agree in all things to submit themselves to such beneficent plans as the Government may provide for them in the selection of a country suitable for a permanent home, where they may live like white men.]

"ARTICLE 5. In consideration of the foregoing cession of territory and rights, and upon full compliance with each and every obligation assumed by the said Indians, the United States does agree to provide all necessary aid to assist the said Indians in the work of civilization; to furnish to them schools and instruction in mechanical and agricultural arts, as provided for by the treaty of 1868. (Also to provide the said Indians with subsistence consisting of a ration for each individual of a pound and a half of beef, (or in lieu thereof, one half pound of bacon,) one-half pound of flour, and one-half pound of corn; and for every one hundred rations, four pounds of coffee, eight pounds of sugar, and three pounds of beans, or in lieu of said articles the equivalent thereof, in the discretion of the Commissioner of Indian Affairs. Such rations, or so much thereof as may be necessary, shall be continued until the Indians are able to support themselves.) Rations shall, in all cases, be issued to the head of each separate family; and whenever schools shall have been provided by the Government for said Indians, no rations shall be issued for children between the ages of six and fourteen years (the sick and infirm excepted) unless such children shall regularly attend school. Whenever the said Indians shall be located upon lands which are suitable for cultivation, rations shall be issued only to the persons and families of those persons who labor, (the aged, sick, and infirm excepted;) and as an incentive to industrious habits the Commissioner of Indian Affairs may provide that such persons be furnished in payment for their labor such other necessary articles as are requisite for civilized life. The Government will aid such Indians as far as possible in finding a market for their surplus productions, and in finding employment, and will purchase such surplus, as far as may be required, for supplying food to those Indians, parties to this agreement, who are unable to sustain themselves; and will also employ Indians, so far as practicable, in the performance of Government work upon their reservation.

"ARTICLE 6. Whenever the head of a family shall, in good faith, select an allotment of said land upon such reservation and engage in the cultivation thereof, the Government shall, with his aid, erect a comfortable house on such allotment; [and if said Indians shall remove to said Indian Territory as hereinbefore provided, the Government shall erect for each of the principal chiefs a good and comfortable dwelling-house.]

"ARTICLE 7. To improve the morals and industrious habits of said Indians, it is agreed that the agent, trader, farmer, carpenter, blacksmith, and other artisans employed or permitted to reside within the reservation belonging to the Indians, parties to this agreement, shall be lawfully married and living with their respective families on the reservation; and no person other than an Indian of full blood, whose fitness, morally or otherwise, is not, in the opinion of the Commissioner of Indian Affairs, conducive to the welfare of said Indians, shall receive any benefit from this agreement or former treaties, and may be expelled from the reservation.

"ARTICLE 8. The provisions of the said treaty of 1868, except as herein modified, shall continue in full force, and, with the provisions of this agreement, shall apply to any country which may hereafter be occupied by the said Indians as a home; and Congress shall, by appropriate legislation, secure to them an orderly government; they shall be subject to the laws of the United States, and each individual shall be protected in his rights of property, person, and life.

"ARTICLE 9. The Indians, parties to this agreement, do hereby solemnly pledge themselves, individually and collectively, to observe each and all of the stipulations herein contained, to select allotments of land as soon as possible after their removal to their permanent home, and to use their best efforts to learn to cultivate the same. And they do solemnly pledge themselves that they will at all times maintain peace with the citizens and Government of the United States; that they will observe the laws thereof and loyally endeavor to fulfill all the obligations assumed by them under the treaty of 1868 and the present agreement, and to this end will, whenever requested by the President of the United States, select so many suitable men from each band to co-operate with him in maintaining order and peace on the reservation as the President may deem necessary, who shall receive such compensation for their services as Congress may provide.

"ARTICLE 10. In order that the Government may faithfully fulfill the stipulations contained in this agreement, it is mutually agreed that a census of all Indians affected hereby shall be taken in the month of December of each year, and the names of each head of family and adult person registered; said census to be taken in such manner as the Commissioner of Indian Affairs may provide.

"ARTICLE 11. It is understood that the term reservation herein contained shall be held to apply to any country which shall be selected under the authority of the United States as the future home of said Indians.

"This agreement shall not be binding upon either party until it shall have received the approval of the President and Congress of the United States.

"Dated and signed at Red Cloud agency, Nebraska, September 26, 1876.

"GEORGE W. MANYPENNY.   SEAL
"HENRY B. WHIPPLE.   SEAL

"J.W. DANIELS   SEAL
"ALBERT G. BOONE.   SEAL
"H.C. BULIS.   SEAL
"NEWTON EDMUNDS.   SEAL
"A.S. GAYLORD.   SEAL

"Attest:
    "CHARLES M. HENDLEY,
       "*Secretary*.

[Here follows the signature of Marpuja-luta, and others of the Oglala Sioux, Arapaho, and Cheyenne.]

"Dated and signed at Spotted Tail agency, Nebraska, September 23, 1876.

[Here follows the signature of Sinta-gleska, and others of the Brule Sioux.]

"The foregoing articles of agreement having been fully explained to us in open council, we, the chiefs and headmen of the various bands of Sioux Indians, receiving rations and annuities at the Cheyenne River agency, in the Territory of Dakota, do hereby consent and agree to all the stipulations therein contained, with the exception of so much of article 4 of said agreement as relates to our visit and removal to the Indian Territory; in all other respects the said article remaining in full force and effect.

"Witness our hands and seals at Cheyenne River agency, Territory of Dakota, this 16th day of October, A.D. 1876.

[Here follows the signature of Kangi-wiyaka, and others.]

"The foregoing articles of agreement having been fully explained to us in open council, we, the undersigned chiefs and headmen of the various bands of Sioux Indians receiving rations and annuities at the Standing Rock agency, in the Territory of Dakota, do hereby consent and agree to all the stipulations therein contained, with the exception of so much of article four of said agreement as relates to our visit and removal to the Indian Territory; in all other respects the said article remaining in full force and effect.

"Witness our hands and seals at Standing Rock agency, Territory of Dakota, this 11th day of October, A.D. 1876.

[Here follows the signature of Mato-nonpa, and others.]

"The foregoing articles of agreement having been fully explained to us in open council, we, the undersigned chiefs and headmen of the Sioux Indians, receiving rations and annuities at Crow Creek agency, in the Territory of Dakota, do hereby consent and agree to all the stipulations therein contained, with the exception of so much of article 4 of said agreement as relates to our visit and removal to the Indian Territory; in all other respects the said article remaining in full force and effect.

"Witness our hands and seals at Crow Creek agency, Territory of Dakota, this 21st day of October, A.D. 1876.

[Here follows the signature of Wanigi-ska, and others.]

"The foregoing articles of agreement having been fully explained to us in open council, we, the undersigned chiefs and headmen of the Sioux Indians, receiving rations and annuities at Lower Brule agency, in the Territory of Dakota, do hereby consent and agree to all the stipulations herein contained, with the exception of so much of article 4 of said agreement as relates to our visit and removal to the Indian Territory; in all other respects the said article remaining in full force and effect.

Witness our hands and seals at Lower Brule agency, Territory of Dakota, this 24th day of October, A.D. 1876.

[Here follows signatures of Maza-oyate, and others.]

"The foregoing articles of agreement having been fully explained to us in open council, we, the undersigned chiefs and headmen of the Sioux Indians, receiving rations and annuities at the Santee reservation, in Knox County, in the State of Nebraska, do hereby consent and agree to all the stipulations therein contained, saving, reserving, and excepting all our rights, both collective and individual, in and to the said Santee reservation, in said Knox County and State of Nebraska, upon which we, the undersigned, and our people are now residing.

"Witness our hands and seals at Santee agency, county of Knox, State of Nebraska, this 27th day of October, A.D. 1876.

[Here follows signature of Joseph Wabashaw, and others.]

Approved, February 28, 1877.

ACT OF FORTY-NINTH CONGRESS, SECOND SESSION, 1887

CHAP. 119 — An act to provide for the allotment of lands in severalty to Indians on the various reservations, and to extend the protection of the laws of the United States and the Territories over the Indians, and for other purposes.

Be it enacted, &c., [For substitute for section 1, see 1891, Feb. 28, c. 383.]

SEC. 2. That all allotments set apart under the provisions of this act shall be selected by the Indians, heads of families selecting for their minor children, and the agents shall select for each orphan child, and in such manner as to embrace the improvements of the Indians making the selection.

Where the improvements of two or more Indians have been made on the same legal subdivision of land, unless they shall otherwise agree, a provisional line may be run dividing said lands between them, and the amount to which each is entitled shall be equalized in the assignment of the remainder of the land to which they are entitled under this act:

Provided, That if any one entitled to an allotment shall fail to make a selection within four years after the President shall direct that allotments may be made on a particular reservation, the Secretary of the Interior may direct the agent of such tribe or band, if such there be, and if there be no agent, then a special agent appointed for that purpose, to make a selection for such Indian, which selection shall be allotted as in cases where selections are made by the Indians, and patents shall issue in like manner.

SEC. 3. That the allotments provided for in this act shall be made by special agents appointed by the President for such purpose, and the agents in charge of the respective reservations on which the allotments are directed to be made, under such rules and regulations as the Secretary of the Interior may from time to time prescribe, and shall be certified by such agents to the Commissioner of Indian Affairs, in duplicate, one copy to be retained in the Indian Office and the other to be transmitted to the Secretary of the Interior for his action, and to be deposited in the General Land Office.

SEC. 4. That where any Indian not residing upon a reservation, or for whose tribe no reservation has been provided by treaty, act of Congress or executive order, shall make settlement upon any surveyed or unsurveyed lands of the United States not otherwise appropriated, he or she shall be entitled, upon application to the local land-office for the district in which the lands are located, to have the same allotted to his or her, and to his or her children, in quantities and manner as provided in this act for Indians residing upon reservations; and when such settlement is made upon unsurveyed lands, the grant to such Indians shall be adjusted upon the survey of the lands so as to conform thereto; and patent shall be issued to them for such lands in the manner and with the restrictions as herein provided.

And the fees to which the officers of such local land-office would have been entitled had such lands been entered under the general laws for the disposition of the public lands shall be paid to them, from any moneys in the Treasury of the United States not otherwise appropriated, upon a statement of an account in their behalf for such fees by the Commissioner of the General Land Office and a certification of such account to the Secretary of the Treasury by the Secretary of the Interior.

SEC. 5. That upon the approval of the allotments provided for in this act by the Secretary of the Interior, he shall cause patents to issue therefor in the name of the allottees, which patents shall be of the legal effect, and declare that the United States does and will hold the land thus allotted for the period of twenty-five years, in trust for the sole use and benefit of the Indian to whom such allotment shall have been made, or, in case of his decease, of his heirs according to the laws of the State or Territory where such land is located, and that at the expiration of said period the United States will convey the same by patent to said Indian, or his heirs as aforesaid, in fee, discharged of said trust and free of all charge or incumbrance whatsoever: *Provided*, That the President of the United States may in any case in his discretion extend the period.

And if any conveyance shall be made of the lands set apart and allotted as herein provided, or any contract made touching the same, before the expiration of the time above mentioned, such conveyance or contract shall be absolutely null and void:

Provided, That the law of descent and partition in force in the State or Territory where such lands are situate shall apply thereto after patents therefor have been executed and delivered, except as herein otherwise provided; and the laws of the State of Kansas regulating the descent and partition of real estate shall, so far as practicable, apply to all lands in the Indian Territory which may be allotted in severalty under the provisions of this act:

And provided further, That at any time after lands have been allotted to all the Indians of any tribe as herein provided, or sooner if in the opinion of the President it shall be for the best interest of said tribe, it shall be lawful for the Secretary of the Interior to negotiate with such Indian tribe for the purchase and release by said tribe, in conformity with the treaty or statute under which such reservation is held, of such portions of its reservation not allotted as such tribe shall, from time to time, consent to sell, on such terms and conditions as shall be considered just and equitable between the United States and said tribe of Indians, which purchase shall not be complete until ratified by Congress, and the form and manner of executing such release shall also be prescribed by Congress:

Provided however, That all lands adapted to agriculture, with or without irrigation so sold or released to the United States by any Indian tribe shall be held by the United States for the sole purpose of securing homes to actual settlers and shall be disposed of by the United States to actual and bona fide settlers only in tracts not exceeding one hundred and sixty acres to any one person, on such terms as Congress shall prescribe, subject to grants which Congress may make in aid of education:

And provided further, That no patents shall issue therefor except to the person so taking the same as and for a homestead, or his heirs, and after the expiration of five years occupancy thereof as such homestead; and any conveyance of said lands so taken as a homestead, or any contract touching the same, or lien thereon, created prior to the date of such patent, shall be null and void.

And the sums agreed to be paid by the United States as purchase money for any portion of any such reservation shall be held in the Treasury of the United States for the sole use of the tribe or tribes of Indians to whom such reservations belonged; and the same, with interest thereon at three per cent per annum, shall be at all times subject to appropriation by Congress for the education and civilization of such tribe or tribes of Indians or the members thereof.

The patents aforesaid shall be recorded in the General Land Office, and afterward delivered, free of charge, to the allottee entitled thereto.

And if any religious society or other organization is now occupying any of the public lands to which this act is applicable, for religious or educational work among the Indians, the Secretary of the Interior is hereby authorized to confirm such occupation to such society or organization, in quantity not exceeding one hundred and sixty acres in any one tract, so long as the same shall be so occupied, on such terms as he shall deem just; but nothing herein contained shall change or alter any claim of such society for religious or educational purposes heretofore granted by law.

And hereafter in the employment of Indian police, or any other employees in the public service among any of the Indian tribes or bands affected by this act, and where Indians can perform the duties required, those Indians who have availed themselves of the provisions of this act and become citizens of the United States shall be preferred.

SEC. 6. That upon the completion of said allotments and the patenting of the lands to said allottees, each and every member of the respective bands or tribes of Indians to whom allotments have been made shall have the benefit of and be subject to the laws, both civil and criminal, of the State or Territory in which they may reside; and no Territory shall pass or enforce any law denying any such Indian within its jurisdiction the equal protection of the law.

And every Indian born within the territorial limits of the United States to whom allotments shall have been made under the provisions of this act, or under any law or treaty, and every Indian born within the territorial limits of the United States who has voluntarily taken up, within said limits, his residence separate and apart from any tribe of Indians therein, and has adopted the habits of civilized life, [*and every Indian in Indian Territory,*] is hereby declared to be a citizen of the United States, and is entitled to all the rights, privileges, and immunities of such citizens, whether said Indian has been or not, by birth or otherwise, a member of any tribe of Indians within the territorial limits of the United States without in any manner impairing or otherwise affecting the right of any such Indian to tribal or other property.

SEC. 7. That in cases where the use of water for irrigation is neccessary to render the lands within any Indian reservation available for agricultural purposes, the Secretary of the Interior be, and he is hereby, authorized to prescribe such rules and regulations as he may deem necessary to secure a just and equal distribution thereof among the Indians residing upon any such reservations; and no other appropriations or grant of water by any riparian proprietor shall be authorized or permitted to the damage of any other riparian proprietor.

SEC. 8. That the provision of this act shall not extend to the territory occupied by the Cherokees, Creeks, Choctaws, Chickasaws, Seminoles, and Osage, Miamies and Peorias, and Sacs and Foxes, in the Indian Territory, nor to any of the reservations of the Seneca Nation of New York Indians in the State of New York, nor to that strip of territory in the State of Nebraska adjoining the Sioux Nation on the south added by executive order.

SEC. 9. That for the purpose of making the surveys and resurveys mentioned in section two of this act, there be, and hereby is, appropriated, out of any moneys in the Treasury not otherwise appropriated, the sum of one hundred thousand dollars, to be repaid proportionately out of the proceeds of the sales of such land as may be acquired from the Indians under the provisions of this act.

SEC. 10. That nothing in this act contained shall be so construed as to affect the right and power of Congress to grant the right of way through any lands granted to an Indian, or a tribe of Indians, for railroads or other highways, or telegraph lines, for the public use, or to condemn such lands to public uses, upon making just compensation.

SEC. 11. That nothing in this act shall be so construed as to prevent the removal of the Southern Ute Indians from their present reservation in the Southwestern Colorado to a new reservation by and with the consent of a majority of the adult male members of said tribe. [*February 8, 1887.*]

ACT OF FIFTIETH CONGRESS, SECOND SESSION, 1889

CHAP. 422 — An act to provide for allotment of land in severalty to United Peorias and Miamies in Indian Territory, and for other purposes.

Be it enacted by the Senate and House of Representatives of the United States of America in Congress assembled, That the provisions of chapter One hundred and Nineteen of the acts of eighteen hundred and eighty seven, entitled "An act to provide for the allotment of lands in severalty to Indians on the various reservations, and to extend the protection of the laws of the United States and the Territories over the Indians, and for other purposes," are hereby declared to extend to and are made applicable to the Confederated Wea, Peoria, Kaskaskia, and Piankeshaw tribes of Indians, and the Western Miami tribe of Indians, now located in the northeastern part of the Indian Territory and to their reservation, in the same manner and to the same extent as if said tribes had not been excepted from the provisions of said act, except as to section 6 of said act, and as otherwise hereinafter provided.

That the Secretary of the Interior is hereby authorized and directed, within ninety days from and after the passage of this act, to cause to be allotted to each and every member of the said Confederated Wea, Peoria, Kaskaskia, and Piankeshaw tribes of Indians, and the Western Miami tribe of Indians, upon lists to be furnished him by the chiefs of said tribes, duly approved by them, and subject to the approval of the Secretary of the Interior, an allotment of land not to exceed two hundred acres, out of their common reserve, to each person entitled thereto by reason of their being members of said tribes by birth or adoption; all allotments to be selected by the Indians, heads of families selecting for their minor children, and the chiefs of their respective tribes for each orphan child. All differences arising between members of said tribes, in making said allotments, shall be settled by the chiefs of the respective tribes, subject to the approval of the Secretary of the Interior; *Provided,* That before any of the allotments herein provided for shall be made, there shall be set apart, not to exceed twenty acres in all, for school, church, and cemetery purposes; the location of the same to be selected by the chiefs of said tribes, subject to the approval of the Secretary of the Interior, in such quantities and at such points as they shall deem best, which, together with all improvements now existing or that may hereafter be made by the tribes thereon, shall be held as common property of the respective tribes. If in making the selections as herein provided for, the sites of present school buildings should not be retained, then all improvements thereon may be removed. If not removed, then they shall be sold after appraisement by the chiefs of the tribes; the sale to be approved by the Secretary of the Interior and the proceeds placed to the credit of the proper tribe. If any religious denomination, with the consent of either or both of said tribes, should erect any building for church or school purposes upon any of the land selected for church use, the said building, together with the land, shall be held the property of such religious denomination so long as they shall occupy the same for religious or school purposes. And should such denomination at any time desire to move said church or school house to any other place on their reservation, they may do so; or, if they prefer, may sell the same with or without the lands upon which said house is situate, and apply the proceeds to their new building.

The land so allotted shall not be subject to alienation for twenty five years from the date of the issuance of patent therefor, and said lands so allotted and patented shall be exempt from levy, sale, taxation, or forfeiture for a like period of years. As soon as all the allotments or selections shall have been made as herein provided, the Secretary of the Interior shall cause a patent to issue to each and every person so entitled, for his or her allotment, and such patent shall recite in the body thereof that the land therein described and conveyed shall not be alienated for twenty-five years from the date of said patent, and shall also recite that such land so allotted and patented is not subject to levy, sale, taxation, or forfeiture for a like period of years, and that any contract or agreement to sell or convey such land or allotments so patented entered into before the expiration of said term of years shall be absolutely null and void.

SEC. 2. That in making allotments under this act no more in the aggregate than the seventeen thousand and eighty-three acres of said reservation shall be allotted to the Miami Indians, nor more than thirty-three thousand two hundred and eighteen acres in the aggregate to the United Peoria Indians; and said amounts shall be treated in making said allotments in all respects as the extent of the reservation of each of said tribes, respectively. If, in making said allotments any difference shall arise between said tribes, all such matters of difference shall be determined by the Secretary of the Interior. After the allotments herein provided for shall have been completed, the residue of the lands, if any, not alloted, shall be held in common under present title by said United Peorias and Miamies in the proportion that the residue, if any of each of the said allotments shall bear to the other. And said United Peorias and Miamies shall have power, subject to the approval of the Secretary of the Interior, to lease for grazing, agricultural, or mining purposes from time to time and for any period not exceeding ten years at any one time, all of said residue, or any part thereof, the proceeds or rental to be divided between said tribes in proportion to their respective interests in said residue. And after said allotments are completed each allottee may lease or rent his or her individual allotment for any period not exceeding three years, the father acting for his minor children, and in case of no father then the mother, the chief acting for orphans of the tribe to which said orphans may belong.

At the expiration of twenty-five years from the date of the passage of this act, all of said remaining or unallotted lands may be equally divided among the members of said tribes, according to their respective interests, or the same may be sold on such terms and conditions as the President and the adult members of said tribe may hereafter mutually agree upon, and the proceeds thereof divided according to ownership as hereinbefore set forth: *Provided*, That before any division of the land is made, or sale had, that three-fourths of the bona fide adult members of said tribes shall petition the Secretary of the Interior for such division or sale of said land: *Provided further*, That sections one and two of this act shall not take effect until the consent thereto of each of said tribes separately shall have been signified by three-fourths of the adult male members thereof, in manner and form satisfactory to the President of the United States.

SEC. 3. That any act or part of acts of Congress heretofore passed that may conflict with the provisions of this act, either as to land or money, are hereby repealed.

SEC. 4. That full jurisdiction is hereby conferred upon the Court of Claims, subject to an appeal to the Supreme court of the United States, as in other cases, to hear and determine what are the just rights at law, or in equity, of those Wea, Peoria, Kaskaskia, and Piankeshaw Indians and of their children, or heirs at law, or legal representatives, who became citizens of the United States under the provisions of article twenty-eight of the treaty of February twenty-third, eighteen hundred and sixty-seven, made with the confederated tribes of Peorias, Kaskaskias, Weas, and Piankeshaw in the invested funds and other common property of the said confederated tribes. And the exercise of such jurisdiction shall not be barred by any lapse of time heretofore, nor shall the rights of said Indians be impaired by any ruling or determination upon such rights heretofore made. Suit may be instituted against the United States in said court of Claims within twelve months after the passage of this act, but not later, on behalf of said Indians who so become citizens of the United States, their heirs and legal representatives, in the name and style of "The Citizen Wea, Peoria, Kaskaskia, and Piankeshaw Indians," in accordance with the practice of said Court, for the hearing and determination of such rights at law and in equity as are claimed for said citizen Indians, or any of them, in such suit, which rights or equities arise out of the provisions of said treaty, or any law of the United States relating to the invested funds and common property of said confederated tribes. Said "confederated tribes of Peorias, Kaskaskias, Weas, and Piankeshaws" may be made a party defendant in said suit, on petition in that name to be made such party defendant, to be filed within three months from the date of the bringing of such suit, but the United States, through its proper officers, shall defend said suit on behalf of said Indians, whether or not they shall become parties to the same. Said courts shall determine what are the legal and equitable rights and interests of the Indians who separated from the tribes to which they belonged, and became citizens of the United States under said treaty, and of the heirs and legal representatives of such of them as are dead, and shall ascertain the value thereof, after deducting what has been paid to each of said Indians on account of such invested funds and common property. And such sums shall be paid to the persons who are respectively entitled to the same out of any money or funds held in trust by the United States for and on account of said confederated tribes of Peoria, Kaskaskia, Wea, and Piankeshaw Indians. Out of the funds so found due to said citizen Indians said Court of Claims may allow a reasonable compensation to the counsel or attorneys of such Indians, to be ratably apportioned upon and paid out of the sums due them, respectively; and the court may ascertain the reasonable value of the services of counsel employed by said confederated tribes to represent the tribes on such examination, not to exceed ten per centum of the aggregate sum actually in controversy, and the Secretary of the Interior shall cause to be paid to said counsel so much of the sum so ascertained as in equity and justice he may consider to be due them for such services, out of any money in the Treasury of the United States now due to such tribes arising from the sale of lands of said tribe in Kansas.

SEC. 5. That the Secretary of the Interior shall transmit to said Court of Claims, upon its request, certified copies of any records, documents, or papers that relate to the rights of any of said Indians involved in such suit.

Approved, March 2, 1889.

ACT OF FIFTY-FIRST CONGRESS, SECOND SESSION, 1891

CHAP. 383. — An act to amend and further extend the benefits of the act approved February eighth, eighteen hundred and eighty-seven entitled "An act to provide for the allotment of land in severalty to Indians on the various reservations, and to extend the protection of the laws of the United States over the Indians, and for other purposes."

Be it enacted, &c., That section one of the act entitled "An act to provide for the allotment of lands in severalty to Indians on the various reservations, and to extend the protection of the laws of the United States and the Territories over the Indians, and for other purposes," approved February eighth, eighteen hundred and eighty-seven, be, and the same is hereby, amended so as to read as follows:

"SEC. 1. That in all cases where any tribe or band of Indians has been, or shall hereafter be, located upon any reservation created for their use, either by treaty stipulation or by virtue of an Act of Congress, or Executive order setting apart the same for their use, the President of the United States be, and he hereby is, authorized, whenever in his opinion any reservation, or any part thereof, of such Indians is advantageous for agricultural or grazing purposes, to cause said reservation, or any part thereof, to be surveyed, or resurveyed, if necessary, and to allot to each Indian located thereon one-eighth of a section of land:

Provided, That in case there is not sufficient land in any of said reservations to allot lands to each individual in quantity as above provided the land in such reservation or reservations shall be alloted to each individual pro rata, as near as may be, according to legal subdivisions:

Provided further, That where the treaty or act of Congress setting apart such reservation provides for the allotment of lands in severalty to certain classes in quantity in excess of that herein provided the President, in making allotments upon such reservation, shall allot the land to each individual Indian of said classes belonging thereon in quantity as specified in such treaty

160

or act, and to other Indians belonging thereon in quantity as herein provided:

Provided further, That where existing agreements or laws provide for allotments in accordance with the provisions of said act of February eighth, eighteen hundred and eighty-seven, or in quantities substantially as therein provided, allotments may be made in quantity as specified in this act, with the consent of the Indians, expressed in such manner as the President, in his discretion, may require:

And provided further, That when the lands allotted, or any legal subdivision thereof, are only valuable for grazing purposes, such lands shall be allotted in double quantities."

SEC. 2. That where allotments have been made in whole or in part upon any reservation under the provisions of said act of February eighth, eighteen hundred and eighty-seven, and the quantity of land in such reservation is sufficient to give each member of the tribe eighty acres, such allotments shall be revised and equalized under the provisions of this act:

Provided, That no allotments heretofore approved by the Secretary of the Interior shall be reduced in quantity.

SEC. 3. That whenever it shall be made to appear to the Secretary of the Interior that, by reason of age or other disability, any allottee under the provisions of said act, or any other act or treaty can not personally and with benefit to himself occupy or improve his allotment or any part thereof the same may be leased upon such terms, regulations and conditions as shall be prescribed by such Secretary, for a term not exceeding three years for farming or grazing, or ten years for mining purposes:

Provided, That where lands are occupied by Indians who have bought and paid for the same, and which lands are not needed for farming or agricultural purposes, and are not desired for individual allotments, the same may be leased by authority of the Council speaking for such Indians, for a period not to exceed five years for grazing, or ten years for mining purposes in such quantities and upon such terms and conditions as the agent in charge of such reservation may recommend, subject to the approval of the Secretary of the Interior.

SEC. 4. That where any Indian entitled to allotment under existing laws shall make settlement upon any surveyed or unsurveyed lands of the United States not otherwise appropriated, he or she shall be entitled, upon application to the local land office for the district in which the lands are located, to have the same allotted to him or her and to his or her children, in quantities and manner as provided in the foregoing section of this amending act for Indians residing upon reservations; and when such settlement is made upon unsurveyed lands the grant to such Indians shall be adjusted upon the survey of the lands so as to conform thereto; and patents shall be issued to them for such lands in the manner and with the restrictions provided in the act to which this is an amendment.

And the fees to which the officers of such local land office would have been entitled had such lands been entered under the general laws for the disposition of the public lands shall be paid to them from any moneys in the Treasury of the United States not otherwise appropriated, upon a statement of an account in their behalf for such fees by the Commissioner of the General Land Office, and a certification of such account to the Secretary of the Treasury by the Secretary of the Interior.

SEC. 5. That for the purpose of determining the descent of land to the heirs of any deceased Indian under the provisions of the fifth section of said act, whenever any male and female Indian shall have co-habited together as husband and wife according to the custom and manner of Indian life the issue of such co-habitation shall be, for the purpose aforesaid, taken and deemed to be the legitimate issue of the Indians so living together, and every Indian child, otherwise illegitimate, shall for such purpose be taken and deemed to be the legitimate issue of the father of such child:

Provided, That the provisions of this act shall not be held or construed as to apply to the lands commonly called and known as the "Cherokee Outlet":

And provided further, That no allotment of lands shall be made of annuities of money paid to any of the Sac and Fox of the Missouri Indians who were not enrolled as members of said tribe on January first, eighteen hundred and ninety; but this shall not be held to impair or otherwise affect the rights or equities of any person whose claim to membership in said tribe is now pending and being investigated.

[*February 28, 1891.*]

ACT OF FIFTY-NINTH CONGRESS, FIRST SESSION, 1906

CHAP. 2348. — An act to amend section six of an act approved February eighth, eighteen hundred and eighty-seven, entitled "An act to provide for the allotment of lands in severalty to Indians on the various reservations, and to extend the protection of the laws of the United States and the Territories over the Indians, and for other purposes."

Be it enacted by the Senate and House of Representatives of the United States of America in Congress assembled, That section six of an act approved February eighth, eighteen hundred and eighty-seven, entitled "An act to provide for the allotment of land in severalty to Indians on the various reservations, and to extend the protection of the laws of the United States and the Territories over the Indians, and for other purposes," be amended to read as follows:

"SEC. 6. That at the expiration of the trust period and when the lands have been conveyed to the Indians by patent in fee, as provided in section five of this act, then each and every allottee shall have the benefit of and be subject to the laws, both civil and criminal, of the State or Territory in which they may reside; and no Territory shall pass or enforce any law denying any such Indian within its jurisdiction the equal protection of the law. And every Indian born within the territorial limits of the United States to whom allotments shall have been made and who has received a patent in fee simple under the provisions of this act, or under any law or treaty, and every Indian born within the territorial limits of the United States who has voluntarily taken up within said limits his residence, separate and apart from any tribe of Indians therein, and has adopted the habits of civilized life, is hereby declared to be a citizen of the United States, and is entitled to all the rights, privileges, and immunities of such citizens, whether said Indian has been or not, by birth or otherwise, a member of any tribe of Indians within the territorial limits of the United States without in any manner impairing or otherwise affecting the right of any such Indian to tribal or other property: *Provided,* That the Secretary of the Interior may, in his discretion, and he is hereby authorized, whenever he shall be satisfied that any Indian allottee is competent and capable of managing his or her affairs, at any time to cause to be issued to such allottee a patent in fee simple, and thereafter all restrictions as to sale, incumbrance, or taxation of said land shall be removed and said land not be liable to the satisfaction of any debt contracted prior to the issuing of such patent: *Provided further*, That until the issuance of fee-simple patents all allottees to whom trust patents shall hereafter be issued shall be subject to the exclusive jurisdiction of the United States: *And provided further*, That the provisions of this act shall not extend to any Indians in the Indian Territory."

That hereafter, when an allotment of land is made to any Indian and any such Indian dies before the expiration of the trust period, said allotment shall be cancelled and the land shall revert to the United States, and the Secretary of the Interior shall ascertain the legal heirs of such Indian, and shall cause to be issued to said heirs and in their names, a patent in fee simple for said land, or he may cause the land to be sold as provided by law and issue a patent therefor to the purchaser or purchasers, and pay the net proceeds to the heirs, or their legal representatives, of such deceased Indian. The action of the Secretary of the Interior in determining the legal heirs of any deceased Indian, as provided herein, shall in all respects be conclusive and final.

Approved; May 8, 1906.

ACT OF SIXTY-EIGHTH CONGRESS, FIRST SESSION, 1924

CHAP. 233. — An Act To authorize the Secretary of the Interior to issue certificates of citizenship to Indians.

Be it enacted by the Senate and House of Representatives of the United States of America in Congress assembled, That all noncitizen Indians born within the territorial limits of the United States be, and they are hereby, declared to be citizens of the United States: *Provided,* That the granting of such citizenship shall not in any manner impair or otherwise affect the right of any Indian to tribal or other property.

Approved, June 2, 1924.

ACT OF SEVENTY-THIRD CONGRESS, SECOND SESSION, 1934

CHAP. 576.—An Act To conserve and develop Indian lands and resources; to extend to Indians the right to form business and other organizations; to establish a credit system for Indians; to grant certain rights of home rule to Indians; to provide for vocational education for Indians; and for other purposes.

Be it enacted by the Senate and House of Representatives of the United States of America in Congress assembled, That hereafter no land of any Indian reservation, created or set apart by treaty or agreement with the Indians, Act of Congress, Executive order, purchase, or otherwise, shall be allotted in severalty to any Indian.

SEC. 2. The existing periods of trust placed upon any Indian lands and any restriction on alienation thereof are hereby extended and continued until otherwise directed by Congress.

SEC. 3. The Secretary of the Interior, if he shall find it to be in the public interest, is hereby authorized to restore to tribal ownership the remaining surplus lands of any Indian reservation heretofore opened or authorized to be opened, to sale, or any other form of disposal by Presidential proclamation, or by any of the public-land laws of the United States: *Provided, however,* That valid rights or claims of any persons to any lands so withdrawn existing on the date of the withdrawal shall not be affected by this Act: *Provided further,* That this section shall not apply to lands within any reclamation project heretofore authorized in any Indian reservation: *Provided further,* That the order of the Department of the Interior signed, dated, and approved by Honorable Ray Lyman Wilbur, as Secretary of the Interior, on October 28, 1932, temporarily withdrawing lands of the Papago Indian Reservation in Arizona from all forms of mineral entry or claim under the public land mining laws, is hereby revoked and rescinded, and the lands of the said Papago Indian Reservation are hereby restored to exploration and location, under the existing mining laws of the United States, in accordance with the express terms and provisions declared and set forth in the Executive orders establishing said Papago Indian Reservation: *Provided further*, That damages shall be paid to the Papago Tribe for loss of any improvements on any land located for mining in such a sum as may be determined by the Secretary of the Interior but not to exceed the cost of said improvements: *Provided further*, That a yearly rental not to exceed five cents per acre shall be paid to the Papago Tribe for loss of the use or occupancy of any land withdrawn by the requirements of mining operations, and payments derived from damages or rentals shall be deposited in the Treasury of the United States to the credit of the Papago Tribe: *Provided further*, That in the event any person or persons, partnership, corporation, or association, desires a mineral patent, according to the mining laws of the United States, he or they shall first deposit in the Treasury of the United States to the credit of the Papago Tribe the sum of $1.00 per acre in lieu of annual rental, as hereinbefore provided, to compensate for the loss or occupancy of the lands withdrawn by the requirements of mining operations: *Provided further*, That patentee shall also pay into the Treasury of the United States to the credit of the Papago Tribe damages for the loss of improvements not heretofore paid in such a sum as may be determined by the Secretary of the Interior, but not to exceed the cost thereof; the payment of $1.00 per acre for surface use to be refunded to patentee in the event that patent is not acquired.

Nothing herein contained shall restrict the granting or use of permits for easements or rights-of-way; or ingress or egress over the lands for all proper and lawful purposes; and nothing contained herein, except as expressly provided, shall be construed as authority for the Secretary of the Interior, or any other person, to issue or promulgate a rule or regulation in conflict with the Executive order of February 1, 1917, creating the Papago Indian Reservation in Arizona or the Act of February 21, 1931 (46 Stat. 1202).

SEC. 4. Except as herein provided, no sale, devise, gift, exchange or other transfer of restricted Indian lands or of shares in the assets of any Indian tribe or corporation organized hereunder, shall be made or approved: *Provided, however*, That such lands or interests may, with the approval of the Secretary of the Interior, be sold, devised, or otherwise transferred to the Indian tribe in which the lands or shares are located or from which the shares were derived or to a successor corporation; and in all instances such lands or interests shall descend or be devised, in accordance with the then existing laws of the State, or Federal laws where applicable, in which said lands are located or in which the subject matter of the corporation is located, to any member of such tribe or of such corporation or any heirs of such member: *Provided further*, That the Secretary of the Interior may authorize voluntary exchanges of lands of equal value and the voluntary exchange of shares of equal value whenever such exchange, in his judgement, is expedient and beneficial for or compatible with the proper consolidation of Indian lands and for the benefit of cooperative organizations.

SEC. 5. The Secretary of the Interior is hereby authorized, in his discretion, to acquire through purchase, relinquishment, gift, exchange, or assignment, any interest in lands, water rights or surface rights to lands, within or without existing reservations, including trust or otherwise restricted allotments whether the allottee be living or deceased, for the purpose of providing land for Indians.

For the acquisition of such lands, interests in lands, water rights, and surface rights, and for expenses incident to such acquisition, there is hereby authorized to be appropriated, out of any funds in the Treasury not otherwise appropriated, a sum not to exceed $2,000,000 in any one fiscal year: *Provided*, That no part of such funds shall be used to acquire additional land outside of the exterior boundaries of Navajo Indian Reservation for the Navajo Indians in Arizona and New Mexico, in the event that the proposed Navajo boundary extension measures now pending in Congress and embodied in the bills (S. 2499 and H.R. 8927) to define the exterior boundaries of the Navajo Indian Reservation in Arizona, and for other purposes, and the bills (S. 2531 and H.R. 8982) to define the exterior boundaries of the Navajo Indian Reservation in New Mexico and for other purposes, or similar legislation, become law.

The unexpended balances of any appropriations made pursuant to this section shall remain available until expended.

Title to any lands or rights acquired pursuant to this Act shall be taken in the name of the United States in trust for the Indian tribe or individual Indian for which the land is acquired, and such lands or rights shall be exempt from State and local taxation.

SEC. 6. The Secretary of the Interior is directed to make rules and regulations for the operation and management of Indian forestry units on the principle of sustained-yield management, to restrict the number of livestock grazed on Indian range units to the estimated carrying capacity of such ranges, and to promulgate such other rules and regulations as may be necessary to protect the range from deterioration, to prevent soil erosion, to assure full utilization of the range, and like purposes.

SEC. 7. The Secretary of the Interior is hereby authorized to proclaim new Indian reservations on lands acquired pursuant to any authority conferred by this Act, or to add such lands to existing reservations: *Provided*, That lands added to existing reservations shall be designated for the exclusive use of Indians entitled by enrollment or by tribal membership to residence at such reservations.

SEC. 8. Nothing contained in this Act shall be construed to relate to Indian holdings of allotments or homesteads upon the public domain outside of the geographic boundaries of any Indian reservation now existing or established hereafter.

SEC. 9. There is hereby authorized to be appropriated, out of any funds in the Treasury not otherwise appropriated, such sums as may be necessary, but not to exceed $250,000 in any fiscal year, to be expended at the order of the Secretary of the Interior, in defraying the expenses of organizing Indian chartered corporations or other organizations created under this Act.

SEC. 10. There is hereby authorized to be appropriated, out of any funds in the Treasury not otherwise appropriated, the sum of $10,000,000 to be established as a revolving fund from which the Secretary of the Interior, under such rules and regulations as he may prescribe, may make loans to Indian chartered corporations for the purpose of promoting the economic development of such tribes and of their members, and may defray the expenses of administering such loans. Repayment of amounts loaned under this authorization shall be credited to the revolving fund and shall be available for the purposes for which the fund is established. A report shall be made annually to Congress of transactions under this authorization.

SEC. 11. There is hereby authorized to be appropriated, out of any funds in the United States Treasury not otherwise appropriated, a sum not to exceed $250,000 annually, together with any unexpended balances of previous appropriations made pursuant to this section, for loans to Indians for the payment of tuition and other expenses in recognized vocational and trade schools: *Provided*, That not more than $50,000 of such sum shall be available for loans to Indian students in high schools and colleges. Such loans shall be reimbursable under rules established by the Commissioner of Indian Affairs.

SEC. 12. The Secretary of the Interior is directed to establish standards of health, age, character, experience, knowledge, and ability for Indians who may be appointed, without regard to civil-service laws, to the various positions maintained, now or hereafter, by the Indian Office, in the administration of functions or services affecting any Indian tribe. Such qualified Indians shall hereafter have the preference to appointment to vacancies in any such positions.

SEC. 13. The provisions of this Act shall not apply to any of the Territories, colonies, or insular possessions of the United States, except that sections 9, 10, 11, 12, and 16, shall apply to the Territory of Alaska: *Provided*, That Sections 2, 4, 7, 16, 17, and 18 of this Act shall not apply to the following-named Indian tribes, the members of such Indian tribes, together with members of other tribes affiliated with such named tribes located in the State of Oklahoma, as follows: Cheyenne, Arapaho, Apache, Comanche, Kiowa, Caddo, Delaware, Wichita, Osage, Kaw, Otoe, Tonkawa,

Pawnee, Ponca, Shawnee, Ottawa, Quapaw, Seneca, Wyandotte, Iowa, Sac and Fox, Kickapoo, Pottawatomi, Cherokee, Chickasaw, Choctaw, Creek, and Seminole. Section 4 of this Act shall not apply to the Indians of the Klamath Reservation in Oregon.

SEC. 14. The Secretary of the Interior is hereby directed to continue the allowance of the articles enumerated in section 17 of the Act of March 2, 1889 (23 Stat.L. 894), or their commuted cash value under the Act of June 10, 1896 (29 Stat.L. 334), to all Sioux Indians who would be eligible, but for the provisions of this Act, to receive allotments of lands in severalty under section 19 of the Act of May 29, 1908 (25 (35) Stat.L. 451), or under any prior Act, and who have the prescribed status of the head of a family or single person over the age of eighteen years, and his approval shall be final and conclusive, claims therefor to be paid as formerly from the permanent appropriation made by said section 17 and carried on the books of the Treasury for this purpose. No person shall receive in his own right more than one allowance of the benefits, and application must be made and approved during the lifetime of the allottee or the right shall lapse. Such benefits shall continue to be paid upon such reservation until such time as the lands available therein for allotment at the time of the passage of this Act would have been exhausted by the award to each person receiving such benefits of an allotment of eighty acres of such land.

SEC. 15. Nothing in this Act shall be construed to impair or prejudice any claim or suit of any Indian tribe against the United States. It is hereby declared to be the intent of Congress that no expenditures for the benefit of Indians made out of appropriations authorized by this Act shall be considered as offsets in any suit brought to recover upon any claim of such Indians against the United States.

SEC. 16. Any Indian tribe, or tribes, residing on the same reservation, shall have the right to organize for its common welfare, and may adopt an appropriate constitution and bylaws, which shall become effective when ratified by a majority vote of the adult members of the tribe, or of the adult Indians residing on such reservation, as the case may be, at a special election authorized and called by the Secretary of the Interior under such rules and regulations as he may prescribe. Such constitution and bylaws when ratified as aforesaid and approved by the Secretary of the Interior shall be revocable by an election open to the same voters and conducted in the same manner as hereinabove provided. Amendments to the constitution and bylaws may be ratified and approved by the Secretary in the same manner as the original constitution and bylaws.

In addition to all powers vested in any Indian tribe or tribal council by existing law, the constitution adopted by said tribe shall also vest in such tribe or its tribal council the following rights and powers: To employ legal counsel, the choice of counsel and fixing of fees to be subject to the approval of the Secretary of the Interior; to prevent the sale, disposition, lease, or encumbrance of tribal lands, interests in lands, or other tribal assets without the consent of the tribe; and to negotiate with the Federal, State, and local Governments. The Secretary of the Interior shall advise such tribe or its tribal counsel of all appropriation estimates or Federal projects for the benefit of the tribe prior to the submission of such estimates to the Bureau of the Budget and the Congress.

SEC. 17. The Secretary of the Interior may, upon petition by at least one-third of the adult Indians, issue a charter of incorporation to such tribe: *Provided*, That such charter shall not become operative until ratified at a special election by a majority vote of the adult Indians living on the reservation. Such charter may convey to the incorporated tribe the power to purchase, take by gift, or bequest, or otherwise, own, hold, manage, operate, and dispose of property of every description, real and personal, including the power to purchase restricted Indian lands and to issue in exchange therefor interests in corporate property, and such further powers as may be incidental to the conduct of corporate business, not inconsistent with law, but no authority shall be granted to sell, mortgage, or lease for a period exceeding ten years any of the land included in the limits of the reservation. Any charter so issued shall not be revoked or surrendered except by Act of Congress.

SEC. 18. This Act shall not apply to any reservation wherein a majority of the adult Indians, voting at a special election duly called by the Secretary of the Interior, shall vote against its application. It shall be the duty of the Secretary of the Interior, within one year after the passage and approval of this Act, to call such an election, which election shall be held by secret ballot upon thirty days' notice.

SEC. 19. The term "Indian" as used in this Act shall include all persons of Indian descent who are members of any recognized Indian tribe now under Federal jurisdiction, and all persons who are descendants of such members who were, on June 1, 1934, residing within the present boundaries of any Indian reservation, and shall further include all other persons of one-half or more Indian blood. For the purposes of this Act, Eskimos and other aboriginal peoples of Alaska shall be considered Indians. The term "tribe" wherever used in this Act shall be construed to refer to any Indian tribe, organized band, pueblo, or the Indians residing on one reservation. The words "adult Indians" wherever used in this Act shall be construed to refer to Indians who have attained the age of twenty-one years.

Approved, June 18, 1934.

ACT OF SEVENTY-NINTH CONGRESS, SECOND SESSION, 1946

CHAP. 959. — To create an Indian Claims Commission to provide for the powers, duties, and functions thereof, and for other purposes.

Be it enacted by the Senate and House of Representatives of the United States of America in Congress assembled, That there is hereby created and established an Indian Claims Commission, hereafter referred to as the Commission.

JURISDICTION

SEC. 2. The Commission shall hear and determine the following claims against the United States on behalf of any Indian tribe, band, or other identifiable group of American Indians residing within the territorial limits of the United States or Alaska: (1) claims in law or equity arising under the Constitution, laws, treaties of the United States, and Executive orders of the President; (2) all other claims in law or equity, including those sounding in tort, with respect to which the claimant would have been entitled to sue in a court of the United States if the United States was subject ot suit; (3) claims which would result if the treaties, contracts, and agreements between the claimant and the United States were revised on the ground of fraud, duress, unconscionable consideration, mutual or unilateral mistake, whether of law or fact, or any other ground cognizable by a court of equity; (4) claims arising from the taking by the United States, whether as the result of a treaty of cession or otherwise, of lands owned or occupied by the claimant without the payment for such lands of compensation agreed to by the claimant; and (5) claims based upon fair and honorable dealings that are not recognized by any existing rule of law or equity. No claim accruing after the date of the approval of this Act shall be considered by the Commission.

All claims hereunder may be heard and determined by the Commission notwithstanding any statute of limitations or laches, but all other defenses shall be available to the United States.

In determining the quantum of relief the Commission shall make appropriate deductions for all payments made by the United States on the claim, and for all other offsets, counterclaims, and demands that would be allowable in a suit brought in the Court of Claims under section 145 of the Judicial Code (36 Stat. 1136; 28 U.S.C. sec. 250), as amended; the Commission may also inquire into and consider all money or property given to or funds expended gratuitously for the benefit of the claimant and if it finds that the nature of the claim and the entire course of dealings and accounts between the United States and the claimant in good conscience warrants such action, may set off all or part of such expenditures against any award made to the claimant, except that it is hereby declared to be the policy of Congress that monies spent for the removal of the claimant from one place to another at the request of the United States, or for agency or other administrative, educational, health or highway purposes, or for expenditures made prior to the date of the law, treaty or Executive Order under which the claim arose, or for expenditures made pursuant to the Act of June 18, 1934 (48 Stat. 984), save expenditures made under section 5 of that Act, or for expenditures under any emergency appropriation or allotment made subsequent to March 4, 1933, and generally applicable throughout the United States for relief in stricken agricultural areas, relief from distress caused by unemployment and conditions resulting therefrom, the prosecution of public work and public projects for the relief of unemployment or to increase employment, and for work relief (including the Civil Works Program) shall not be a proper offset against any award.

MEMBERSHIP APPOINTMENT; OATH; SALARY

SEC. 3. (a) The Commission shall consist of a Chief Commissioner and two Associate Commissioners, who shall be appointed by the President, by and with the advice and consent of the Senate, and each of whom shall receive a salary of $10,000 per year. At all times at least two members of the Commission shall be members of the bar of the Supreme Court of the United States in good standing: *Provided further*, That not more than two of the members shall be of the same political party. Each of them shall take an oath to support the Constitution of the United States and to discharge faithfully the duties of his office.

TERM OF OFFICE; VACANCIES; REMOVAL

(b) The Commissioners shall hold office during their good behavior until the dissolution of the Commission as hereinafter provided. Vacancies shall be filled in the same manner as the original appointments. Members of the Commission may be removed by the President for cause after notice and opportunity to be heard.

NOT TO ENGAGE IN OTHER VOCATIONS OR REPRESENT TRIBES

(c) No Commissioner shall engage in any other business, vocation, or employment during his term of office nor shall he, during his term of office or for a period of two years thereafter, represent any Indian tribe, band, or group in any matter whatsoever, or have any financial interest in the outcome of any tribal claim. Any person violating the provisions of this subdivision shall be fined not more than $10,000 or imprisoned not more than two years, or both.

QUORUM

(d) Two members shall constitute a quorum, and the agreement of two members shall be necessary to any and all determinations for the transaction of the business of the Commission, and, if there be a quorum, no vacancy shall impair or affect the business of the Commission, or its determinations.

STAFF OF COMMISSION

SEC. 4. The Commission shall appoint a clerk and such other employees as shall be requisite to conduct the business of the Commission. All such employees shall take oath for the faithful discharge of their duties and shall be under the direction of the Commission in the performance thereof.

OFFICES

SEC. 5. The Principal office of the commission shall be in the District of Columbia.

EXPENSES OF COMMISSION

SEC. 6. All necessary expenses of the Commission shall be paid on the presentation of itemized vouchers therefor approved by the Chief Commissioner or other member or officer designated by the Commission.

TIME OF MEETINGS

SEC. 7. The time of the meetings of the Commission shall be prescribed by the Commission.

RECORD

SEC. 8. A full written record shall be kept of all hearings and proceedings of the Commission and shall be open to public inspection.

CONTROL OF PROCEDURE

SEC. 9. The Commission shall have power to establish its own rules of procedure.

PRESENTATION OF CLAIM

SEC. 10. Any claim within the provisions of this Act may be presented to the Commission by any member of an Indian tribe, band, or other identifiable group of Indians as the representative of all its members; but wherever any tribal organization exists, recognized by the Secretary of the Interior as having authority to represent such tribe, band, or group, such organization shall be accorded the exclusive privilege of representing such Indians, unless fraud, collusion, or laches on the part of such organization be shown to the satisfaction of the Commission.

TRANSFER OF SUITS FROM COURT OF CLAIMS

SEC. 11. Any suit pending in the Court of Claims or the Supreme Court of the United States or which shall be filed in the Court of Claims under existing legislation, shall not be transferred to the Commission: *Provided*, That the provisions of section 2 of this Act, with respect to the deduction of payments, offsets, counterclaims and demands, shall supersede the provisions of the particular jurisdictional Act under which any pending or authorized suit in the Court of Claims has been or will be authorized: *Provided further*, That the Court of Claims in any suit pending before it at the time of the approval of this Act shall have exclusive jurisdiction to hear and determine any claim based upon fair and honorable dealings arising out of the subject matter of any such suit.

LIMITATIONS

SEC. 12. The Commission shall receive claims for a period of five years after the date of the approval of this Act and no claim existing before such date but not presented within such period may thereafter be submitted to any court or administrative agency for consideration, nor will such claim thereafter be entertained by the Congress.

NOTICE AND INVESTIGATION

SEC. 13. (a) As soon as practicable the Commission shall send a written explanation of the provisions of this Act to the recognized head of each Indian tribe and band, and to any other identifiable groups of American Indians existing as distinct entities, residing within the territorial limits of the United States and Alaska, and to the superintendents of all Indian agencies, who shall promulgate the same, and shall request that a detailed statement of all claims be sent to the Commission, together with the names of aged or invalid Indians from whom depositions should be taken immediately and a summary of their proposed testimonies.

(b) The Commission shall establish an Investigation Division to investigate all claims referred to it by the Commission for the purpose of discovering the facts relating thereto. The Division shall make a complete and thorough search for all evidence affecting each claim, utilizing all documents and records in the possession of the Court of Claims and the several Government departments, and shall submit such evidence to the Commission. The Division shall make available to the Indians concerned and to any interested Federal agency any data in its possession relating to the rights and claims of any Indian.

CALLS UPON DEPARTMENTS FOR INFORMATION

SEC. 14. The Commission shall have the power to call upon any of the departments of the Government for any information it may deem necessary, and shall have the use of all records, hearings, and reports made by the committees of each House of Congress, when deemed necessary in the prosecution of its business.

At any hearing held hereunder, any official letter, paper, document, map, or record in the possession of any officer or department, or court of the United States or committee of Congress (or a certified copy thereof), may be used in evidence insofar as relevant and material, including any deposition or other testimony of record in any suit or proceeding in any court of the United States to which an Indian or Indian tribe or group was a party, and the appropriate department of the Government of the United States shall give to the attorneys for all tribes or groups full and free access to such letters, papers, documents, maps, or records as may be useful to said attorneys in the preparation of any claim instituted hereunder, and shall afford facilities for the examination of the same and, upon written request by said attorneys, shall furnish certified copies thereof.

REPRESENTATION BY ATTORNEYS

SEC. 15. Each such tribe, band, or other identifiable group of Indians may retain to represent its interests in the presentation of claims before the Commission an attorney or attorneys at law, of its own selection, whose practice before the Commission shall be regulated by its adopted procedure. The fees of such attorney or attorneys for all services rendered in prosecuting the claim in question, whether before the Commission or otherwise, shall, unless the amount of such fees is stipulated in the approved contract between the attorney or attorneys and the claimant, be fixed by the Commission at such amount as the Commission, in accordance with standards obtaining for prosecuting similar contingent claims in courts of law, finds to be adequate compensation for services rendered and results obtained, considering the contingent nature of the case, plus all reasonable expenses incurred in the prosecution of the claim; but the amount so fixed by the Commission, exclusive of reimbursements for actual expenses, shall not exceed 10 per centum of the amount recovered in any case. The attorney or attorneys for any such tribe, band, or group as shall have been organized pursuant to section 16 of the Act of June 18, 1934 (48 Stat. 987; 25 U.S.C., sec. 476), shall be selected pursuant to the constitution and bylaws of such tribe, band, or group. The employment of attorneys for all other claimants shall be subject to the provisions of sections 2103 to 2106, inclusive, of the Revised Statutes (25 U.S.C., secs. 81, 82–84).

The Attorney General or his assistants shall represent the United States in all claims presented to the Commission, and shall have authority, with the approval of the Commission, to compromise any claim presented to the Commission. Any such compromise shall be submitted by the Commission to the Congress as a part of its report as provided in section 21 hereof in the same manner as final determinations of the Commission, and shall be subject to the provisions of section 22 hereof.

NO MEMBER OF CONGRESS TO PRACTICE BEFORE COMMISSION

SEC. 16. No Senator or Member of or Delegate to Congress shall, during his continuance in office, practice before the Commission.

HEARING

SEC. 17. The Commission shall give reasonable notice to the interested parties and an opportunity for them to be heard and to present evidence before making any final determination upon any claim. Hearings may be held in any part of the United States or in the Territory of Alaska.

TESTIMONY

SEC. 18. Any member of the Commission or any employee of the Commission, designated in writing for the purpose by the Chief Commissioner, may administer oaths and examine witnesses. Any member of the Commission may require by subpena (1) the attendance and testimony of witnesses, and the production of all necessary books, papers, documents, correspondence, and other evidence, from any place in the United States or Alaska at any designated place of hearing; or (2) the taking of depositions before any designated individual competent to administer oaths under the laws of the United States or of any State or Territory. In the case of a deposition, the testimony shall be reduced to writing by the individual taking the deposition or under his direction and shall be subscribed by the deponent. In taking testimony, opportunity shall be given for cross-examination, under such regulations as the Commission may prescribe. Witnesses subpenaed to testify or whose depositions are taken pursuant to this Act, and the officers or persons taking the same, shall severally be entitled to the same fees and mileage as are paid for like services in the courts of the United States.

FINAL DETERMINATION

SEC. 19. The final determination of the Commission shall be in writing, shall be filed with its clerk, and shall include (1) its findings of the facts upon which its conclusions are based; (2) a statement (a) whether there are any just grounds for relief of the claimant and, if so, the amount thereof; (b) whether there are any allowable offsets, counterclaims, or other deductions, and, if so, the amount thereof; and (3) a statement of its reasons for its findings and conclusions.

REVIEW BY COURT OF CLAIMS

SEC. 20. (a) In considering any claim the Commission at any time may certify to the Court of Claims any definite and distinct questions of law concerning which instructions are desired for the proper disposition of the claim; and thereupon the Court of Claims may give appropriate instructions on the questions certified and transmit the same to the Commission for its guidance in the further consideration of the claim.

(b) When the final determination of the Commission has been filed with the clerk of said Commission the clerk shall give notice of the filing of such determination to the parties to the proceeding in manner and form as directed by the Commission. At any time within three months from the date of the filing of the determination of the Commission with the clerk either party may appeal from the determination of the Commission to the Court of Claims, which Court shall have exclusive jurisdiction to affirm, modify, or set aside such final determination. On said appeal the Court shall determine whether the findings of fact of the Commission are supported by substantial evidence, in which event they shall be conclusive, and also whether the conclusions of law, including any conclusions respecting "fair and honorable dealings", where applicable, stated by the Commission as a basis for its final determination, are valid and supported by the Commission's findings of fact. In making the foregoing determinations, the Court shall review the whole record or such portions thereof as may be cited by any party, and due account shall be taken of the rule of prejudicial error. The Court may at any time remand the cause to the Commission for such further proceedings as it may direct, not inconsistent with the foregoing provisions of this section. The Court shall promulgate such rules of practice as it may find necessary to carry out the foregoing provisions of this section.

(c) Determinations of questions of law by the Court of Claims under this section shall be subject to review by the Supreme Court of the United States in the manner prescribed by section 3 of the Act of February 13, 1925 (43 Stat. 939; 28 U.S.C., sec. 288), as amended.

REPORT OF COMMISSION TO CONGRESS

SEC. 21. In each claim, after the proceedings have been finally concluded, the Commission shall promptly submit its report to Congress.

The report to Congress shall contain (1) the final determination of the Commission; (2) a transcript of the proceedings or judgment upon review, if any, with the instructions of the Court of Claims; and (3) a statement of how each Commissioner voted upon the final determination of the claim.

EFFECT OF FINAL DETERMINATION
OF COMMISSION

SEC. 22. (a) When the report of the Commission determining any claimant to be entitled to recover has been filed with Congress, such report shall have the effect of a final judgement of the Court of Claims, and there is hereby authorized to be appropriated such sums as are necessary to pay the final determination of the Commission.

The payment of any claim, after its determination in accordance with this Act, shall be a full discharge of the United States of all claims and demands touching any of the matters involved in the controversy.

(b) A final determination against a claimant made and reported in accordance with this Act shall forever bar any further claim or demand against the United States arising out of the matter involved in the controversy.

DISSOLUTION OF THE COMMISSION

SEC. 23. The existence of the Commission shall terminate at the end of ten years after the first meeting of the Commission or at such earlier time after the expiration of the five-year period of limitation set forth in section 12 hereof as the Commission shall have made its final report to Congress on all claims filed with it. Upon its dissolution the records of the Commission shall be delivered to the Archivist of the United States.

FUTURE INDIAN CLAIMS

SEC. 24. The jurisdiction of the Court of Claims is hereby extended to any claim against the United States accruing after the date of the approval of this Act in favor of any Indian tribe, band, or other identifiable group of American Indians residing within the territorial limits of the United States or Alaska whenever such claim is one arising under the Constitution, laws, treaties of the United States, or Executive orders of the President, or is one which otherwise would be cognizable in the Court of Claims if the claimant were not an Indian tribe, band, or group. In any suit brought under the jurisdiction conferred by this section the claimant shall be entitled to recover in the same manner, to the same extent, and subject to the same conditions and limitations, and the United States shall be entitled to the same defenses, both at law and in equity, and to the same offsets, counterclaims, and demands, as in cases brought in the Court of Claims under section 145 of the Judicial Code (36 Stat. 1136; 28 U.S.C., sec. 250), as amended: *Provided, however*, That nothing contained in this section shall be construed as altering the fiduciary or other relations between the United States and the several Indian tribes, bands, or groups.

EFFECT ON EXISTING LAWS

SEC. 25. All provisions of law inconsistent with this Act are hereby repealed to the extent of such inconsistency, except that existing provisions of law authorizing suits in the Court of Claims by particular tribes, bands, or groups of Indians and governing the conduct or determination of such suits shall continue to apply to any case heretofore or hereafter instituted thereunder save as provided by section 11 hereof as to the deduction of payments, offsets, counterclaims, and demands.

SEC. 26. If any provision of this Act, or application thereof, is held invalid, the remainder of the Act, or other applications of such provisions, shall not be affected.

Approved August 13, 1946.

ACT OF EIGHTY-SIXTH CONGRESS, FIRST SESSION, 1959

CHAP. 322. — To provide for the division of the tribal assets of the Catawba Indian Tribe of South Carolina among the members of the tribe and for other purposes.

Be it enacted by the Senate and House of Representatives of the United States of America in Congress assembled, That when a majority of the adult members of the Catawba Indian Tribe of South Carolina, according to the most reliable information regarding membership that is available to the Secretary of the Interior, have indicated their agreement to a division of the tribal assets in accordance with the provisions of this Act, the Secretary shall publish in the Federal Register a notice of that fact. The membership roll of the Catawba Indian Tribe of South Carolina shall thereupon be closed as of midnight of the date of such notice, and no child born thereafter shall be eligible for enrollment. The Secretary of the Interior with advice and assistance of the tribe shall prepare a final roll of the members of the tribe who are living at such time, and when so doing shall provide a reasonable opportunity for any person to protest against the inclusion or omission of any name on or from the roll. The Secretary's decisions on all protests shall be final and conclusive. After all protests are disposed of, the final roll shall be published in the Federal Register.

SEC. 2. Each member whose name appears on the final roll of the tribe as published in the Federal Register shall be entitled to receive an approximately equal share of the tribe's assets that are held in trust by the United States in accordance with the provisions of this Act. This right shall constitute personal property which may be inherited or bequeathed, but it shall not otherwise be subject to alienation of encumbrance.

SEC. 3. The tribe's assets shall be distributed in accordance with the following provisions:

(a) If the State of South Carolina by legislation authorizes assets that are held by the State in trust for the tribe to be included in the distribution plan prepared by the Secretary in accordance with the provisions of this Act, they may be included.

(b) The tribal council shall designate any part of the tribe's land that is to be set aside for church, park, playground, or cemetery purposes and the Secretary is authorized to convey such tracts to trustees or agencies designated by the tribal council for that purpose and approved by the Secretary.

(c) The remaining tribal assets shall be appraised by the Secretary and the share of each member shall be determined by dividing the total number of enrolled members into the total appraisal. The tribal assets so appraised shall not include any improvements that were placed on the part of an assignment that is selected by an assignee, or his wife or children, pursuant to subsection (d) of this section. Such improvements shall be property of the assignee.

(d) Subject to the provisions of this subsection, each member who is an adult under the laws of the State and who has an assignment shall be given the option of selecting and receiving title to any part of his assignment that has an appraised value not in excess of his share of the tribe's assets. A wife, husband, or child of such adult member may select and receive title to any part of such assignment that has an appraised value not in excess of her or his share of the tribe's assets; and, if the child is a minor under the laws of the State, the option on his behalf may be exercised by such adult member. Each selection shall be subject to the approval of the Secretary of the Interior, who shall consider the effect of the selection on the total value of the property. The title to any part of an assignment so selected may be taken in the name of the person entitled thereto, or the title to all of the parts of an assignment so selected may be taken in the names of the persons entitled thereto as tenants in common.

(e) Each member who has no assignment may select and receive title to any part of the tribal land that is not selected pursuant to subsection (d) of this section and that has an appraised value not in excess of his share of the tribe's assets.

(f) All assets of the tribe that are not selected and conveyed to members pursuant to subsections (d) and (e) of this section shall be sold and the proceeds distributed to the members in accordance with their respective interests. Such sales shall be by competitive bid and any member shall have the right to purchase property offered for sale for a price not less than the highest acceptable bid therefor. If more than one member exercises such right, the property shall be sold to the member exercising the right who offers the highest price. Any tribal assets that are not sold by the Secretary within two years from the date of the notice provided for in section 1 of this Act shall be conveyed to a trustee selected by the Secretary for disposition in accordance with this subsection, and the fees and expenses of such trustee shall be paid out of funds appropriated for the purposes of this Act.

SEC. 4. The Secretary of the Interior is authorized to make such land surveys and to execute such conveyancing instruments as he deems necessary to convey marketable and recordable titles to the tribal assets disposed of pursuant to this Act. Each grantee shall receive an unrestricted title to the property conveyed.

SEC. 5. The constitution of the tribe adopted pursuant to the Act of June 18, 1934 (48 Stat. 984), as amended, shall be revoked by the Secretary. Thereafter, the tribe and its members shall not be entitled to any of the special services performed by the United States for Indians because of their status as Indians, all statutes of the United States that affect Indians because of their status as Indians shall be inapplicable to them, and the laws of the several States shall apply to them in the same manner they apply to other persons or citizens within their jurisdiction. Nothing in this Act, however, shall affect the status of such persons as citizens of the United States.

SEC. 6. Nothing in this Act shall affect the rights, privileges, or obligations of the tribe and its members under the laws of South Carolina.

SEC. 7. No property distributed under the provisions of this Act shall at the time of distribution be subject to any Federal or State income tax. Following any distribution of property made under the provisions of this Act, such property and income derived therefrom by the distributee shall be subject to the same taxes, State and Federal, as in the case of non-Indians: *Provided*, That for the purpose of capital gains or losses the base value of the property shall be the value of the property when distributed to the grantee.

SEC. 8. Prior to the revocation of the tribal constitution provided for in this Act, the Secretary is authorized to undertake, within the limits of available appropriations, a special program of education and training designed to help the members of the tribe to earn a livelihood, to conduct their own affairs, and to assume their responsibilities as citizens without special services because of their status as Indians. Such program may include language training, orientation in non-Indian community customs and living standards, vocational training and related subjects, transportation to the place of training or instruction, and subsistence during the course of training or instruction. For the purposes of such program, the Secretary is authorized to enter into contracts or agreements with any Federal, State, or local governmental agency, corporation, association, or persons. Nothing in this section shall preclude any Federal agency from undertaking any other program for the education and training of Indians with funds appropriated to it.

Approved September 21, 1959.

INDEX

Apache 170
Arapaho, also Arrapahoe 2, 90, 91, 93, 123, 133, 145, 149, 170
Arrickara, also Arrickaree 90, 91, 92
Assinaboine 90, 91, 92, 99, 100
Aunce-pa-pas 99

Blackfeet, also Blackfoot 2, 91, 99, 100, 101, 104, 123, 136
Blood 99, 101, 104
Bosque Redondo reservation 120
Boundaries, setting of 6, 18, 24, 25, 26, 27, 30, 33, 34, 39, 40, 43, 52, 53, 54, 57, 58, 63, 65, 71, 72, 84, 85, 91, 94, 95, 99, 100, 106, 110, 117, 124, 146, 168
Brulé 2, 123, 130, 135, 149

Caddo 170
Canada 9, 14
Canayiahaga 12, 14
Catawba 2, 16, 18, 182
Cayugas 24, 25, 33, 42, 43
Cherokee 2, 16, 51, 52, 53, 54, 55, 69–82, 154, 170
"Cherokee Outlet" 162
Cheyenne 90, 91, 92, 145, 149, 170
Chickesaw, also Chickasaw 3, 16, 59–68, 84, 85, 111, 154, 170
Chippewa 26
Choctaw, also Chactaw, also, Choctow 16, 29, 30, 31, 32, 71, 84, 85, 111, 154, 170
Christianization, 102

Churches, or Missions 37, 101, 114, 117, 125, 157, 183
Citizenship 154, 159, 163, 165
Civil Works Program 173
Comanche 170
Confederate States 108, 114
Cree 99
Creek 16, 18, 52, 57, 108, 109, 110, 111, 112, 114, 115, 154, 170
Crow 90, 91, 92, 99, 100
Cuthead 2, 123, 136

Dahcotah 90, 91
Delaware 20, 21, 22, 26, 27, 28, 170

English 10, 11, 12, 13, 14, 15, 17, 18, 19
Eskimos 171

Fishing rights 1, 2, 40, 92, 95, 100
Flathead 99, 104
Forts, and Posts: Fort Defiance 117; Post of Detroit 27; Fort Gibson 57, 72, 85; Fort Harmar 33, 34; Fort Laramie 90, 130, 131, 134; Fort Lawrence 26; Fort Lyon 117; Post of Michillimachenac 28; Fort M'Intosh 26; Fort Oswego 25, 34; Fort Pitt 23; Fort Schlosser 43, 44; Fort Smith 108; Fort Stanwix 24, 33, 34; Fort Sumner 116, 121; Fort Towson 84, 85; Fort Wachitta 85

Fox 154, 162, 170
France 16
Franklin, Benjamin 4, 15
French 10, 13, 14, 27

Great Britain 16, 30, 36, 43, 47, 49, 78
Gros-Ventre 90, 91, 92, 99, 101, 104

Historical Society of Pennsylvania 4, 15
Hunkpapa 2, 123
Hunting rights 1, 2, 18, 27, 29, 30, 92, 95, 99, 100, 101, 103, 119, 121, 128, 129, 146

Indian Appropriations Act of March 3, 1871 1
Indian Claims Commission 172–180
Iowa 170
Ireland 16

Jackson, Andrew 51, 65

Kappler, Charles J. 4, 44
Kaskaskia 156, 158, 159
Kaughnawaugas 36
Kaw 170
Kikapoo 170
King George the Third 16, 17, 18, 19
Kiowa 170
Klamath 170
Kootenay 99

Land, exchange of 142, 143
Land, sale of 141, 154, 158, 164, 171, 183
Land-book 118, 125
Land claims 1, 2
Liquor 5, 96, 102

Mandan 90, 91, 92
Miamie 154, 156, 157, 158
Military posts, establishment of 54, 72, 88, 90, 101, 105, 120, 129
Miniconjou, also Minneconjon 2, 123, 132
Mohawk 24, 25, 33, 34, 47

Navajo, also Navaho 116, 117, 118, 120, 121, 168
Navajo land-book 118
Navigation, right of 146
Nez Percés 2, 99, 104, 138, 139
Nisqualli 2, 94

Oglala, also Ogallalah 2, 123, 131, 135, 149
Omaha 94
Oneida 24, 25, 33, 34, 36, 37, 38, 42, 43
Onondaga 24, 25, 33, 42, 43
Osage 72, 73, 81, 154, 170
Otoe 170
Ottawa 26, 27, 170

Papago 166, 177
Passamaquoddy 2, 39
Pawnee 170
Peace and friendship 9, 16, 17, 20, 21, 24, 31, 32, 33, 42, 44, 45, 49, 59, 70, 73, 87, 90, 99, 105, 108, 109, 116, 123, 128
Penn, William 5, 6, 7, 8
Penobscot 2
Peorias 154, 156, 157, 158, 159
Piankeshaw 156, 158, 159
Piegan 99, 101, 103, 104
Ponca 170
Pottawatomi 170
Praying 10, 13
Puyallup 2, 94

Quapaws 72, 170

Railroads, establishment of 106, 111, 119, 120, 128, 129, 155
Red Cloud 134
Removal 47, 48, 51, 52, 53, 54, 57, 58, 59, 72, 74, 75, 76, 77, 78, 79, 82, 95, 96, 121, 138, 142, 143, 145, 148, 149, 150, 155
Reservation, assigning of allotments 55, 61, 62, 63, 64, 118, 125, 138, 139, 147, 148, 151, 152, 154, 156, 157, 158, 160, 161, 163, 170
Reservation, establishment of 27, 30, 34, 42, 43, 55, 88, 95, 106, 117, 124, 138, 146, 148, 155, 168
Reservation, termination of allotment policy 166
Roads 44, 54, 72, 90, 95, 101, 120, 129, 146, 155

Sacs 154, 162, 170
Sa-heh-wamish 94
Sans Arcs 2, 99, 123, 137
Santee 2, 123, 137
Scalping 120, 128
Schools, establishment of 65, 75, 97, 101, 114, 117, 118, 125, 126, 138, 139, 147, 157
Self-government 2, 170
Seminole 57, 58, 111, 112, 154, 170
Senecas, also Senekas 24, 25, 33, 43, 44, 71, 154, 170
Seneka Abeal 25
Shawnee 170
S'Homamish 94
Shoshoni, also Shoshonee 2, 105, 106
Sioux, or Sioux Nation 2, 49, 90, 91, 92, 123, 130–137, 145, 149, 150, 154, 170
Sioux land-book 125
Sitting Bull 132
Six Nations 9, 13, 14, 24, 25, 33, 34, 35, 42–45
Slaves 22, 29, 61, 68, 97, 109
Snakes 99
Squawskin 94
Squi-aitl 94
State, territory, or province: Alabama 64, 76; Alaska 169, 171, 178; Arizona 168; California 107; Colorado 155; Dakota 130, 149, 150; Florida 57;

Georgia 16, 18, 19, 69, 78, 81; Kansas 152; Maine 2, 39; Massachusetts 39; Mississippi 64; Missouri 72; Montana 130; Nebraska 99, 124, 148, 149, 150, 154; Nevada 2, 105, 107; New Mexico 88, 89, 121, 168; New York 14, 47, 154; North Carolina 2, 19, 76; Oklahoma 170; Oregon 170; Pennsylvania 5, 6, 9, 13, 15, 23, 24, 25, 28, 33, 43; South Carolina 2, 19, 182, 184; South Dakota 2; Tennessee 51, 64, 76; Virginia 19, 23; Washington 2, 138
Stehchass 94
Steilacoom 94
Stockbridge 36, 37, 38

Tonkawa 170
T'Peeksin 94
Trade 140
Trading posts, establishment of 27, 30
Treaty making, termination of 144
Treaty of Laramie 100
Treaty of Pontitock 65, 67, 68
Tuscarora, also Tuscorora 24, 25, 33, 34, 36, 37, 38
Two Kettle 2, 123, 136

Uncpapa 135
Upper Pend d'Oreille 99
Utah 87, 88, 89
Ute 155

Vancouver's Island 97

Wagon trains 105, 120, 128
Wampum 7, 11, 13, 14
Wea 156, 158, 159
Wichita 170
Wyandot, also Wiandot, also Wyandotte 26, 27, 28, 170

Yanktonai 2, 123, 133